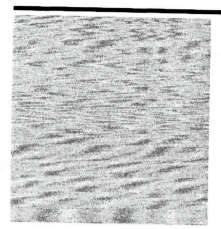

D0074072

Scheduling Construction Projects

Principles and Practices

Sandra Christensen Weber
Arizona State University

PEARSON
Prentice
Hall

Upper Saddle River, New Jersey
Columbus, Ohio

Library of Congress Cataloging in Publication Data

Weber, Sandra Christensen.
   Scheduling construction projects : principles and practices / Sandra Christensen
Weber.—1st ed.
     p. cm.
   Includes bibliographical references and index.
   ISBN 0-13-114870-2
   1. Building industry—Management. 2. Building—Superintendence. 3. Production
scheduling. I. Title.
   TH438.4 W43 2005
   690'.068'5—dc22

                                                2004015326

Executive Editor: Ed Francis
Editorial Assistant: Jennifer Day
Production Editor: Christine Buckendahl
Project Coordination: Carlisle Publishers Services
Design Coordinator: Diane Ernsberger
Cover Designer: Jeff Vanik
Cover art: Superstock
Production Manager: Deidra Schwartz
Marketing Manager: Mark Marsden

This book was set in Times Roman by Carlisle Communications, Ltd. It was printed and bound by R. R. Donnelley &
Sons Company. The cover was printed by The Lehigh Press, Inc.

Pearson Prentice Hall™ is a trademark of Pearson Education, Inc.
Pearson® is a registered trademark of Pearson plc
Prentice Hall® is a registered trademark of Pearson Education, Inc.

Pearson Education Ltd
Pearson Education Singapore Pte. Ltd
Pearson Education Canada, Ltd
Pearson Education—Japan

Pearson Education Australia Pty. Limited
Pearson Education North Asia Ltd.
Pearson Educación de Mexico, S.A. de C.V.
Pearson Education Malaysia Pte. Ltd.

10 9 8 7 6 5 4 3 2 1
0-13-114870-2

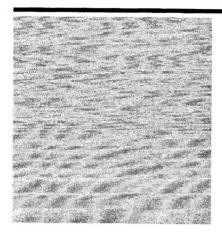

Dedication

Sandra Weber *was my good friend, a friend who was always there to lend a helping hand or simply a kind word. Our paths first crossed in the early 1980s as members of the American Society of Civil Engineers' Committee on Construction Equipment and Techniques. In those years, we shared the joys and trials of heavy construction with our respective companies, she with the Guy F. Atkinson Construction Company. Later she joined the Arizona State University construction faculty and soon convinced me to also enter teaching. At the Del E. Webb School of Construction, we enjoyed the triumphs of our former students who entered the world of construction and went on to work on so many interesting projects. Her legacy lives with those students who first learned construction scheduling from a professional who radiated her love of construction.*

Cliff Schexnayder

The Publisher wishes to acknowledge Cliff Schexnayder for his vital assistance in reviewing edited manuscript and page proofs. This allowed the project to go forward to publication so that Professor Weber's hard work could come to fruition.

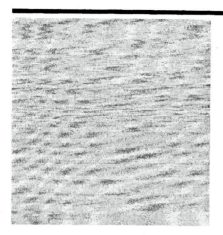

Contents

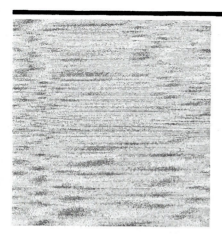

Preface

This book is intended for university students and industry professionals. The varied concepts of construction planning and scheduling are presented, along with illustrations and examples designed to make even difficult concepts easily understood. Both theory and application are given in support of each concept and scheduling technique. Particular attention is given to the concepts used most frequently in industry practice, such as precedence network diagramming; resource allocation, monitoring, and control; and report generation and interpretation.

In addition to typical pedagogical tools, such as chapter-ending problems and numerous graphics, the text uses examples from the three most frequently used scheduling software packages (Primavera Project Planner®, Microsoft Project®, and Sure Trak®), provides a glossary of words and phrases commonly used in the industry, uses photographs of construction activities in support of text examples, and has appendices that include an example scheduling specification, a sample narrative, and a sample request for payment.

The text is organized into four main sections, totaling nineteen chapters. Section 1 covers scheduling basics, including an historical sketch; the identification of tasks; finding task durations and identifying relationships; bar charts; and the creation of precedence networks, diagramming, and calculations. Section 2 covers resource management from the allocation and assignment of resources to activities to the determination of which activities to shorten or which to delay in order to shorten a project's duration or achieve a more uniform resource profile. Section 3 includes the notion of schedule manipulation with constraints, progress assessment and replanning via the update, measuring the project status using earned value reporting, using and interpreting reports, and computer applications. In addition, the use of schedules in support of claims and change orders is also covered. All of the concepts covered in Section 3 are essential to good field scheduling practice. Section 4 covers some advanced topics typical of university teaching at the junior level and above. These topics include linear scheduling, activity on arrow networking, project evaluation and review technique (a statistical approach to scheduling), and resource leveling using the minimum moment method and leveling multiple resources with the Burgess method. Last, the topic of scheduling multiple projects is discussed. Although some of the topics could have been placed in other locations in the text, Section 4 is reserved for topics most commonly taught at the university level.

The text is designed to support the planning and scheduling course at the college or university level, as well as for the construction industry practitioner wanting to amplify his or her knowledge of the topic. An accompanying instructor's manual provides classroom examples of all text topics. The examples and solved problems are suitable for use as teaching aids.

Acknowledgments

Thanks to the following reviewers for their helpful comments and suggestions: H. Rocky Gerber, University of Washington, Seattle; John Jarchow, Pima Community College; and James J. Stein, Eastern Michigan University.

SECTION
ONE

SCHEDULING BASICS

CHAPTER 1

Introduction

Goal

Emphasize the importance of scheduling to the successful completion of a construction project.

Objectives

- Define planning and scheduling in the construction context.
- Give examples of how scheduling can be used in addition to pre-planning and historical record keeping.
- Provide a historical sketch of the development of construction scheduling techniques.
- Briefly define project success and show the role of the schedule in achieving success.

Planning and scheduling are basic to most things we, as humans, do. Planning is the way we organize and sequence the tasks needed to accomplish a goal. There are plans for meeting common goals, such as getting to work on time, and more formal plans, such as those used by companies (such as a strategic plan, business plan, financial plan, and marketing plan). The planning required to construct an office building requires the identification of the tasks needed to complete the building and then the sequencing of those tasks in their logical order. Scheduling is one component of the plan and aids in visualizing the plan.

The scheduling part of the construction plan requires that the *tasks* or *activities* are assigned a duration corresponding to the anticipated productivity of the *crews* doing the work. The words *task* and *activity* will be used interchangeably throughout this text. When tasks have durations and are put in their proper order by identifying the *relationships* they have with one another, a construction schedule is created. Scheduling is just one part of construction planning, which may also include plans for safety, community relations, material storage and handling, and environmental protection along with the schedule to create the overall *construction plan*.

The construction schedule has many uses, beginning with its representation of the initial construction plan. To be effective, plans must be monitored for progress. A comparison of the progressed, or *updated*, schedule with the project *baseline*, or original, plan enables the manager to identify problems early. Adjustments can be made when needed, and the effect of proposed changes can be *simulated* in the schedule, so that the results can be assessed.

Advantages of Construction Schedules

The use of scheduling tools enables the constructor to

- Effectively visualize the planned construction work,
- Use computerized what-if capabilities to analyze alternatives and make schedule adjustments,
- Effectively allocate *resources*, and
- Compare budgeted and actual costs, *productions*, and durations.

Schedule Generation

When a project is determined to fit the contractor's *work profile* (e.g., type, size, and location of the project) and appears to be a project that the company will bid, the *contract documents* are carefully reviewed. These documents contain the information needed for planning the work. The plans or drawings and specifications explain and show how the various elements of the project are to be assembled. These documents are the foundation of the construction plan. The estimator will use them to help visualize the construction process and work sequences. The contract *special conditions* usually establish contractural time limits on the *contract duration*, or the amount of time allocated to complete the project. The professional judgment of the estimator translates these facts into a project bid and, frequently, a construction schedule. When the time-related tasks have been joined in their proper or expected sequence, *forward and backward pass calculations* can be performed to determine the *critical path*, or longest path through the network of tasks. These calculations will show the project duration and the amount of *total float* available to network activities.

Converting the construction plan into a construction schedule will help the construction manager and estimator determine whether the selected plan and work task productivity estimates will provide a construction duration that is within the time limits established by the contract.

Several methods can be used to display the resulting network and its logic. The *bar chart* is perhaps the most recognizable of these methods. It is a pictorial display of each project activity with rectangles, or "bars," used to indicate the estimated activity-time duration. Most bar charts do not convey activity relationship information. Bar charts decorate the walls of many construction trailers because they are easily understood. *Logic diagrams,* unlike bar charts, show how activities are related. They have traditionally come in two varieties, the activity on arrow (AOA) or the activity on node (AON) *critical path* representation. The AOA method was developed first and uses *dummy activities* to help depict logic and maintain the network-required uniqueness of activity numbering. This type of network diagram has been virtually replaced by the AON diagram. The AON network omits 15% or more of the extra activities attributed to the use of dummies in the AOA network.

Schedule Use in Pre-Planning

Pre-project planning of on-site construction, as described in 1989,[1] is the vehicle by which project management can organize its thoughts about the organization and prosecution of the project and by which the project's operational system is developed. In their book, Oglesby, Parker, and Howell note that,

> Formal preplanning, done correctly, involves five steps or phases, which are:
> 1. Planning the planning process
> 2. Gathering information
> 3. Preparing the preplan
> 4. Disseminating the pertinent information in the plan to all affected parties
> 5. Evaluating the results of the planning efforts and its consequences[2]

The text goes on to state

> Preplanning without scheduling has little merit. Only with a suitable schedule in appropriate detail and worked out sufficiently in advance can job management function effectively, because, without a suitable schedule, many questions about what, why, when, where, how, and who will go unanswered.[3]

The value of the schedule in pre-planning is as a communication device, aiding the project manager in disseminating his or her vision of the work to project staff; owners and their representatives; construction company management; and lenders, insurers, and bonding companies.

In the mid-1990s, pre-project planning was described as a tool for owners that would help them make critical decisions about the commitment of resources and would help them improve the likelihood of project success. It was described as "the project-development interface between business and engineering in terms of capital expenditures."[4]

The concept embodied by most planning, if not all planning, is that early intervention provides the best opportunity for constructive and cost-effective change. Although the work by Gibson, Kaczmarowski, and Lore links the pre-project planning process to the owner, constructors can make use of what they have learned.

First, the pre-project plan prior to construction must be tied to the company's business plan. Sometimes, the focus on the project budget leads the project management team to focus on cost-cutting measures that they believe will improve the project's bottom line. However, an effective construction plan that is well thought out by the project team and has their buy-in is important to channeling the project team's efforts on the construction sequence, methods, and risk reduction strategies and to improving communication. A schedule that illustrates the proposed construction approach, as described by the tasks and relationships it embodies, is a reminder of where the team wants to go and how it plans to get there. Because schedules can be presented graphically, they often bridge the boundaries between contractors and subcontractors, contractors and owner, and contractors and their material and equipment suppliers.

Second, in making the pre-project plan meet the company's business needs, many points of view should be included in the planning process. The time dedicated to participation in the pre-project planning effort must be supported by management at all levels, acknowledging that the process will bring rewards that, although tangible, may not be immediately realized. Like all team exercises, it is important that there be a facilitator to keep the team moving in the right direction. However, care should be taken to include all opinions and avoid hierarchical patterns of authority, so that consensus can be reached. The resulting plan and the process of getting to the plan should be documented.

Third, once formed, the team should stay together throughout the construction of the project. The team should meet regularly to discuss the project progress toward the goals initially established and comment on changes to the plan and to the planning process. In each of the three elements of this pre-project planning process, the schedule and scheduler are elemental. They will record the work of the team in a unique and communicable way.

History of Scheduling

Although scheduling has likely been a part of human, and perhaps animal, existence since lunar cycles were observed for hunting and gathering, modern scheduling perhaps began when Henry L. Gantt developed bar charts in 1917. Henry Gantt (1861–1919) was a pioneer of management science who is almost as well known in management sciences circles for his views on productivity and employee compensation as for the bar chart. He developed a means of depicting industrial tasks in a way that easily communicated the tasks, their durations, and their timing to each project participant. Construction borrowed and embraced this technique. A complete discussion of how bar charts are constructed and used appears in Chapter 3.

Two companies, DuPont and Remington Rand, collaboratively developed the *critical path method (CPM)* in the 1950s for the renovation, construction, and maintenance of chemical plants. "DuPont's goal was to optimize and balance the lost opportunity costs of a refinery's downtime with the increased costs of accelerating the renovation."[5] At nearly the same time, the *program evaluation and review technique (PERT)* was developed by the U.S. Navy, in collaboration with Booz Allen Hamilton and Lockheed, to manage the multiple contractors developing the Polaris missile for use in submarines. "The object of this effort was to identify trouble spots quickly and take appropriate action, thus utilizing time and resources as efficiently as possible."[6]

This critical path method evolved into what is known as the arrow diagramming method (ADM) or activity on arrow (AOA) method. The ADM removed the statistical component from the PERT critical path method and replaced it with a deterministic method for assigning activity durations. Later, the *precedence diagramming method (PDM)* evolved replacing the single *finish-to-start relationship* found in the ADM with multiple types of relationships. Each advance has given the planner and scheduler better tools for modeling reality. PDM is discussed fully beginning in Chapter 4, whereas ADM and PERT are covered in Chapters 14 and 15, respectively.

John Fondahl, emeritus faculty at Stanford University and winner of the American Society of Civil Engineer's (ASCE) Peurifoy Construction Research Award in 1990, has been noted as the originator of the modern, deterministic CPM scheduling method. His work has helped constructors effectively model their projects in more flexible and less cumbersome ways than were previously available.

Computerization

One or more of the network diagramming methods can be used to help each project participant visualize the work plan. Analysts can use these tools to identify conflicts and resource allocation problems before work begins, or when there is ample time to develop alternate plans. The use of computers to calculate and display construction project information is an important tool used by today's construction planner. By producing multiple computerized schedules based on different assumptions the construction manager can simulate a variety of corrective actions, analyze the results, and select a solution. The processing speed of the computer, coupled with the sophistication of many construction scheduling programs, provides needed information to managers quickly and efficiently. These programs allow managers to compare the original plan with the current plan at any time during the life of the project. However, this assumes that the original information is updated with actual data on a regular basis. All of these tasks required to provide schedule information are simplified with the computer. It was not until the early 1980s that PC-based construction planning software became available commercially that rivaled large, expensive, and costly to maintain *mainframe* scheduling programs used by large construction companies during the 1970s. Today, we are beginning to see the advent of truly mobile project data-entry tools; collaboration and data sharing that are not location-sensitive; and a variety of Internet, intranet, and extranet applications to aid in planning and scheduling tasks.

Schedule as a Monitor of Project Success

For construction projects, success is typically measured by achieving budget projections while completing the project on time. Other measures of project success include safety, positive customer and public relations, and experiential gains by project personnel. No matter which party—the constructor, the owner, the public—views the project and comments on project success, being on time and on budget is always a primary indication of success.

Although cost and schedule are closely allied, they are often managed by different people and analyzed with different pieces of software. Programs such as Primavera Project Planner® (P3) allow financial data to be tied to activities and can report on their use with respect to time. Even though many P3 users do not cost-load their schedules, schedules are still the best way to monitor timely project completion, to test what-if scenarios when changes are needed, to justify the effects of change orders, to make claims for payment based on time percent complete, and to monitor project success.

When cost and schedule are tied to one another, time/cost comparisons can be made. Graphs and charts can be prepared and can be used to claim payment based on cost percent complete, to project cash needs, and to compare current costs with budgeted costs as a means of monitoring project success.

Conclusion

Scheduling has been used for plan implementation and execution from time immemorial, but it was not until the 1950s that the beginning of modern construction scheduling dawned. Modern schedules help constructors improve their bottom line by identifying problems early that arise from changes to the original plan and by enabling managers to test or simulate their solutions, so that the best plan revision can be selected.

Historical scheduling records can be used to improve future estimates and provide support for change orders and claims. Actual productivities for common activities can be indexed and/or updated based on historical scheduling records. Productivities, which relate directly to activity durations, are influenced by the construction method, crew composition, project location, and local work rules. The use of historical scheduling records in support of change orders and claims is discussed in Chapter 11.

Computerization has made all forms of construction scheduling far easier than when hand-generated reports were the norm. Scheduling programs for today's PCs have improved over the past 20 years, and new electronic technologies have given construction managers the tools to be more profitable (e.g., PDAs and cell phones).

Notes

1. C. H. Oglesby, H. W. Parker, and G. A. Howell, *Productivity Improvement in Construction.* New York: McGraw-Hill, 1989.
2. Ibid., p. 85.
3. Ibid., p. 100.
4. G. E. Gibson, J. H. Kaczmarowski, and H. E. Lore, Jr., "Preproject-Planning Process for Capital Facilities," *Journal of Construction Engineering and Management, 121*(3) (1995): 312.
5. B. L. Bright, A. F. Nagorzanski, and D. F. Sweeney, "Critical Path Method Scheduling and Its Use in Supporting Construction Claims," *Proceedings of 7th Annual Construction Law Conference* (February 10–11, 1994), Houston, TX, found at *http://www.constlaw.org/papers/bright7.pdf* (2003), p. 1 (last accessed 9/12/2003).
6. Ibid.

CHAPTER 2

Activities, Tasks, and Production

Goal

Demonstrate how activities and their elemental components are determined and create a task list.

Objectives

- Discuss level of control and how it manifests in the creation of activities.
- Demonstrate how activity I.D.s are created and used.
- Categorize activities.
- Demonstrate the creation of useful activity descriptions.
- Show how productivity determines activity duration.
- Create an activity list.

Planning and scheduling require that the planner consider the level of control needed to track progress, to identify problems quickly, and to incorporate changes easily. A construction manager could look at building a house or a subdivision of houses and use but one activity or task—"build a house" or "build a subdivision." Managers discarded this level of detail early because there is no intermediate control of time or money. As the work progresses, it is difficult, if not impossible, to tell if the project will finish on time and within budget when only one activity is used to represent the entire project. There are no intermediate *benchmarks,* or markers, with which to measure outcomes.

Task Identification and Level of Detail/Control

As the plans and specifications are examined, the estimator and the project management team develop a plan for construction, based on their individual visualizations for the sequential ordering of needed tasks. Identifying tasks may seem trivial; however, consider the construction of a house. Again, one activity or task can be used to describe the entire house or project—"build a house." Conversely, the activities used to describe the construction might include all of the details, such as purchasing nails, installing individual light fixtures, and sealing ceramic tile grout. At this level of detail, there can be hundreds of activities. The purpose of identifying tasks is to select those activities that are critical to project success and those that are required to control the construction process effectively. Fifty to a hundred activities are generally used for describing the construction of a single house; however, there is no correlation between the number of activities needed to represent a project and the project's size or cost. Controlling the time and cost is the primary issue when selecting activities to represent the project.

Each project manager must determine the appropriate level of detail for describing the project. The resulting activities are used to prepare the initial schedule. As the project progresses, management may also determine that certain areas of the project require more detail, more activities, to achieve the needed control. Management may find other areas that need fewer activities. Changes can, and should, be made to the schedule as needed throughout the life of the project.

Activities and tasks consume time and may use any or all of the resources needed for construction: *permanent or expendable materials;* salaried or hourly labor; rented, leased, or owned equipment; and money. There are three typical types of tasks or activities: *procurement, production,* and *management* activities.[1] Procurement activities represent the purchase and delivery of long lead-time items, such as large or unique pieces of equipment or specialized materials. Procurement activities are very important when they represent owner-furnished equipment. Delays in owner-furnished items can create project delays. Nonowner-furnished procurement activities, or contractor-furnished materials and equipment, require time and have an associated cost. *Fabrication, order,* and *delivery* are words often associated with procurement activities.

Production activities are those needed to accomplish the work and generally include an action verb in their description, such as *install, set, erect, paint, clean,* and *place.* Production activities are the heart of the construction schedule. These activities usually consume the diverse set of resources needed to construct the project.

Management activities are those such as required submittals, owner or engineer approvals, testing, and delays, or activities imposed for more efficient scheduling. These activities take time, sometimes cost the contractor money, and often require input, work, or review by others.

Sometimes, the contract specifications require that the contractor not only stay within the allowed project duration but also meet intermediate deadlines. These events are frequently known as *milestones*. Milestones have no duration and use no resources; they merely mark a point in time. Some milestones mark the end of events, such as project completion, building enclosed, substantial completion, and unit online. These are known as *finish milestones*. *Start milestones* mark the beginning of a specific set of activities, such as notice to proceed, area available for (sub)contractor mobilization, detour open, or building ready for electrification. When many activities begin or end a PDM network, milestones are often used to preserve the one start, one finish convention used in critical path scheduling.

Programs such as Primavera Project Planner® (P3) have a variety of other ways of identifying "activities." P3 uses flags, meetings, and hammocks, among others, whereas Microsoft Project® uses fixed duration, fixed units, or fixed work to identify activities, events, and groups of activities. However, the most common classification is the task.

Activity Descriptions and Identifications

Activity descriptions for production activities should include action-related verbs. Each project activity should have a distinct description. Having multiple activities with the description "Place Concrete Slab" does nothing to identify the location of the slab or to distinguish one slab from another. Therefore, carefully consider how to identify each activity distinctly—"Place Slab-on-Grade, Building 1," "Form 3rd Floor Slab, Recreation Room," and "Install Reinforcing 2nd Floor Cantilever Slab, Forebay" are far more descriptive activity identifications. Each of these descriptions effectively describes the location of the task as well as what is to be done.

In addition to descriptions, activities usually have activity identifications (I.D.s) that are alphanumeric shorthand for the activity. Some schedules use consecutive numbers (1, 2, 3 or 10, 20, 30) as activity I.D.s. Numeric identifications such as these are difficult to read as shorthand; descriptions are needed to make sense of the identifications. Some projects, especially large ones, create more elaborate identification schemes. Figure 2.1 shows how a nine-digit identification might be created to better describe an activity.

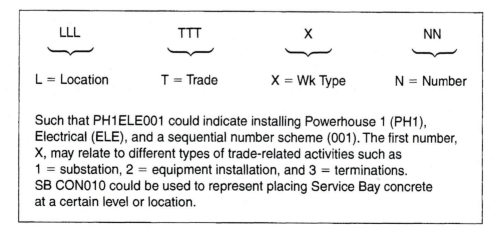

Figure 2.1
Informative alphanumeric shorthand activity identification.

Sometimes, the identifications are assigned to coincide with bid item numbers or with cost account numbers. Any identification scheme that helps the schedule reviewer to identify the activity quickly, especially in a large network, is acceptable.

Durations

Once the activities are identified, their durations must be determined. Estimating activity durations is a matter of evaluating the measurable quantity that the activity represents, determining all of the subtasks included in the activity and their quantities, and estimating *crew* productivities. The term *crew* is meant to include both labor and equipment.

For example, consider the construction of an at-grade concrete slab, often termed slab-on-grade (SOG). Although the slab activity may contain reinforcing and formwork, the primary, measurable quantity is the number of cubic yards or surface area square yards of concrete. What remains is to determine the anticipated productivity, because the productivity and quantity will determine the duration. How many cubic yards can be placed per hour or day?

Then the duration becomes

$$Duration = \frac{Quantity(cubic\_yards)}{Productivity(cubic\_yards\_per\_hour)} = hours; \qquad (2\text{-}1)$$

$$Duration = \frac{total\_hours}{hours\_worked\_per\_day} = days \qquad (2\text{-}2)$$

Many references are available to the constructor for determining production rates for activities. Some of the common commercial references are *Walker's Building Estimator's Reference Book, Richardson's General Construction Estimating Standards,* and R. S. Means construction cost indexes or cost data books. Some of these references incorporate the required subtasks in great detail when providing productivities and costs.

Activities must be broken into identifiable tasks that allow the constructor to control time and cost. For example, if a project requires sixteen 48-inch-diameter drilled and cast-in-place (CIP) piles that are each 35 feet long, the schedule may contain two activities: one for drilling the shafts and another for the forms (if needed), rebar, and concrete placement necessary for constructing the piles. The productivity of the drilling operation and *spoil* removal, obtained from a commercial reference or the company estimator, might be 3 feet per hour for the type of soil encountered and a move, setup, and dismantle time of 3 hours each time a new shaft is drilled, based on the speed of movement for the drill rig and the distance from one hole to the next. Concrete placement rates are determined to average 20 cubic yards (cy) per hour, whereas forming and setting prefabricated rebar cages will take 2 days per pier.

$$Actual\ Drilling\ Time\ Duration = \frac{16\_holes \times 35\_ft\_per\_hole}{3\_ft\_per\_hour} = 186.67\_hours$$

$$Move/setup/dismantle \ Duration = 15 \ moves \times 3 \ hours \ per \ move$$
$$= 45 \ hours$$

There are only 15 move/setup/dismantle subtasks, as it is assumed that the mobilization of the equipment at the first hole and the demobilization at the last hole are accounted for elsewhere. If the drilling crew works 8 hours per day at 100% efficiency, the total drilling duration in days = 186.67 + 45 = 231.67 hours/8 hours per day = 28.96 days. To keep whole-day durations, say 29 days. It is assumed that the removal of the excavated soil or spoil is done concurrently with the drilling. Therefore, there is no additional time duration required, although additional cost is added to the cost of the drilling for the removal of this material.

The concrete placement duration is dependent on the concrete quantity per hole.

$$\text{The concrete Quantity per Drilled Pier} = \frac{\pi}{4}\left(\frac{48 \ in.}{12 \ in. \ per \ ft}\right)^2 \times 35 \ ft \times \frac{1}{27 \ cy \ per \ ft^3} = 16.3 \ cy$$

$$\text{Then the concrete Duration} = \frac{16.3 \ cy}{20cy/hr} = 0.815 \ hours$$

The short duration for placing the concrete does not control the concrete duration because it takes 2 days to fabricate and place the rebar cages and any needed formwork. Therefore, each pier takes 2 days and about 1 hour to complete. If the durations were added, there would be 29 days (drilling) + 32 days (rebar and forms) + 2 days (concrete) = 63 days. This makes an assumption, however, that all the piers are drilled before any forming, reinforcing, or concrete can be installed. The actual sequencing of the subtasks can change this assumption and it may be possible to cut the overall activity duration nearly in half. Chapters 3 and 4 describe how this can be done.

Most computerized scheduling systems generally use whole days for durations. However, some systems allow scheduling by the hour. Unless the majority of the activities have durations of less than 1 day, daily scheduling should be used. It would be difficult to graphically represent an hourly schedule for a project of a month or more in total duration. However, hourly schedules are often used when power plants or manufacturing facilities, such as microprocessor plants, are losing revenue during any construction-related shutdown. Weeks and months may also be used for very long duration projects with long duration activities.

Once tasks have been identified to control the construction and durations have been established, a task list can be developed. The list can be developed similar to an outline, so that more and more detail emerges as each new level of the outline is reached (Fig. 2.2).

Relationships among the activities should be considered, so that the timing and sequencing of all of the activities can be diagrammed. Relationships will be discussed in more detail in future chapters. However, the bar chart information in Chapter 3 relies on activities and when they occur during the project duration. To be effective, this typically requires knowledge of the sequence of the tasks that represent work.

I. Site work

   A. Clear and grub

   B. Survey

   C. Excavation

      1. Common excavation

         a. Bulk excavation

         b. Hand excavation

      2. Rock excavation

Figure 2.2
Task list in outline format.

Activity List Example

The following is an example list of the activities and their *workday durations* needed to build a modest house.

Activity	Duration	Activity	Duration
Clear and *Grub* Site	1	Rough-In HVAC	2
Level and Lay Out Site	2	Plumbing Top Out	1
Excavate Foundation	1	Rough-In Gas/ Electrical	3
Form and Reinforce Foundation	2	Roof Dry-In	1
Place Foundation Concrete	1	Load Roof	0
Place Underground Utilities	1	Exterior Insulation and Vapor Barrier	3
Form, Reinforce, and Place or Set Stem Walls	3	Interior Insulation	2
Place Slab-on-Grade	4	Apply Stucco	5
Place Interior and Exterior Framing	10	Hang, Texture, and Sand Drywall	5
Set Roof Trusses	3	Install Trim Carpentry	3
Install Windows and Doors	1	Exterior Paint	3
		Roofing	2
		Interior Paint	2

Activity	Duration	Activity	Duration
Install Subflooring	1	Test and Adjust All Systems	1
Cabinetry	2		
HVAC Trim	2	Install Flooring (Tile, Carpet, and Wood)	2
Electrical Trim	2		
Plumbing Trim	2	Cleanup	1
Install Countertops	2	Punch List	2
Install Appliances	1	Final Cleanup	1

Durations can be determined through production rates and quantities or from an estimator's experience. The estimator's experience provided the activity durations (minimum 1 day) for the example typical house activity list.

If the activities were to be put into an outline, they might look like this:

I. Site Work

    A. Clear and Grub

    B. Level and Lay Out Site

    C. Excavate Foundation

    D. Place Underground (U/G) Utilities (Fig. 2.3)

II. Concrete Work

    A. Foundation

        1. Form and Reinforce

        2. Place Concrete

    B. Form, Reinforce, and Place (FRP) Stem Walls

    C. FRP Slab-on-Grade (SOG)

Figure 2.3
Place underground (U/G) utilities.

Figure 2.4
Set roof trusses.

III. Structure

    A. Erect Framing

        1. Exterior

        2. Interior

    B. Set Roof Trusses (Fig. 2.4)

    C. Install Insulation

        1. Exterior and Vapor Barrier

        2. Interior

    D. Apply Stucco

    E. Erect Roof

        1. Dry-In (Fig. 2.5)

        2. Load

        3. Apply Roofing

    F. Set Windows and Doors

    G. Install Drywall

    H. Install Subfloor

IV. Electrical/Mechanical

    A. Rough-In

        1. Plumbing (Fig. 2.6)

        2. Heating, Ventilating, and Air Conditioning (HVAC)

        3. Electrical and Gas

    B. Finish Trim

        1. Plumbing

Figure 2.5
Erect roof, dry-in.

Figure 2.6
Rough-in plumbing.

2. HVAC

3. Electrical and Gas

V. Finishes

   A. Paint

      1. Exterior

      2. Interior

   B. Finish Carpentry

   C. Install Cabinets

   D. Install Countertops

   E. Install Appliances

   F. Install Flooring

      1. Carpet

      2. Tile

      3. Wood

VI. Management

   A. Test and Adjust Systems and Appliances

   B. Cleanup

   C. Punch List

   D. Final Cleanup

Conclusion

Identifying tasks that provide the construction manager with an appropriate level of control is essential to implementing a construction plan; however, for unique projects with durations longer than a year, details may only be known in the near term. As these long duration projects progress, more detail can be added to improve planning, response, and control. A list of project tasks can be developed. Durations for each activity can be derived from the plan quantities and expected production rates or from the experience of estimators.

No matter the number of activities or the level of detail selected, a task list is a good place to begin. Using the contract documents and estimate as a guide, the scheduler will develop the most complete task list possible. Some companies prefer to list activities under predetermined headings, so that few omissions occur.

The outline task list can help the scheduler get to an appropriate level of detail while creating the activity list. The outline can later serve as the mechanism for successive levels of project aggregation for reporting, as with a *work breakdown structure* or when using *activity codes* or summary activities. As in the example, the sample project might have thirty-six detail activities, or it might be grouped into the seven upper-level Roman numeral activities. Thus, there is detail for those needing detail and summary for those able to work at the summary level.

Problems and/or Questions

1. Develop an activity list for placing 4-inch outside diameter (O.D.) underground process piping (you choose the material). The pipe run looks like that shown in Figure 2.7, with all lengths in feet and all pipe 4-inch O.D. There is one valve (Fig. 2.8) and one 90° elbow (Fig. 2.9). Assume that the pipe is buried a depth of 4 feet below existing grade and that all nonspecified ground conditions are typical of vacant land in your home state and locality. The diagram is not to scale.

2. Show the calculation(s) required for obtaining the excavation duration for the problem 1 situation.

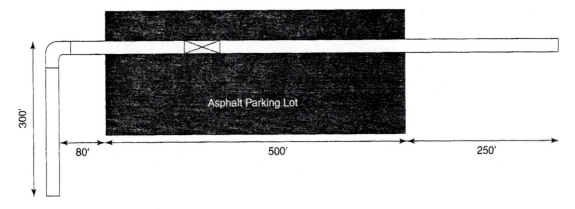

300'

Asphalt Parking Lot

80'   500'   250'

Figure 2.7
Underground pipe run.

Figure 2.8
In-line gate valve.

Figure 2.9
90° elbow.

3. Discuss the procurement and management activities needed for problem 1.

4. Discuss the tie between estimating and scheduling in a company with which you are familiar.

5. Create an activity list for changing a flat tire. State all assumptions.

6. Create an activity list and provide durations for the preparation of a spaghetti dinner. Keep duration units consistent (e.g., all minutes).

7. Obtain a construction schedule from a company (construction or owner) and determine what percentage of the activities are procurement, production, and management. Note if you find any additional activity categories. Submit the schedule with your solution.

8. Find a journal article that comments on the use of management activities. Present a copy of the article and your synopsis.

9. Take a picture of a small structure, such as a bus stop shelter, tree house, built-in-place shed, or swimming pool, and list all of the activities that you would use to control the construction. Include the picture in your presentation.

10. Create an activity list for constructing the bridge in the following diagram. The photos illustrate some of the construction tasks.

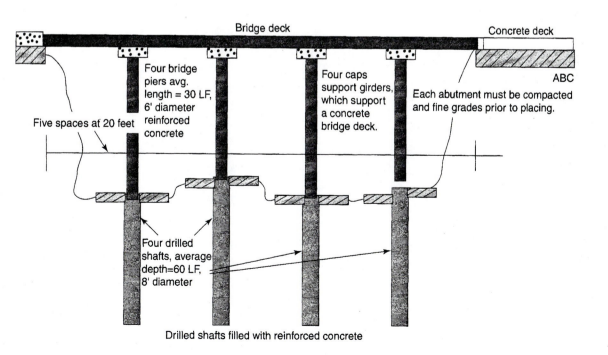

Bridge deck

Concrete deck

Four bridge piers avg. length = 30 LF, 6' diameter reinforced concrete

Four caps support girders, which support a concrete bridge deck.

ABC

Five spaces at 20 feet

Each abutment must be compacted and fine grades prior to placing.

Four drilled shafts, average depth=60 LF, 8' diameter

Drilled shafts filled with reinforced concrete

Shaft drilling.
Photo courtesy of Cliff Schexnayder.

Concrete placement for piers.
Photo courtesy of Cliff Schexnayder.

Bridge piers supported by drilled
shaft piles.

Bridge piers, pier caps, and beams.

Bridge deck prior to concrete placement.

11. Find the duration for the drilled shafts in problem 10 using the text example and productivities.

12. Discuss how to create an activity identification system for a current project. If you have already created the system, justify its strengths and critique its weaknesses. The answer will require a brief description of the project.

Notes

1. Robert B. Harris, *Precedence and Arrow Networking Techniques for Construction.* New York: Wiley, 1978, p. 12.

CHAPTER 3

Bar Charts

Goal

Present the components of a bar chart, a histogram, and an s-curve.

Objectives

- Show bar chart basics:
  - Descriptive attribute columns
  - Time scale
  - Title
  - Legend
  - Bars
- Discuss the distribution of resources.
- Develop a histogram.
- Develop an s-curve.

Introduction

One of the oldest scheduling methods used in construction is the bar, or Gantt, chart. Henry Gantt developed the bar chart to plan and track the progress of manufacturing operations. Recent computerized scheduling techniques have virtually

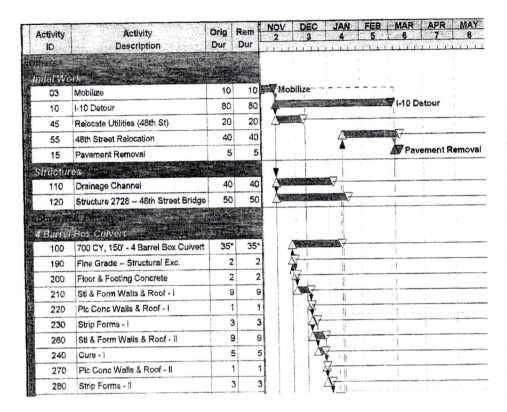

Activity ID	Activity Description	Orig Dur	Rem Dur	NOV 2	DEC 3	JAN 4	FEB 5	MAR 6	APR 7	MAY 8
Others										
Initial Work										
03	Mobilize	10	10	Mobilize						
10	I-10 Detour	80	80					I-10 Detour		
45	Relocate Utilities (48th St)	20	20							
55	48th Street Relocation	40	40							
15	Pavement Removal	5	5					Pavement Removal		
Structures										
110	Drainage Channel	40	40							
120	Structure 2728 -- 48th Street Bridge	50	50							
4 Barrel Box Culvert										
100	700 CY, 150' - 4 Barrel Box Culvert	35*	35*							
190	Fine Grade -- Structural Exc.	2	2							
200	Floor & Footing Concrete	2	2							
210	Stl & Form Walls & Roof - I	9	9							
220	Plc Conc Walls & Roof - I	1	1							
230	Strip Forms - I	3	3							
260	Stl & Form Walls & Roof - II	9	9							
240	Cure - I	5	5							
270	Plc Conc Walls & Roof - II	1	1							
280	Strip Forms - II	3	3							

Figure 3.1
Example bar chart.

eliminated the drafting tasks once required to create, update, and maintain a bar chart schedule.

Bar charts resemble horizontal bar graphs. Each horizontal bar represents a project activity or task, whereas each bar's length represents its duration.

Once a list of tasks has been made and activity durations have been established, it is time to decide how the tasks relate to one another. For a bar chart, the relationships among the activities will define the placement of the bars on the chart. Although relationships must be understood in order to place the activities, the relationships are not usually included on the diagram. However, Figure 3.1 shows a computer-generated bar chart from Primavera® that does show relationships.

Bar Chart Graphical Techniques

Activities are represented as horizontal bars, which are plotted beneath a corresponding time scale. The longer the project, the larger the calendar units should be. Schedules of about 6 months may use a time scale measured day by day. Schedules of years may be depicted on scales of weeks or months. The partial project bar chart in Figure 3.1 shows an approximately 7-month period of a project. Its scale divisions are in weeks, and titles appear by month, with weekly tick-mark divisions beneath each month.

The length of each bar reflects the activity duration. Consequently, bars of 1-day duration would be difficult to represent on the Figure 3.1 time scale. See Activity I.D. 220 in Figure 3.1. Although activities with longer bars have longer durations than those with shorter bars, it may be difficult to discern small differences in duration when the time scale is large compared to the activity durations. In Figure 3.1, the duration of the activity described as Relocate Utilities (48th St) (Activity I.D. 45, duration 20 days) a short bar compared to that of I-10 Detour (Activity I.D. 10, duration 80 days).

In addition to the activity bars and the time scale, most bar charts contain data in columns to the left of the time-scaled area. The activity information may include the activity's identification number, its description, and its duration, as shown on the left side of Figure 3.1. Other information that sometimes appears includes the start and end dates of the activities and activity attributes, such as material quantities; the required management and trade resources; and the responsible person or company.

Sometimes, bar charts are combined with resource graphics. The resources related to each activity can be totaled to form histograms and line graphs. Figure 3.2 shows one way this can be accomplished.

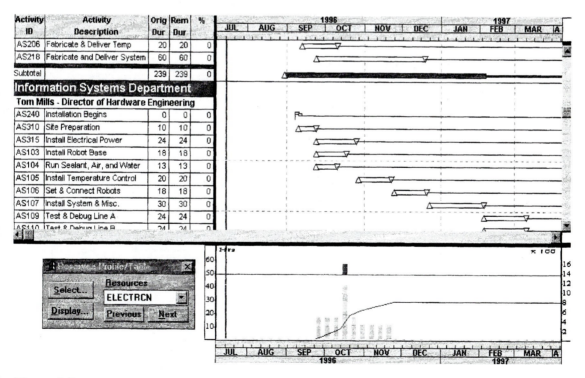

Figure 3.2
Bar chart, histogram, and cumulative curve for electricians.

The resource diagram beneath the bar chart proper in Figure 3.2 shows both a *period histogram* (vertical bars) of needed electrician work hours and a *cumulative curve* (s-curve) of the same resource. The scale to the left of the resource diagram is labeled "hours" and relates to the histogram, whereas the one on the right is "hours × 100" and relates to the cumulative curve. In this diagram, there is a horizontal line at 50 hours indicating a resource limit that has been established for electrician work hours. The horizontal line shows the limit of available electrician work hours. It is clear that there is a week in mid-October when more electrician hours are needed than the number that is available.

Other bar chart diagramming elements include the order in which the activities appear, the chart and column titles, and the legends and other special diagram features. Good diagrams must communicate effectively and be able to stand alone (to be understood if found separated from any supporting documents).

Activities are most understandable when they are ordered by *early start (ES) times*. This means that the activity having the earliest start time is listed and *plotted* first at the top of the diagram. It also means that the activity that happens last is last on the list and diagram. The activities displayed in early start order flow from left to right across the page under the time scale. Figures 3.1 and 3.2 show activities in early start order, cascading from left to right across the time-scale area of the diagram. This type of ordering suggests to the reader the underlying relationships among the activities. Figure 3.2, however, is ordered by ES within subgroups; the information system department subgroup is the most apparent in the figure. This diagram also shows a subgroup *summary activity*.

The effective communication of schedule information often requires groups, subgroups, and summary level activities designed to meet the needs of each schedule reviewer. Construction company senior management may be interested in a summary of

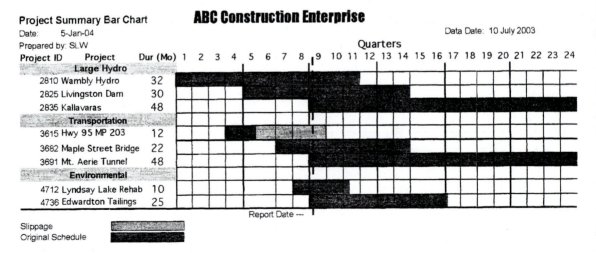

Figure 3.3
Summary bar chart, heavy construction contractor.

all of the company's projects, one bar per project (Figure 3.3). The project manager may want the project detail (Figure 3.4), whereas the electrical supervisor may need to see only the electrical work (Figure 3.5).

The heavy tracked vertical line seen in Figure 3.5 that appears to divide some activities is a *status*, or *data date*, marker. The information to the left of this (end of day 7) line is actual—it has happened—whereas the information to the right (day 8 forward) is planned. Chapter 8 discusses the use of the data date and the impact of actual progress on the schedule.

Each diagram should have a title block, which includes the title (name) of the project, the date of diagram creation, the project start date, and the name of the bar chart creator. Additional information could be included such as revision numbers, chart acceptance information, and a legend. The bar charts in Figures 3.1, 3.2, 3.4, and 3.5 are screen prints generated directly from the scheduling program (Primavera Project Planner®). They are not the printed output that would be submitted to the project management team or the owner. Consequently, they do not have appropriate title and legend information. Figures 3.3 and 3.6 show how title-block entries can appear in either an Excel®-generated or P3-generated bar chart.

The legend identifies the shape, color, and fill characteristics of each bar; when appropriate, the legend also identifies critical activities, those in progress, and those with float. The legend also describes how float is displayed and the meaning of other graphic symbols. For example, some activities are shown in bar charts with the width of the bars narrowed during periods of inactivity. This is known as *necking*. The legend of

Activity ID	Activity Description	Orig Dur	Budgeted Quantity
120	Plumbing Top Out	1	16.00
130	Gas & Electrical Rough-in	3	48.00
140	Roof Dry-in & Load Roof	1	24.00
160	Interior Insultaion	2	16.00
150	Exterior Insulation & Vapor Barrier	3	72.00
180	Hang, Tape, and Seal Drywall	5	80.00
170	Apply Stucco	5	120.00
200	Install Trim Carpentry	3	48.00
190	Exterior Paint	3	48.00
210	Lay Roof Tile	2	48.00
220	Install Cabinets	2	32.00
230	Interior Paint	2	32.00
240	Install Subfloor	1	24.00
250	HVAC Trim	2	32.00
270	Plumbing Trim	2	32.00
280	Install Counter Tops	2	48.00
260	Electrical Trim	2	16.00
290	Install Appliances	1	16.00
300	Test & Adjust All Systems	1	16.00
310	Install Flooring	2	64.00

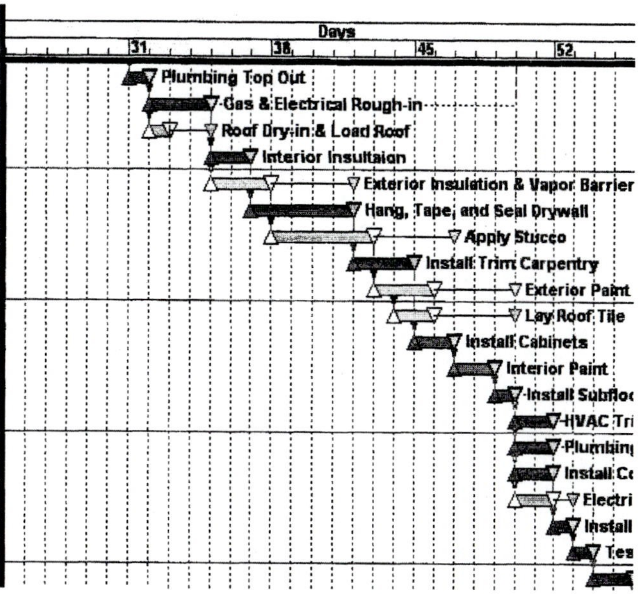

Figure 3.4
Detailed bar chart of a home builder.

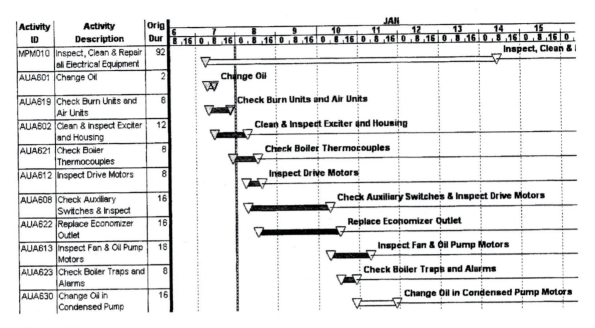

Figure 3.5
Detailed bar chart for power plant shutdown.

Project Start	30OCT00	Early Bar
Project Finish	11APR02	Float Bar
Data Date	30OCT00	Progress Bar
Run Date	13NOV00	Critical Activity

© Primavera Systems, Inc.

202L   Sheet 1 of 2

DEWSC -- ADOT

CON 486 Semester Project

Classic Schedule Layout

Figure 3.6
A bar chart title block, including dates and a legend.

Figure 3.3 also helps the reviewer note a delay of more than one-quarter in the start and finish of project 3615, Hwy 95 MP 203.

All of the bar chart figures also have *horizontal and vertical sight lines*. The horizontal sight lines help the reviewer match the descriptive information on the left of the chart with the bars on the right. Vertical sight lines are used to quickly identify the time periods associated with each activity.

Advantages of Bar Charts

The advantages of using a bar chart include the ease with which they can communicate the project tasks, their durations, and their anticipated start and finish dates to all project participants. Reviewers of the bar chart do not need any special knowledge of scheduling to understand the status of the project, what is expected to be accomplished in the next few time periods, and when the project is expected to end. When schedules are used for simple projects, or for complex projects that can be shown at the summary level or in part, the bar chart is quite suitable. Bar charts are easily constructed for small or simple projects. However, in most cases, bar charts created by a computer program require the construction of the network, including the relationships among the activities.

Disadvantages of Bar Charts

Bar charts typically do not show logic (relationships). P3 requires the user to input the logical framework of the relationships among the activities when constructing the network. After the schedule is calculated, P3 has the option of including or excluding the relationships in the bar chart presentation. Without the logic, or relationships, it is difficult, if not impossible, to determine the downstream effect of changes to activities appearing early in the network. The ability to predict the effects of current changes in the schedule is essential to effective project management. Bar charts for long duration or complex projects are difficult to read when the entire project is shown on one diagram. Bar charts can be used for these types of projects by selecting segments of the project duration or *subsets* of the activities constituting the project.

When bar charts were hand-generated, updating project information was difficult, but now with the use of computer programs it has become easy. Reorganization so that activities can be shown in subsets or in early start order is also simple with computer-generated charts but difficult when done by hand.

Bar Example

The task list developed in Chapter 2 for the construction of a house is presented in this chapter as a bar chart (Figure 3.7). Only a portion of the bar chart is shown because of presentation space limitations. In order to place the bars in their appropriate locations, the underlying logic must be known. In addition, quantities have been added to the activities and are presented as a column to the left of the activity bars. The quantities and logic were derived from experience. When the scheduler lacks the experience to create the logic or to assign the quantities to activities, the estimator, project manager, or superintendent should be consulted.

In Figure 3.7, the vertical sight lines are shown on each day, whereas the horizontal sight lines are shown every five activities. Daily vertical sight lines can be used later to help tabulate resources for the histogram and the cumulative curve.

Activity ID	Activity Description	Orig Dur	Budgeted Quantity	Days
10	Clear and Grub site	1	16.00	
20	Level and Layout site	2	48.00	
30	Excavate Foundation	1	24.00	
40	Form, Rebar, and Place Foundation	3	120.00	
50	Place Underground Utilities	1	24.00	
60	Form, Rebar, & Place Stem Walls	3	120.00	
70	Place Slab on Grade	4	160.00	
80	Erect Framing	10	320.00	
90	Set Trusses	3	96.00	
100	Rough-in HVAC	2	32.00	
110	Set Windows	1	32.00	
120	Plumbing Top Out	1	16.00	
130	Gas & Electrical Rough-in	3	48.00	

Figure 3.7
Example house construction bar chart.

Histograms and S-Curves

Histograms are *period* representations of resource needs or use, whereas s-curves, or *cumulative curves*, show the same information on an accumulated basis. The easiest way to develop a histogram by hand is to begin with the bar chart. Although resources need not be allocated uniformly throughout the duration of an activity, the examples in this section will be confined to the *uniform distribution* of resources. Thus, if an activity requires 1,000 work hours of effort during its 10-day duration, 100 hours per day is required. The bar chart in Figure 3.8 shows how bar charts can be used to tabulate both period and cumulative resources within a project.

The total amount of the analyzed resource can be found at two different locations on the diagram in Figure 3.8. The sum at the bottom of the "Total Resource" column shows 114 resource units. The same total (114) is shown in the "Cumulative Sum" row. The arrows on the bar chart are shown to indicate float (total float) on activities B, D, and F. Activities A, C, and E are shaded to indicate that they are critical. This information, normally found in the legend, is shown above the bar chart, near the title. This bar chart, showing activities and their resource allocations, results in the histogram and s-curve shown in Figures 3.9 and 3.10, respectively.

The histogram is a valuable graphic for use in identifying periods when resources are being used ineffectively. Isolated periods of high resource use suggest a need for the reallocation of resources, if possible, to produce a more uniform profile. If the reallocation of resources is not possible, the manager may need to require overtime work or purchase additional resources. Similarly, if the histogram shows periods when resources are underutilized, such as when labor hours are less than a full crew per day or when only one of three cranes is scheduled for use, the manager may want to rethink the underlying network logic or the reallocation of resources.

Sample Bar Chart						indicates critical activities						⟶ indicates total float			
Activity Information				Work Days											
ID	Desc	Dur	Total Resource	1	2	3	4	5	6	7	8	9	10	11	12	13	14
10	A	4	32	8	8	8	8										
20	B	3	6			2	2	2	⟶								
30	C	7	28			4	4	4	4	4	4	4					
40	D	2	14										7	7	⟶		
50	E	5	25										5	5	5	5	5
60	F	3	9												3	3	3 ⟶
Sum			114														
Period Sum (Early Start)				8	8	14	14	6	4	4	4	4	12	15	8	8	5
Cumulative Sum				8	16	30	44	50	54	58	62	66	78	93	101	109	114

Figure 3.8
Example bar chart tabulation of resources.

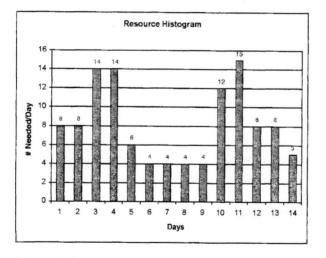

Figure 3.9
Histogram of resources from bar chart shown in Figure 3.8.

The cumulative s-curve is often used to predict cash flow requirements over the life of the project. The s-curve is also a good graphic for comparing the way resources have been used throughout the project with the way they were originally budgeted by plotting both lines on a single graph. Figure 3.10 shows an original budget line with a current project resource line on a cumulative curve. All of these uses of histograms and s-curves are discussed in more detail in Chapters 5 and 6.

The cumulative s-curve generally has a slanted "s" shape, showing slow progress or resource use at the beginning and end of the project and rapid progress during the

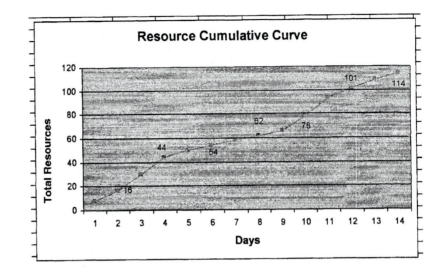

Figure 3.10
s-curve from the Figure 3.8 resources.

middle of the project. The cumulative curve in Figure 3.10 lacks the traditional "s" shape because the underlying histogram in Figure 3.9 is *bi-modal*, not bell-shaped. An s-shaped curve is generated when the corresponding histogram is bell-shaped, or from a normal distribution.

Problems and/or Questions

1. Construct a bar chart for the tasks needed to construct the pipeline construction given in problem 1, Chapter 2. Use all appropriate diagramming techniques.

2. Analyze a bar chart you have used for a company project. Submit the bar chart along with your analysis (compare and contrast the bar chart with best practice for communicating information).

3. Given the bar chart at the top of page 35, draw the corresponding resource histogram and s-curve. Distribute the resources uniformly over each activity duration. Comment on the results (peaks and valley, overall requirement, and duration).

4. Construct a bar chart from your question 5, Chapter 2 information.

5. Construct a bar chart for the project described in question 6, Chapter 2.

6. Create a bar chart based on your knowledge of construction from the following task list for a playhouse.

Question 3 Bar Chart
Use the data below to construct a Resource histogram and s-curve.

Activity	Dur (Days)	Total Resource	Workdays 1	2	3	4	5	6	7	8	9	10	11	12	13	14	15	16
Move to Site	4	2,000																
Clear Site	5	5,000																
Survey Site	3	600																
Grade Site	6	3,000																
Exc. for Sewer	3	6,000																
Exc. for Electric	5	2,000																
Install Sewer	4	1,000																
Install Electric	3	3,000																
Total		22,600																
Period Amount			500	500														
Cumulative Amt.			500	1000														

Playhouse Task List and Information

- Lay out the location for the foundation—1 hour.
- Dig 18″-wide × 12″-deep foundation trench around the 50′ perimeter—8 hours.
- Place and compact aggregate to a nearly full level below a leveled layout string line—2 hours.
- Cut and place treated 2″ × 10″ base plates in the foundation trench. Tamp them into place—3 hours.
- Cut and place treated 6″ × 6″ atop the 2″ × 10″ around the playhouse perimeter. Nail corners together. Square and entire foundation—3 hours.
- Attach 6″ × 6″ to 2″ × 10″ with toed in screws—1 hour.
- Backfill interior of foundation frame with 3″ of aggregate, level, and compact—1 hour.
- Lay 2″ × 16″ × 16″ pavers level with the top of the 6″ × 6″s to fill interior of foundation area. Cut as needed—4 hours.
- Cut and assemble roof trusses (each)—12 hours.
- Cut and assemble exterior walls—16 hours.
- Erect, align, and attach exterior walls—6 hours.
- Add diagonal bracing—1 hour.
- Erect end trusses and align with long roof *purlins*—3 hours.
- Complete the roof framing—5 hours.
- Erect the metal roof cladding, including fascia and drip caps—4 hours.
- Cut and attach exterior plywood sheathing—6 hours.

- Install windows and sills—4 hours.
- Install door—2 hours.
- Install drywall or other interior cladding—10 hours.

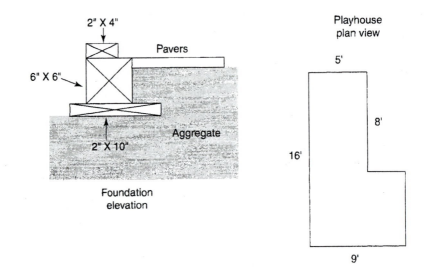

7. From the bar chart shown with the resources provided, construct an early start histogram. Discuss the final profile. Are the peaks and valleys justifiable? Are they good or bad?

Bar Chart Problem 7

Act. I.D.	Activity Description	Dur	Resource Rate per Day	1	2	3	4	5	6	7	8	9	10	11	12	13	14	15	16
10	A	7	300																
20	B	6	250																
30	C	3	400																
60	D	5	125																
40	E	5	300																
50	F	5	400																
70	G	5	300																

Workdays

- Noncritical activity
- Critical activity
- → Float

CHAPTER 4

Precedence Networks

Goal

Present the facets of precedence diagramming and precedence network calculations.

Objectives

- Demonstrate precedence network diagramming, including activities and relationships.
- Discuss all four relationship types and lag values.
- Show how networks are calculated.
- Describe how total and free floats are determined.
- Discuss the importance of float.
- Identify and eliminate redundancies and loops.

Introduction

Precedence networks use the node (rectangular box) to represent an activity, as opposed to the arrow used with activity on arrow (AOA) networks discussed in Chapter 14. Precedence networks are known as activity on node (AON) or the precedence diagramming method (PDM). Relationships among activities are of four different types

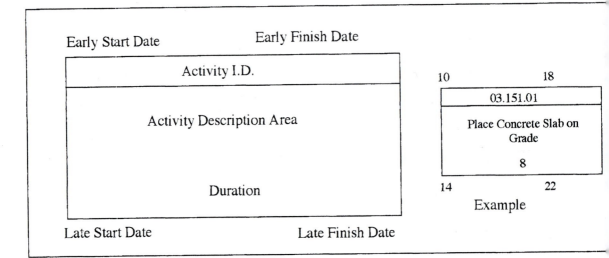

Figure 4.1
Precedence activity box format and an example.

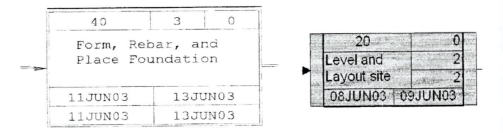

Figure 4.2
P3 nontime-scaled activity box and an on-screen PERT view activity.

including the finish-to-start (FS) as in AOA networks, start-to-start (SS), finish-to-finish (FF), and start-to-finish (SF). Each activity is generally diagrammed with a rectangular box showing all of the pertinent activity data. The activity boxes are then linked together with arrows using one or more of four relationship types. The resulting network fully describes the project to be constructed. Figure 4.1 details the typical precedence activity box as used in this text. Every computer program has its own diagramming convention and may not be faithful to Figure 4.1. Figures 4.2 and 4.3 show activity representations in P3 and MS Project®.

The early and late start and finish dates appear at the bottom of the box in the left-hand activity in Figure 4.2, whereas the I.D., duration, and total float are at the top of the network diagram box. The network diagram has an activity box layout in the legend. The PERT view box on the right of Figure 4.2 shows the early start and early finish at the bottom, the I.D. and the total float across the top, and the *original duration* and *remaining duration* at the right. Formatting in the P3 PERT view allows this layout to be modified.

Mobilization

Start: 6/30/03	ID: 1
Finish: 7/11/03	Dur: 10 days
Res:	

Figure 4.3
A MS Project® on-screen activity box.

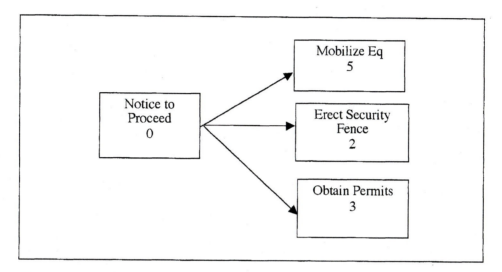

Figure 4.4
Burst from initial activity.

The MS Project ® scheduling program activity box includes labels for the elements of the screen representation, not relying on a legend. The activity I.D. shown in the activity box is established by the program.

All activities except the first one in the network and the last one in the network have logical ties to activities before and after them; they have predecessors and successors. The first activity in the network has no predecessors, and the last activity has no followers, or successors. Any individual activity can be related to multiple activities, thus creating the potential for multiple parallel paths through the network. Bursts, such as the one shown in Figure 4.4, create multiple paths. Merges (Fig. 4.5) are places where multiple paths can recombine. Frequently, the first activity in the network is a burst, whereas the last activity is a merge.

When more than one activity starts or ends the network, a milestone or a pseudo-activity must be added to the precedence network to adhere to the one activity start, one activity finish rule for CPM networks. The milestone start may be "Notice to Proceed," whereas the milestone finish may be "Project Complete." These start and finish activities are shown in Figures 4.4 and 4.5.

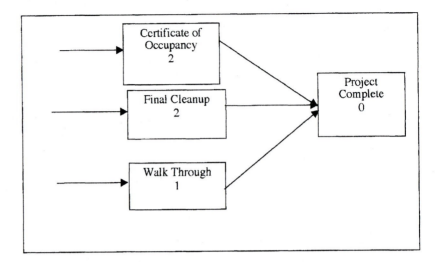

Figure 4.5
Project complete pseudo merge activity.

Network Logic Creation

Computerized precedence scheduling tools allow the user to select from three or four activity relationship types. Each relationship is accompanied by a *lag* value. Lag value indicates the amount of delay between the two elements of the relationship described by the relationship type. A description of activity-linking relationships types and lag values follows. Perhaps the most used logic relationship is the finish-to-start situation, with the most common lag value being zero. Thus, the relationship becomes FS 0, the same as all of the relationships between AOA activities. This means that, as soon as the preceding activity finishes, its successor, or follower, may begin. The activities, shown on the nodes or boxes, are linked together with arrows that have symbols, usually above them, to indicate the relationship and the corresponding lag value between linked activities. Frequently, the FS 0 relationship is excluded from above the arrow because it is the most common. Thus, the arrow is left blank, as shown in Figure 4.6.

Figure 4.6 shows the finish-to-start relationship between Mobilize and Begin Construction. This means that Begin Construction must wait to start until Mobilize has finished. The same is true for activity 30, Site Fencing, which is also related FS 0 with Mobilize. The simplest networks contain only FS 0 relationships. This means that all activities in a FS chain are done in sequence. Portions of a network with such activity chains of this type appears in Figure 4.7. Activities are arranged from left to right without backward (right to left) connecting arrows. When the size of the display is limited, small, circular bubbles act as connectors between the activities. When a bubble is at the right end of an activity box, it contains the activity identification numbers of the following activity. When the bubble appears to the left of the box, it contains the activity

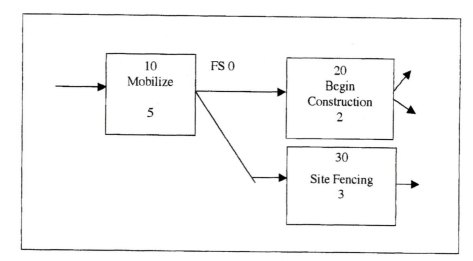

Figure 4.6
Finish-to-start zero lag relationships.

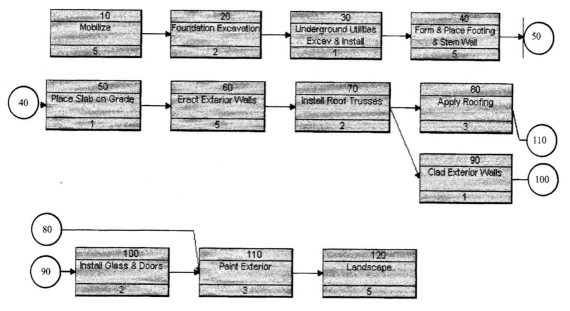

Figure 4.7
Portion of a simple finish-to-start only precedence network.

identification of the preceding activity. Figure 4.7 shows that activity 40 precedes activity 50. It also shows how FS 0 relationships can result in parallel as well as *serial activity placement. Parallel placement* results from one activity proceeding more than one follower, a burst. To return to the serial, or linked, chain of activities, two or more activities must precede or enter one activity, a merge. Figure 4.7 indicates one beginning activity, without a predecessor, and one ending activity, without a successor. The one start, one finish concept is required of good critical path method (CPM) diagramming and calculation techniques, whether AOA or AON.

Good precedence network diagramming uses straight lines with arrowheads, not arcs, to connect the activities. These straight lines can go directly from preceeding activity to follower, as with the lines from activity 70 going to activities 80 and 90 in Figure 4.7. The lines may also proceed diagonally and then terminate in a horizontal line, as in Figure 4.6 between activities 10 and 30.

The first part of this chapter considers only the FS 0 relationship type and lag value. Network calculations and the determination of the project duration are limited to this case initially. Following the initial discussion of networks using finish-to-start zero lag relationships only, the real strength of precedence scheduling is discussed; this being the ability to use multiple relationship types and lag values.

Network Creation Example

Create the network described in Table 4.1. The columns labeled "depends on" indicate the relationship to the activity in the column to the left. Activity A has no predecessor, whereas activity P is preceded by activities A, B, and L. This table contains no activity I.D.s and may contain redundancies. Therefore, I.D.s must be added and redundancies eliminated.

The diagramming of the activities shown in Table 4.1 begins with one activity, and, as there are five activities (A, B, C, E, and F) without predecessors, a milestone or

Table 4.1 Sample of network activities and relationships.

Activity (Dur)	Depends On	Activity (Dur)	Depends On
A (5)	——	M (6)	A and B
B (7)	——	N (10)	M and P
C (8)	——	P (6)	A, B, L
E (3)	——	Q (8)	P
F (12)	——	R (10)	G
G (4)	E	S (3)	K, Q, W
H (3)	C	T (2)	K, Q, W
K (4)	H and F	W (6)	G
L (7)	C		

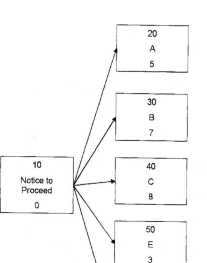

Figure 4.8
Beginning the network for the Table 4.1 data.

pseudo-activity must start the network. Because there are no activity I.D.s, activities will be numbered 10, 20, 30, e.g. by multiples of 10. Figure 4.8 shows how the network begins. Once the network is begun, activities are linked as they appear. Read down the "Depends On" column until all of the "A"s are found. Place an activity box to the right of activity A for all of the activities to which it is linked. In this network, activity A precedes both activity M and P. Activities M and P are also preceded by activity B. Therefore, it may be convenient to position the activity boxes for M and P so that connecting arrows can be drawn from both activities A and B. Place the activity M box to the right of activities A and B first, and then consider activity P. Activity P has another predecessor, activity L, but activity L is not in the first column of activities. When reviewing the list for activity L's predecessor, activity C is found. That means that activity L will go in activity column 3 because C is in activity column 2. And, because activity L goes in activity column 3, activity P must go in activity column 4 to avoid looping, the arrows backward. Figure 4.9 shows the network including the activities described thus far.

The placement of the activities boxes is facilitated by expanding the original table, as shown in Table 4.2. When networks are created without a table, as is often the case, trial and error will lead to the appropriate placement of activities so that the arrows will all go from left to right and the crossing of arrows will be minimized.

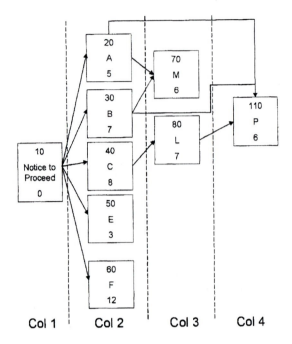

Figure 4.9
Adding activities.

Table 4.2 Activity placement columns.

Activity (Dur)	Depends On	Col	Activity (Dur)	Depends On	Col
A (5)	– 1	2	M (6)	A 2 and B 2	3
B (7)	– 1	2	N (10)	M 3 and P 4	5
C (8)	– 1	2	P (6)	A 2, B 2, L 3	4
E (3)	– 1	2	Q (8)	P 4	5
F (12)	– 1	2	R (10)	G 3	4
G (4)	E 2	3	S (3)	K 4, Q 5, W 4	6
H (3)	C 2	3	T (2)	K 4, Q 5, W 4	6
K (4)	H 3 and F 2	4	W (6)	G 3	4
L (7)	C 2	3			

The predecessor (Notice to Proceed) of all of the activities without dependencies (A, B, C, E, and F) goes in activity placement column 1. If the predecessor is in column 1, the successor activity must go in column 2 to keep the arrows flowing from left to right. If there was only one activity without a predecessor, it would go in column 1, not in column 2. Activity K has predecessors in columns 2 and 3; therefore, it must be

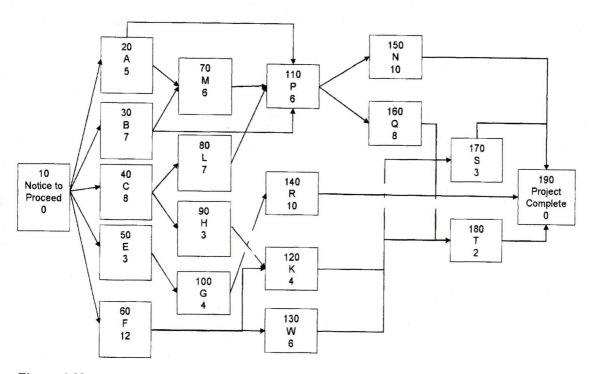

Figure 4.10
Example network.

placed in the next highest column, column 4. Figure 4.10 shows the completed network diagram. Because activities N, R, S, and T have no followers, or successors, a finish milestone has been added to preserve the one start, one finish rule. Note that, when arrows cross, the sense of the direction must be preserved. A break in one of the arrows was used here—for example, in the arrow between activity Q and activity T. Although arrows generally go from the right side or end of one activity box to the left or beginning of another activity box, sometimes the arrows can enter either the top or the bottom of an activity box to help clarify the relationship. In addition, sometimes arrows are merged before reaching the beginning of their predecessor boxes to reduce line clutter in the diagram.

Project Duration Determination

PDM networks are calculated similarly to ADM networks. Forward and backward passes are used to determine the project duration as well as the early and late dates and to provide the information necessary to calculate floats. PDM networks begin at time zero. Therefore, the early start (ES) of the first activity in the network is equal to zero.

Forward Pass

To determine the project duration, a forward pass of calculations must be done. The forward pass establishes the early start (ES) and early finish (EF) dates for each activity. Although only FS 0 relationships have been discussed thus far, each of the four relationship types requires its own calculation to determine the early dates of activities after the first activity. The formulae for all finish-to-start relationships are presented in equations 4-1 and 4-2.

$$Early\_Finish_{activity} = Early\_Start_{activity} + Duration_{activity} \qquad (4\text{-}1)$$

$$Early\_Start_{follower} = \underset{\forall predecessors}{Max} \quad (Early\_Finish_{activity} + Lag\_Value_{between\_them}) \qquad (4\text{-}2)$$

Figure 4.11 shows a sample calculation for the FS relationship type with lag value equal to zero.

In Figure 4.11, if activity 110 begins on day 45 (early start), then its early finish is 50 which is the early start date plus the activity duration. Because the EF of activity 110 is 50, the ES of 120 is also 50 (50 + lag of 0). In addition, the corresponding early finish of activity 120 is 52 (50 + 2 duration).

Remember, when calculating the network by hand, the early start of the first activity in the network is always at the beginning of day zero. Thus, activity 10, Mobilize, in Figure 4.7 begins on day zero and ends on day 5 (EF = ES (0) + Duration (5) = 5). All of the activities in Figure 4.7 are related FS 0. If more than one activity precedes another activity (the merge activity), the early start of the merge activity equals the largest, or maximum, of the early finish dates of its predecessors (Figure 4.12). Here, activity X has 3 predecessors. The latest (maximum value) early finish of the predecessors is workday 45 on activity M. Therefore, the early start of activity X (ES$_X$) equals this maximum, or 45.

Early starts and finishes are calculated from the first activity in the network to the last activity. The early finish (EF) of the last activity in the network is the calculated *project duration.*

Figure 4.13 shows a network with the forward pass completed and its calculated early start and early finish dates shown.

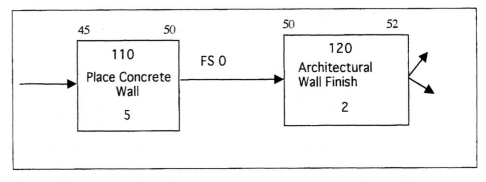

Figure 4.11
Sample activity early start and finish dates.

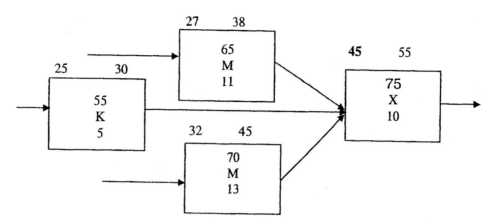

Figure 4.12
Forward pass merge activity, early start calculation.

Backward Pass

The backward pass provides the late start (LS) and late finish (LF) dates for each activity. These dates are shown below each box and are used in conjunction with the early dates to determine the *criticality* of each activity and to identify any available float.

The backward pass begins at the terminal, or last, activity in the network. For the Figure 4.13 network the terminal activity is activity 120, Landscape. For the terminal activity the early dates are simply copied to the late date location, so that the late finish is the same as the early finish and the late start is the same as the early start. Refer to Figure 4.1 for a reminder of the date locations. When proceeding backwards through the network, the forward pass process is conducted in reverse. For the FS 0 relationship, the late finish (LF) of an activity is equal to the earliest LS of all of its follower activities. The late start of an activity is equal to its late finish minus its duration. Equations 4-3 and 4-4 provide backward pass calculation information for all FS relationships. The minimum value is used on the backward pass at a burst.

$$Late\_Finish_{activity} = \underset{\forall\,followers}{Min}\;(Late\_Start_{follower} + Lag\_Value_{between\_them}) \qquad (4\text{-}3)$$

$$Late\_Start_{activity} = Late\_Finish_{activity} - Duration_{activity} \qquad (4\text{-}4)$$

The result of the backward pass is that the LS of the first activity should be zero, just as its ES is zero. Test your backward pass calculation skill on Figure 4.13 and then check the results against Figure 4.14.

Figure 4.14 has four activities that are not critical. Their early start and early finish dates are earlier than their late start and late finish dates. These facts are important in the discussion of float.

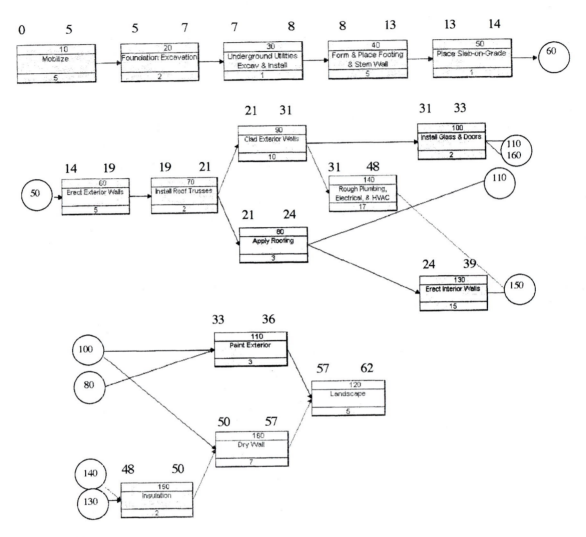

Figure 4.13
Forward pass early start and finish dates.

Finish-to-Start with Lag Value Greater Than Zero

Finish-to-start relationships with a lag value greater than zero are often used to account for resource constraints, such as concrete curing, crane movement, or equipment mobilization, whereas those with a lag value of zero indicate the possibility of an immediate succession of activities. Finish-to-start relationships with a lag value require calculation using the same formulae as those shown with finish-to-start zero lag.

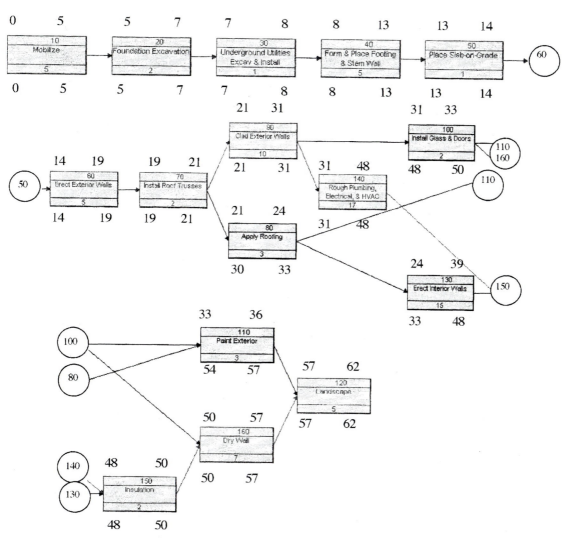

Figure 4.14
Forward and backward pass early start and finish dates, and late start and finish dates.

Figure 4.15 shows the calculation of the forward pass for three finish-to-start activities with lag greater than zero.

In Figure 4.15, the difference between the finish of activity A and the start of activity B is 3, or the value of the lag. Similar observations can be seen with the finish of activity B and the start of activity E, as well as with activities C and G. Note that activity A is related to activity C with an FS 0 relationship.

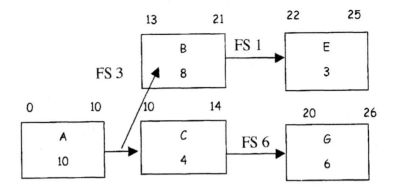

Figure 4.15
FS activity relationship with a lag value greater than zero.

Additional Activity Relationship Types

Besides the finish-to-start activity relationship, there are start-to-start, the finish-to-finish (FF), and the start-to-finish (SF) relationships. Each of these relationship types requires some adaptation to the previously discussed early and late date calculations. Total float calculations are unaffected by the relationship types that join the activities. A discussion of float calculations is provided later in this chapter.

Start-to-Start (SS)

The SS relationship is used for activities whose starts are related. SS relationships are used to relate activities that are done in parallel. For example, when constructing a building of structural steel, it is expected that the steel will be sprayed with fireproofing material before the exterior walls are erected. The fireproofing activity for a multistory building can start before the structural steel is complete on all floors. Therefore, the steel erection can precede the fireproofing with a start-to-start relationship. It is also suggested that other relationships be used to constrain the finish of the fireproofing activity (see the finish-to-finish discussion). For start-to-start relationships, use equations 4-5 and 4-6 to calculate the early dates.

$$Early\_Start_{follower} = \underset{\forall\ preceding\_activities}{Max}\ (Early\_Start_{activity} + Lag_{between\_activities}) \qquad (4\text{-}5)$$

$$Early\_Finish_{follower} = Early\_Start_{follower} + Duration \qquad (4\text{-}6)$$

SS relationships help depict how activities can be done in parallel. The many activities needed to describe paving provide a vivid mental image of how SS relationships can be used.

Using the relationship signifier on the arrow connecting the activities can help the hand-scheduler make appropriate calculations. The dashed arrows in Figure 4.16 show

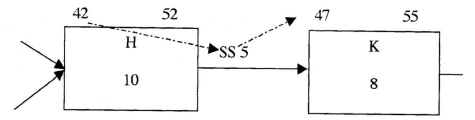

Figure 4.16
Start-to-start activity relationship.

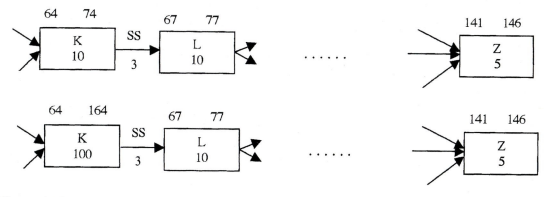

Figure 4.17
SS dramatic activity duration change demonstration.

that the start of H plus the lag value is equal to the start of K ($ES_K = ES_H + lag = 42 + 5 = 47$).

Some computational algorithms calculate the network so that the early finish of the last activity, the one without successors, defines the project duration. This procedure can create problems when the duration of an activity related start-to-start to its follower(s) increases dramatically through either project changes or erroneous reporting. Figure 4.17 demonstrates this point.

In Figure 4.17, the duration of activity K goes from 10 days to 100 days, yet the early dates of activities L and Z are unchanged. To keep the intent of finding the real project duration, activities such as K should also have relationships that tie their finish to another activity, even if K is only tied to the last activity, Z. Misunderstandings about project duration would be avoided if K were also related FS 0 to Z; the result would reflect the change in duration of activity K, as shown in Figure 4.18.

Another precedence diagramming graphical presentation technique shows the arrow for the SS relationship from the start of activity H to the start of activity K in Figure 4.19. In this type of diagramming, the lag type is generally omitted and understood by the way the connecting arrow appears. However, the lag value is still included on the arrow connecting the two activities.

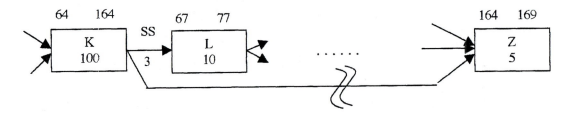

Figure 4.18
Activities with multiple relationships.

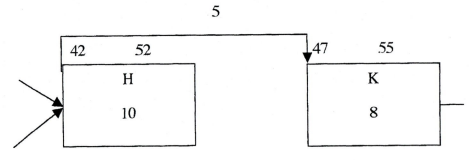

Figure 4.19
Start-to-start activity relationship with alternative diagramming method.

Finish-to-Finish (FF)

With the FF relationship, the finish of one activity controls the finish of another, following activity. FF relationships are similar to SS relationships in that they are frequently used with activities that are performed in parallel. For example, when
constructing a home, it is expected that the drywall cannot be finished until all of the
wall insulation is complete. Although there may be a start-to-start relationship between
these two activities, there can also be a finish-to-finish relationship. The finish of the
wall insulation signals that the drywall may also be completed. For finish-to-finish relationships, use equations 4-7 and 4-8 to calculate the early dates.

$$Early\_Finish_{follower} = \underset{\forall FF\_predecessor\_activities}{Max} (Early\_Finish_{activity} + Lag_{between\_activities}) \quad (4\text{-}7)$$

$$Early\_Start_{follower} = Early\_Finish_{follower} - Duration \quad (4\text{-}8)$$

Figures 4.20 and 4.21 show how finish-to-finish relationships are calculated. In
Figure 4.20, activity L may finish 4 days after activity G finishes. The dashed arrows
can be used to obtain the early finish of activity L. The early finish of activity L is equal
to the early finish of activity G plus the lag between them, or 102 + 4 = 106. The early
start of activity L is obtained by subtracting its duration from its early finish.

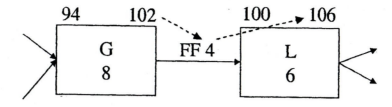

Figure 4.20
A FF activity relationship.

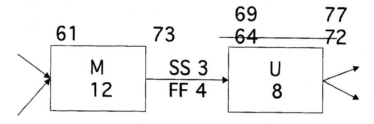

Figure 4.21
Multiple activity relationships.

Figure 4.21 shows multiple activity relationships, both SS and FF. In this example, the FF 4 controls the start and finish of activity U—it creates the latest early start and early finish pair of dates. Some calculation algorithms allow activities to be split (to be discontinuous), starting as early as possible and finishing as late as possible with some nonwork period within the activity's duration. If U were discontinuous, it would begin on day 64 and finish on day 77, with 5 nonworkdays during its duration. This book will focus only on continuous activities. This means that *the latest early date pair* will be used without allowing any nonwork periods during the project duration.

Start-to-Finish (SF)

The SF relationship is used to identify activities whose starts are related to the follower's finish. It is difficult to identify a pair of construction activities that are related SF. Most uses seem to be in the mechanical or electrical construction area. Use equations 4-9 and 4-10 to calculate the early dates of the activities.

$$Early\_Finish_{follower} = \underset{\forall\, predecessor\_activities}{Max} (Early\_Start_{activity} + Lag_{between\_activities}) \qquad (4\text{-}9)$$

$$Early\_Start_{follower} = Early\_Finish_{follower} - Duration \qquad (4\text{-}10)$$

In Figure 4.22, use the dashed arrows to follow the relationship for the calculations. Here, the early start of activity G plus the lag value equals the early finish of

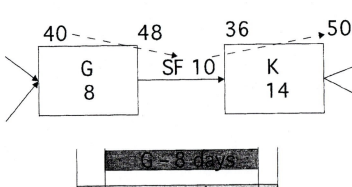

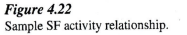

Figure 4.22
Sample SF activity relationship.

activity K (40 + 10 = 50). The early start of activity K is equal to the early finish of activity K minus its duration.

Figure 4.22 shows an SF relationship and its resulting bar chart. The bar chart suggests that activity K precedes activity G instead of being its successor. If the SF lag value is greater than the duration of the predecessor, the start of the follower will be earlier than the ES of the predecessor, as with activities G and K in Figure 4.22. If the initial network activity is tied SF to a follower with a lag value greater than its duration, the follower will start before the project start date. Consequently, it is recommended to use this relationship with care.

Redundancies

When creating schedules and network diagrams, care should be taken to avoid *redundancies*. Some typical redundancy examples are shown in Figures 4.23 and 4.24.

In Figure 4.23, once A is related to B with an FS relationship, no matter whether B goes directly to C or it goes through a chain of activities to reach C, A's relationship to C, which is also FS, is redundant as long as the lag values between A and B and A and C are equal. Redundant relationships are unnecessary. Since the start of activity A controls the start of activity B in Figure 4.24, no matter how B is related to C or any number of activities prior to C, it creates an SS relationship between A and C, redundant as long as the lag values between A and B and A and C are equal.

Increasing the duration of A or B or changing their start dates (Figures 4.23 and 4.24) does not change the activity that pushes activity C, even when there are other relationships between B and C. Redundancies can be demonstrated. Redundant relationships do not cause calculation or logic errors; however, they create unneeded work in maintaining the network and consequently should be avoided.

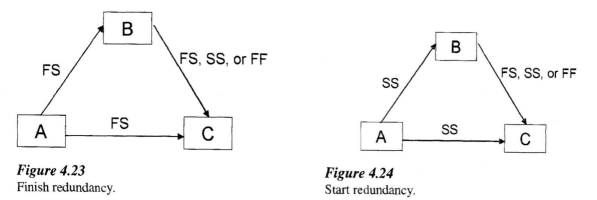

Figure 4.23
Finish redundancy.

Figure 4.24
Start redundancy.

Float

The total float or, in most cases, contingency time, is often, by contract language, shared equally between the contractor and the owner. Specifications often follow or adapt the language found in U.S. Army Corps of Engineers specifications that state that the float is not for the exclusive use of the contractor or the owner. Instead, the float is to be shared.

> Float or slack is defined as the amount of time between the early start date and the late start date, or the early finish date and the late finish date, of any of the activities in the NAS schedule. Float or slack is not time for the exclusive use of or benefit of either the Government or the Contractor.[1]

The word *float*, in its construction context, is consistent with the notion of leeway and flexibility. In general, float in contract documents relates to total float, or the amount of time an activity can be delayed without delaying the project completion. Back in Figure 4.14, the longest path that proceeds from the beginning activity, Mobilize, and terminates at the last activity, Landscape, is the critical path and creates the 62-day project duration. Although there can be more than one critical path in a network, the Figure 4.14 network contains only one such path. The critical path is usually the path with zero *total float*.

Constraints added to activities within the network can create critical paths within the network of negative or positive total float values or abbreviated critical paths not going through the entire network. The constraints topic will be discussed further in Chapter 8.

By definition, delaying any activity on the critical path also delays project completion. Consequently, other activities not on the critical path have float (total float) or flexibility. To calculate the total float of an activity, simply subtract the early finish date from the late finish date. Thus, for activity 60 in Figure 4.14, Erect Exterior Walls, the total float is $19 - 19 = 0$, so this is a critical path activity and has no float.

$$Total\_Float_{activity} = Late\_Finish_{activity} - Early\_Finish_{activity} \qquad (4\text{-}11)$$
$$TF = LF - EF \qquad (4\text{-}12)$$

However, activity 110, Paint Exterior, has a total float of $57 - 36 = 21$ days. This means that the painting activity can be delayed or have its duration extended a maximum of 21 days without creating an impact on the 62-day project duration. Total float is consistent (of the same magnitude) for all activities in a chain of activities, the virtual activity. In Figure 4.11, activities 80 and 130 both have 9 days of total float, but it is apparent that total float is shared among all of the activities in the float chain of activities. If the duration of activity 80 were extended 3 days, the total float in both activities (80 and 130) would be diminished by 3. This means that activity 130 could no longer be delayed 9 days. Instead, it could be delayed only 6 days without a change in the project duration.

Because the specifications often say that float is to be shared between the owner and the contractor, delays created by the owner will not necessarily generate compensatory extensions to the project duration if the path contained ample shared float. This is an important consideration in construction project time management. Total float calculations, equations 4-11 and 4-12, are independent of the relationships between the activities. This is not true of free float.

Free float, another type of float that is often considered in construction, is the amount of time an activity can be delayed without delaying any of its successors or the project completion. For the finish-to-start relationship, free float (FF) is

$$Free\_Float_{activity\_w/FS} = Min\_ES\,(Early\_Start)_{follower} - Lag_{between\_activities} -$$
$$EF\,(Early\_Finish)_{activity} \tag{4-13}$$

Thus, for activity 80 in Figure 4.14, which goes to both activity 110 and 130, the FF is the minimum value calculated using equation 4-13. Between activities 80 and 110, $FF_{80} = 33 - 24 = 9$. However, between activities 80 and 130, $FF_{80} = 24 - 24 = 0$. Therefore, the free float of activity 80 is zero. If activity 80 is delayed just 1 day, activity 130 will also be delayed 1 day. Activity 110 has only one successor, activity 120. Activity 110's FF is 21 days ($57 - 36$). Free float measures the individual flexibility of an activity with its most closely related follower. If an activity has only one predecessor, such as activity 70, then any movement of the predecessor will cause movement in the activity. Therefore, the FF of the predecessor is always zero. All of the activities on the critical path have FF = 0, just as they have TF = 0. When a network has no imposed constraints, FF is always less than or equal to the total float for each activity. When there are no imposed constraints the total and free floats of activities on the critical path (CP) are zero.

The equations for free float with SS lags, FF lags, and SF lags follow:

$$FF_{activity\_wl\_SS} = ES_{follower} - Lag\_Value - ES_{activity} \tag{4-14}$$
$$FF_{activity\_wl\_FF} = EF_{follower} - Lag\_Value - EF_{activity} \tag{4-15}$$
$$FF_{activity\_wl\_SF} = EF_{follower} - Lag\_Value - ES_{activity} \tag{4-16}$$

Fragnets

Fragments of networks or subnetworks that are used repeatedly can be developed and stored for future use. *Fragnets,* as they are called, can represent several activities that are frequently related to one another in the same way and have durations that change very little. Using fragnets can make the construction of a new project schedule much faster than beginning from scratch each time a common project or set of tasks is undertaken. The key is to save only those fragnets that will be used consistently and to adopt a constant activity identification scheme. If the identification scheme is effectively managed, each time two or more fragnets are linked, the numbering schemes mesh and little manipulation is needed. Care should be used when developing a company plan for activity identification, especially if the company expects to merge multiple projects. Multiple project scheduling is addressed in Chapter 18.

Fragnet Example.

The fragnet shown in Figure 4.25 illustrates a chain of five activities that could be repeated more than once in a network or in multiple networks. Fragnets are stored in computer scheduling programs for repeated use.

Loops

When two or more activities are linked in a circular manner, such as those shown in Figure 4.26, the logic cannot proceed from the beginning of the network to the end of the network. Figure 4.26 shows two network logic loops. The first begins with A, goes to C, then to G, and back to A. In addition, activities A, B, F, G, and A again form another loop. Loops are errors in logic and must be fixed before the network can be calculated properly. The logical relationships in a network must not create circular connections.

The errors that create loops are usually found in the relationships where the arrow turns backward. Perhaps the follower of activity G should not be activity A.

Figure 4.25
A fragnet for major equipment purchases.

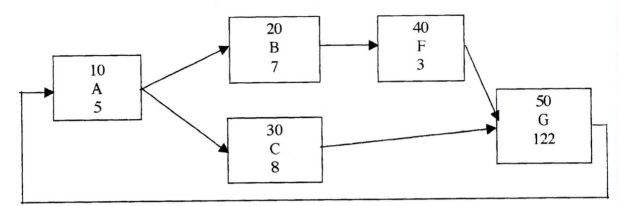

Figure 4.26
Two loops.

Problems and/or Questions

1. Draw a precedence network diagram to represent the activities shown in the table below.

2. Answer the following:
   a. What is the project duration?
   b. List the activities on the critical path.
   c. What is the free float on activity N?
   d. What is the total float on activity F?
   e. What are the early start and finish dates on activity H?
   f. What are the late dates on activity D?
   g. What activity(ies) has (have) the largest amount of total float and how much is it?
   h. What activity(ies) has (have) the most free float and how much is it?

Activity	Duration	Follower	Relationship
A	7	B, D	FS 0
		C	FS 2
B	3	E	SS 1
		F	FF 0
C	8	F	SS 5
		G	FS 3
D	7	H	SF 10
		K	FS 0

E	10	L	FS 0
F	4	L	FS 4
		M	FS 0
G	2	M	FS 0
H	5	M	FF 3
		N	FS 0
K	2	N	FS 2
L	8	P	FS 0
M	7	P	SS 2 and FF 1
N	4	P	FS 0
P	6		

3. Discuss how the understanding of float on construction activities can improve project management practices.

4. Develop a fragnet that would be used frequently for the projects you manage. Show all relationships and durations. Indicate what precedes the fragnet and what follows in general terms. Estimate the percentage of the projects done each year for which this fragnet would apply.

5. Calculate the dates and floats for the network diagram below. Identify the critical path.

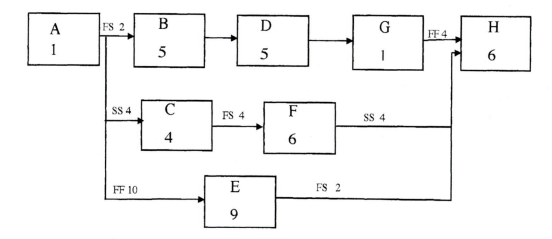

6. Using the network on the next page, answer the questions that follow.
   a. What are the early start and early finish of activity N?
   b. What are the late start and late finish of activity M?
   c. What are the total and free floats on activity P?

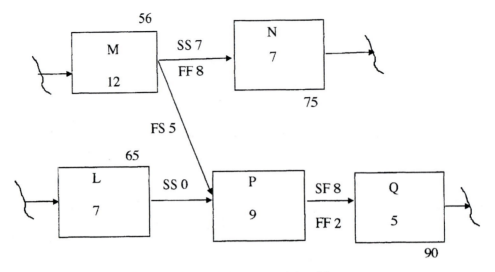

d. What is the total float on activity Q?

e. What is the free float on activity L?

1. Draw a precedence network diagram from the following activity information. Determine the project duration and identify the critical path. Note: The relationship between the activities flows from predecessor to successor.

Activity	Duration	Successor	Relationship
		B	FF 8
A	8	C	SF 6
		D	FS 0
B	12	E	FS 4
C	5	E	FS 0
		F	FS 0
D	8	F	FS 0
		G	FS 0
E	6	H	FS 0
F	11	H	SS 5
		I	FS 0
G	5	J	SS 7
H	7	K	FS 0
I	6	K	FS 0
J	15	K	FF 8
K	12		

7. For the following PDM network, perform forward and backward pass and determine the project duration. Highlight the critical path and tabulate the ES, LS, EF, LF, TF, and FF for each activity.

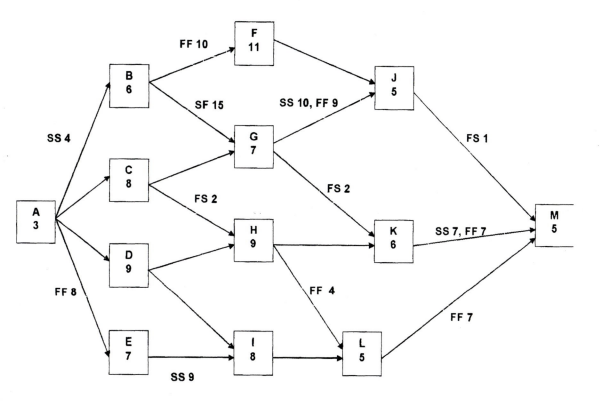

8. From the information in the following table,

    a. Draw a PDM network diagram.

    b. Draw the bar chart and highlight the critical path.

    c. Draw a histogram and a cumulative s-curve for the resources provided.

Activity	Duration	Depends On	Resources
A	5	——	2,000
B	6	——	6,000
C	5	A	7,500
D	4	A	6,000
E	6	A	4,200
F	3	B	3,600

Activity	Duration	Depends On	Resources
G	5	B	4,000
H	9	C	4,500
I	4	C	3,600
J	3	G, H	4,800
K	4	F, H, E, D	2,400
L	6	I, J	4,800
M	5	H, E, D	6,000

9. Answer the questions about the diagram that follows:

    a. What is the project duration?

    b. What is the free float on activity G?

    c. What is the total float on activity E?

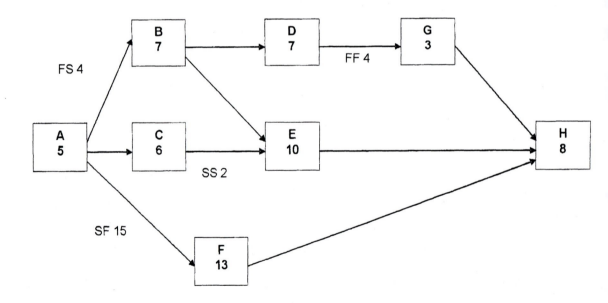

Notes

1. *http://www.law.gwu.edu/asbca/decision/pdf2000/50136.pdf.* p. 2 "Armed Services Board of Contract Appeals, Opinion by Administrative Law Judge Younger.

SECTION TWO

RESOURCE MANAGEMENT

CHAPTER 5

Resource Allocation

Goal

Link cost and schedule, so that the time value of money and use of other resources is clear to the user of the schedule.

Objectives

- Describe resource allocation to activities.
- Identify resource units.
- Provide cost theory:
  - Duration distributions versus deterministic durations
  - Crash and normal costs, and durations
  - Cost slope matrices
  - Project costs
    - Direct cost
    - Indirect cost
    - Total cost
  - Fondahl's envelope of costs
- Describe and demonstrate the Modified Siemens' Method for crashing.

Introduction

Each activity uses time and usually one or more of the following resources: money, labor, materials, and equipment. Even subcontracted work and procurement, shown as activities in the project schedule, have a cost and duration. Some companies track resources other than time in their schedules because resources are generally limited and costly. Understanding the aggregated project resource demands can help the manager identify where resource needs outstrip supply. These demands are produced by the activity sequences in the network and this is usually done before the project begins. Work sequences can be changed, work hours per week increased, or additional resources obtained to meet demands higher than planned supply. On some projects, major pieces of equipment play an important role in schedule arrangement and preparation. In some geographic locations, specially trained or limited labor availability can critically influence schedule decisions.

The resources considered the most critical should be assigned to each applicable activity, and a histogram that tabulates each resource on an appropriate time scale should be constructed. This graphic representation must use a time scale that allows the reviewer to clearly identify resource demands in excess of supply. For example, if only one crew is available, using a weekly time frame for resource accumulation might hide an overallocation. If two crews are required on day 1 and one crew for the next 3 days, but no crew the 5th day, the result is a weekly total of 5 crew-days, or an average of one crew per day. It would appear that one crew per day would meet resource availability limits. However, the two crews demanded on day one would be hidden. Because the limit in the example is one crew and seems quite small, the over allocation may not seem problematic. This 1-day overage could be solved by a second shift that day, with overtime, by extending the activity duration or by finding an additional crew for 1 day. All of these potential solutions come with an increased cost, and at least one solution may lead to a delay in the project completion. Additionally, overallocation may not be limited to 1-day durations amid an entire project.

If crews worked 8-hour days and there were three crews, 24 crew hours would be available each day. The histogram in Figure 5.1 suggests that, on 4 days (day 5 through day 8) the resource requirement exceeds crew availability. The histogram also demonstrates more about the distribution of the resource. On many days, less than one crew is required and there are only 4 days on which nearly the full complement of three crews is required within the 22-day project duration. Underallocation or oversupply of available resources is also problematic and costly. If many projects are merged into a *master schedule,* it is important to balance the crew resource so that every day, or nearly every day, all three crews are fully employed. Of course, this means that the reduced productivity due to new work environments and, potentially, from travel time to new locations must be factored into the need and duration associated with the activities using these crews. This topic will be covered in more detail in Chapters 6 and 18.

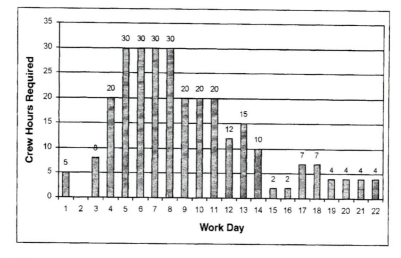

Figure 5.1
Periodic resource histogram.

Resource and Cost Descriptions

The description of resources should include the unit of measure, such as CY concrete, carpenter hour, crew hour, crane hour, and pounds rebar. Even if the resource that is described is money, dollars are not necessarily enough of a description. Instead, the scheduler may want to use direct cost or bid-value to identify the resource clearly and so that new entries for added activities or updates of existing-activity resource data use appropriate units.

Costs can be allocated as a function of each resource such that the hourly cost of a crew is assigned to *costs* and the hourly use of the crew per day is assigned as a *resource* to the appropriate activity. Costs can be broken up into cost categories, such as labor and materials, and cost accounts representing a subset of each category, or they can be kept as simple resources.

Resource Assignments to Schedule

Resources may be assigned to each activity in a uniform fashion such that, if there were ten periods during the duration, each would receive 10% of the resource allocation (Figure 5.2). This most common method of distribution, and the Primavera® and MS Project® default is the uniform distribution across the entire duration. In addition, the shape of the resource distribution can vary such that all of the resources and costs are distributed to 1 day or in a variety of other distributions.

Figure 5.3 shows a normal distribution for the ten periods of an activity and the resulting cumulative curve. The cumulative curve is s-shaped. Similarly, if 100% of

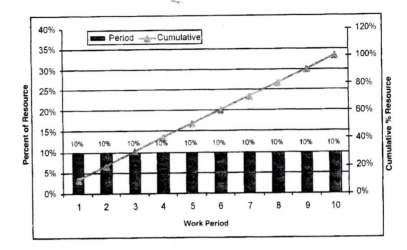

Figure 5.2
Uniform resource allocation and resulting cumulative curve.

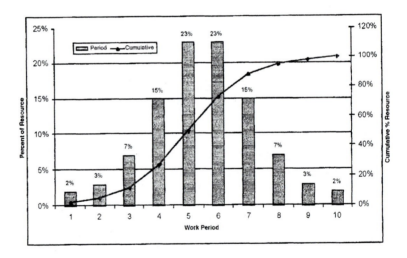

Figure 5.3
Normal resource distribution and resulting cumulative curve.

activity resource were used in the first 10% of the activity duration, there would be one histogram spike and the cumulative curve would go from zero to 100% in the first period and then plateau there for the remaining time periods.

There are several ways to look at resources throughout the life of the project. Comparing the budgeted resources on an activity or a project with those actually used is the most common resource comparison. The initial schedule that has resources assigned to activities reflects the budget quantities. If this schedule is stored or saved as the *baseline*, or original, schedule, the budgeted resources can be compared with those in the *current* schedule. The current schedule is the result of each periodic update, which includes progress reporting for all resources, including time.

Activity Cost Theory

Each activity has a cost and duration and these attributes are not deterministic. In reality cost and duration are statistical distributions that describe the variability inherent in the construction process. In other words, if the same task were performed on several projects, the productivity and duration of the same quantity of work would vary from project to project. Unlike manufacturing, construction frequently requires work to be done outside, thus making it susceptible to the vagaries of the weather. Each construction project is unique, even when the design of the project components is the same as that of a prior project; the total design is nearly always unique, as is the location where the project is built. Even though there is variability that can be statistically viewed, constructors usually use deterministic durations based on *average productivities* and *expected quantities*. However, some other factors create variability when making an activity cost and duration comparison. For example, holding the number of resources constant but using a crew with all journeymen will produce project costs and durations different from those produced using a crew consisting of predominantly apprentices. Changes in the cost related to each activity-duration can also be seen if the construction method is changed, which means changes in the mix of labor and equipment. Figure 5.4

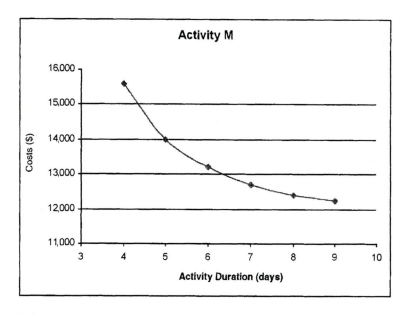

Figure 5.4
Activity cost-duration curve.

is the graph of a typical activity direct cost-duration chart. Charts such as these are derived for activities in which the resource quantity may vary but the construction method remains the same.

Notice in Figure 5.4 that there are both minimum (4) and maximum (9) durations for activity M. Time/cost graphs for activities take into account the variability resulting from factors related to the physical characteristics of the project, human factors, environmental variables, and resource efficiencies. These factors create minimum and maximum duration limits to a generic hyperbolic curve. For example, the highest cost–shortest duration end of the curve for the activity results when increases in crew size and composition have no effect on duration, only on cost, as in overcrowding. Similarly, at the other end of the duration scale, no matter how unqualified the crew or how few the workers, the task must still be completed. There are task-consistent lower limits to crew size. For example, many tasks require more than one crew member because of the physical constraints of the task. Minimum and maximum durations, as with other duration-related statistics, can be obtained from historical records but are frequently not kept by the company in the detail needed to derive curve information. To use the activity data properly, it may be necessary to convert the curve to a piecewise linear representation. Figure 5.5 is the same information as is shown in Figure 5.4, but with linear line segments used to mimic the smooth curve of Figure 5.4.

The resulting line segments each have a slope equivalent to cost per unit time. These slopes, or change in cost per unit change in time ($\Delta C/\Delta T$), provide a convenient method of making least-cost comparisons when activities must be shortened, or *crashed*. Some terminology related to the graph includes the crash cost (CC), or maximum cost at the

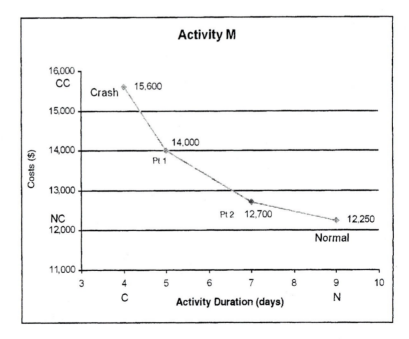

Figure 5.5
Piecewise linear resource representation.

crash or minimum duration (CD). Most companies attempt to assign activity durations at their minimum, or *normal*, cost (NC). This point relates to the maximum duration on the graph, or the normal duration (ND). Points at line-segment junctions, not at the normal or crash points, are intermediate points and labeled as such (e.g., Pt 1, Pt 2). Some evaluations of minimum and maximum duration assume no intermediate points, merely a constant slope line connecting the crash point to the normal point (Figure 5.6).

However, when two or more individual line segments are drawn, a cost/slope matrix can be developed. Sometimes, the slope between crash and normal closely mirrors the actual curve. When this happens, there is a constant change between points, and, no matter how many days the activity is compressed, it costs the same amount each day.

Figure 5.7 shows a comparison among the curve shown in Figure 5.4, the linear representation in Figure 5.5, and the straight-line linear slope from crash to normal in Figure 5.6. Notice that the difference between the cost and duration at day 6 between the straight line and the line segments may be considered substantial (more than 13%).

Figure 5.8 shows a matrix developed for the Figure 5.7 activity M. The matrix is constructed using the slope ($\Delta C/\Delta T$) of each segment such that the cells contain a daily rate of change in cost when moving from point to point on the graph. Notice that the matrix is developed on a "from," "to" set of points with corresponding durations. Because there is neither a change in cost nor a change in time when going from crash (C) to crash, or any other pair of common points, the diagonal of the matrix is filled with zeros. When moving down the curve from crash to point 1 (Pt1), the corresponding matrix cell has a negative value and becomes

$$\frac{\Delta C}{\Delta T} = \frac{\$14,000 - \$15,600}{|5-4| \, day} = \$-1,600/day$$

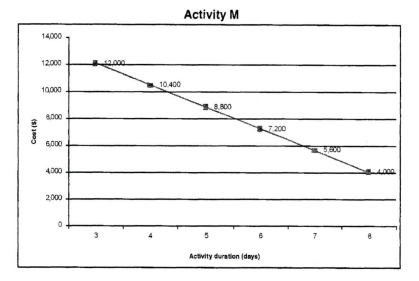

Figure 5.6
Single slope crash-normal graph.

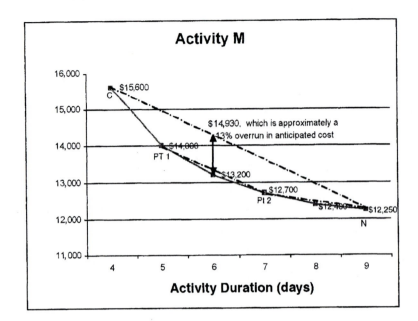

Figure 5.7
Piecewise linear versus strictly linear.

	To	C	Pt 1	Pt 2	N
		4	5	7	9
From					
C	4	0	-1600	-966	-670
Pt 1	5	1600	0	-650	-437.5
Pt 2	7	966	650	0	-225
N	9	670	437.5	225	0

Figure 5.8
Cost/slope matrix for activity M.

because this indicates a reduction in cost when increasing the duration. When moving from point 1 to C, or up the curve, the cost per day will increase. Thus,

$$\frac{\Delta C}{\Delta T} = \frac{\$15,600 - \$14,000}{|4-5| \ day} = \$1,600/day$$

It is clear that, if the ΔT were shown as reducing, in the equation, the cost per day would once again be negative. It is also apparent that moving up the curve means that the cost is increasing for every reduction in duration, so the result must be positive. Thus, always using the absolute value of the change in time gives an appropriate result.

When measuring the slope between Pt1 and normal, the line connecting the points could give a misleading value, just as shown in Figure 5.7. When trying to find an intermediate point, the scheduler should follow each line segment and not use the long, bridging linear span unless the activity is being shortened the entire duration between the two points they span.

The matrix and the linear crash-normal slopes enable the manager to compare and contrast the cost of reducing the duration of activities when the duration of the network needs to be reduced. Sometimes, there is a trade-off to consider when contemplating shortening the project duration. The cost of liquidated damages versus the cost of crashing, or the incentive for early completion versus crashing costs, can be analyzed using the crash costs for the critical activities that are chosen to effect the project duration reduction.

Day-at-a-Time Crashing

Consider the network in Figure 5.9 and suppose that it must be shortened 4 days. To shorten, or crash, the network, the scheduler must begin by considering the activities on the critical path.

Crashing the network means that activity A, D, G, K, L, or N will be considered first because these activities form the critical path. If there are paths that have less than

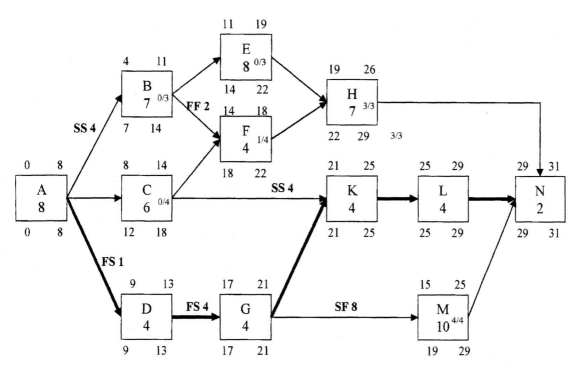

Figure 5.9
Network for crashing.

4 days of float (in this example), these may become critical and, ultimately, control the project duration. Each day that the network is crashed, the network should be re-calculated to determine the changes in float until the analyst feels confident in understanding the changes in float without the calculations. Care should be taken when considering crashing the first or last activity on the critical path. Normally, these activities are good choices because, when they are crashed, the paths with float seldom lose any of their floats. However, when the start activity is related start-to-start with its followers or the finish activity has predecessors related finish-to-finish, changes in duration in the start or the finish activity may make no difference in the project duration.

Activities are not always scheduled at their minimum cost or normal value. When evaluating critical activities to crash, consider those that are cheapest first, then those that have ample duration for crashing.

Given the crash information in Figure 5.10, plus the facts that activity G may be crashed a minimum of 2 days at a constant rate of $3,000 per day and activity E can be shortened 2 days at a cost of $3,500 per day, consider which activity to crash first.

To answer such a crashing question, consider the critical path activities first. Since all three activities, A, K, and G, are critical, analyze each one. Activity A currently has an 8 days' duration. Thus, to crash it 1 day, it would be on the slope from 8 days to 6 days, or $2,500 per day $\left(\dfrac{\$54,000 - \$49,000}{|6-8|\ day} \right)$. This would increase the cost of the project by $2,500 for 1 day. Activity K is currently at 4 days' duration; to go from 4 days to 3 days costs $8,500 (Figure 5.11). Crashing activity G, which can be crashed up to 2 days, costs $3,000 per day, and activity E can be shortened 2 days, at a cost of $3,500 per day. Thus, the cheapest activity to crash first would be A, at a cost of $2,500.

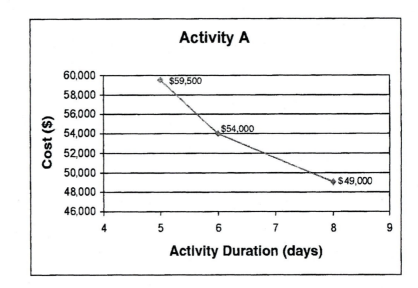

Figure 5.10
Activity A time-cost curve.

	To	C	Pt 1	N
From		3	4	6
C	3	$ 0	$ -8,500	$-4,333.33
Pt 1	4	$ 8,500	$ 0	$ -2,250
N	6	$4,333.33	$ -2,250	$ 0

Figure 5.11
Cost/slope matrix for activity K.

The scheduler may have other choices, such as changing relationships, lag values, or constraints. When activities are in a series, there may be ways of changing one or more relationships to perform activities in parallel. Sometimes, the lag values are too large. For example, if a lag is meant to signify concrete curing and the activity is confined to a 5-day workweek, a weekend or two may be included and not counted in the cure time. Thus, the lag value may be diminished or the calendar changed to more accurately reflect the true nature of the activity. Constraints may be used to specify when events will occur, such as an anticipated winter shutdown. These dates are often targets that can be changed to improve schedule acceptability when the change better predicts reality.

Capturing each successive crash in a table, which also has columns for tracking changes in duration and cost, enables the scheduler to make the most inexpensive choices at each iteration. Table 5.1 will be used to tabulate the reductions to achieve the 4-day project duration reduction in Figure 5.9 in the network. The first move is to reduce activity A by 1 day, at a cost of $2,500.

In Table 5.1, after iteration 1, the duration of the critical path is reduced by 1 day, and the total floats on activities B, E, F, and H are reduced by 1 day. Iteration 2, crash activity A again, reduces the duration of activity A by 1 more day, as it is still the cheapest. In iteration 3, the slope on activity A changes to $5,500 $\left(\dfrac{\$59,500-\$54,000}{|5-6|} \right)$. Therefore, activity G, which is now the cheapest, is crashed 1 day. Once the activities in the first three iterations have been crashed, activities B, E, and H are critical too, as the early finish of H is 26 and the early start of N has now been reduced to 26. In the last iteration, activity G is crashed 1 more day to shorten the *original critical* path, and activity E is crashed to shorten the second critical path. The result is a network that has been crashed a total of 4 days and has a new project duration of 27 days. The overall increase in cost is $14,500. Figure 5.12 shows the crashed network.

The one-day-at-a-time crashing method uses the following steps:

1. Calculate the network and identify the critical path and all floats.
2. Identify the paths that may become critical—those with total float less than the number of days to be crashed.
3. Determine which of the activities identified can be crashed based on normal and crash cost for single slope activities, activities with cost slope matrices, and activities with cost-duration graphs.

Table 5.1 Crashing the network in Figure 5.6.

Iteration	Crashing Possibilities	Available Reduction	Current Project Duration	Incremental Cost	Cumulative Cost
1	Act. A—$2,500	2	30	$2,500	$2,500
		1			
		2			
2	Act. A—$2,500	1	29	$2,500	$5,000
		1			
		2			
3	Act. G—$3,000	1	28	$3,000	$8,000
		1			
		1			
4	Act. G—$3,000	1	27	$3,000	$14,500
	Act. E—$3,500	1		$3,500	
		0			
		1			

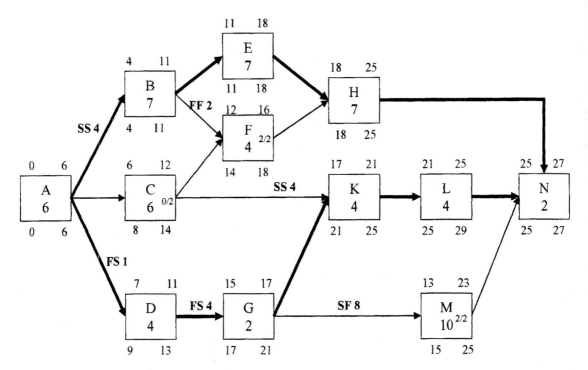

Figure 5.12
Crashed network—result.

4. Determine which activity on the critical path should be crashed based on least cost to reduce the duration. Ties can be broken if more than one activity has the least cost by selecting the activity with the most available days for reduction.

5. Check the relationships to ensure that crashing an activity's duration will have the desired effect on the project duration.

6. Reduce the project duration one day at a time, noting all changes in duration and float.

7. Continue to crash the critical path until the desired duration is reached by starting again at step 4. When there is more than one path, activities on all critical paths must be crashed until the desired duration is reached.

8. When the desired project duration is achieved, stop. Check the results by updating the network diagram with the revised, crashed durations. Because crashing can be an iterative process, 3 days of shortening during one update and 2 days on the next one, check activities not crashed to see if they can be lengthened, a process that will reduce total float and cost when activities are not at their normal cost-duration.

Modified Siemens' Algorithm for Crashing

This method for crashing or shortening activities and the project, presented by Moder, Phillips, and Davis,[1] is processed in a tabular format. The process begins by constructing a table that lists all of the paths through the network that exceed the desired and/or crashed project duration, T_S. Using the network in Figure 5.9, again crash it 4 days, or so that T_S equals 27 days.

The critical path, A, D, G, K, L, and N, is a path that must be reduced 4 days. The path A, B, E, H, and N has only 3 days of total float and therefore may need to be crashed 1 day, too. Recognize that both activities A and N are on both paths. Thus, crashing them may eliminate the need to crash any other activity in the secondary path. The relationships between activities may be important to crashing considerations.

Steps 1 and 2 place the paths in the columns for "Paths Requiring Reduction" and then list every activity in these paths once in the rows under the column "Activity." These first two steps are shown in Table 5.2.

The "cost slope" ($\Delta C/\Delta T$) and "time reduction available" (Current Duration – Crash Duration) are also listed in the appropriate columns adjacent to their activities (Table 5.3). The paths that each activity exists in are indicated by leaving blanks in the "Paths Requiring Reduction" column, and those not included are crossed out (Table 5.3). At the bottom of these path columns, after all of the activities are listed, the "Initial Path Length," or path duration, is recorded. Notice that activities B, D, H, L, and N are not found in Table 5.3 because they have no crash information.

The "effective" cost slopes for all activities are listed in the column labeled "Iteration 1" aligned with the corresponding activity (Table 5.3). An "effective" cost slope, EC_{ij}, is then defined by Siemens as the cost slope divided by the number of inadequately

Table 5.2   Modified Siemens' algorithm.

Activity	Paths Requiring Reduction		Cost Slope $/day	Time Reduction Available	Iteration
	AD	AB			
	GK	EH			
	LN	N			
A					
B					
D					
E					
G					
H					
K					
L					
N					

Initial Path Length	Iteration	Action	Iteration Cost	Cumulative Cost
Remaining Time Reduction Required				

shortened paths, N_{ij}, which contain activity $(i–j)$.[2] N_{ij} is equal to the sum of the paths requiring reduction for each activity (ij). In this example, not all activities have cost slopes. Therefore, not all activities have entries in the "Iteration 1" column. Note that activity A appears in two rows in Table 5.3. When an activity has more than one cost slope segment, all segments must be listed in the order they will be crashed. Reductions in the duration of activity A have no impact on the subcritical path, A, B, E, H, and N, because the relationship between A and B is SS. Changing the duration of activity A will not change the start date of activity B. Therefore, the effective cost slope is the full $2,500 for each of the first 2 days activity A can be crashed. If activity A did impact both paths, its effective cost slope would be 2,500/2 = $1,250. The second example problem shows effective slopes that are not equal to cost slopes.

For the path(s) with the most remaining time reduction required, select the activity with the lowest effective cost slope. Break ties by considering the following ordered criteria

Table 5.3 Updated Table 5.2 with solution.

Activity	Paths Requiring Reduction		Cost Slope $/day	Time Reduction Available	Iteration		
	ADG	AB					
	KLN	EHN			1	2	3
A	2		$ 2,500	0	$ 2,500	——————————→	
A			$ 5,500	1	$ 5,500	$ 5,500	$ 5,500
E		1	$ 3,500	1	$ 3,500	$ 3,500	$ 3,500
G	2		$ 3,000	0	$ 3,000	$ 3,000	———→
K			$ 8,500	0	$ 8,500	$ 8,500	$ 8,500

Initial Path Length	31	28	Iteration	Action	Iteration Cost	Cumulative Cost
Remaining Time Reduction Required	4	1	0	——	——	——
	2	1	1	Cut Act. A by 2 days	$ 5,000	$ 5,000
	0	1	2	Cut Act. G by 2 days	$ 6,000	$ 11,000
	0	0	3	Cut Act. E by 1 day	$ 3,500	$14,500

1. Give preference to the activity that lies on the greatest number of inadequately shortened paths.
2. Give preference to the activity that permits the greatest amount of shortening.
3. Choose an activity at random.[3]

The selected activity, from step 4, is shortened as much as possible to the minimum limit of the "unallocated time remaining" or "the smallest demand of those inadequately shortened paths containing the activity."[4] Any paths shortened too much must be elongated, if possible. The process is complete if all paths requiring reduction have reached their desired length. If this is not the case at the end of the current iteration, return to step 4.

In Table 5.3, activity A is crashed from N to Pt1 (6 to 4 days) because the critical path needs to be crashed 4 days total and activity A can be crashed a total of 3 days. On the cost slope from N to Pt1, the lowest effective slope on the critical path, activity A can be crashed 2 days. This is iteration 1. In iteration 2, activity A's cost slope is higher than activity G's, which is also on the critical path. Crash activity G 2 days as the minimum of its available crash duration and the critical reduction requirement is equal: 2. At the end of iteration 2, the original critical path is fully crashed, but the subcritical path needs to be reduced 1 day. The minimum effective slope is found on activity E at $3,500. Actually, it is the only activity with cost slope information on this path. Therefore, in iteration 3, crash activity E by 1 day. The result is a crash cost $14,500 higher than the original, uncrashed project cost as shown in Table 5.3. Figure 5.12 shows the resulting crashed network. Notice that there are now two critical paths. The results of the Modified Siemens' Method are the same as those found in the Day-at-a-Time Method.

Modified Siemens' Algorithm Example

Using the Modified Siemens' Method, reduce the Figure 5.13 project duration to 30 days at the least cost. Table 5.4 shows activity crashing cost information.

Begin by calculating the network and finding the floats. The critical path, A-B-C-F-K, has a duration equal to the project duration, 35 days. Thus, this path is listed in column "Paths Requiring Reduction" (Table 5.5). Its duration is listed in the row labeled "Initial Path Length." The path A-B-D-F-K is 1 day shorter than the critical path. This is because C has a duration of 7 days, whereas D has a duration of 6 days—the total

Using the Modified Siemens' Method, reduce the Figure 5.13 project duration to 30 days at the least cost.

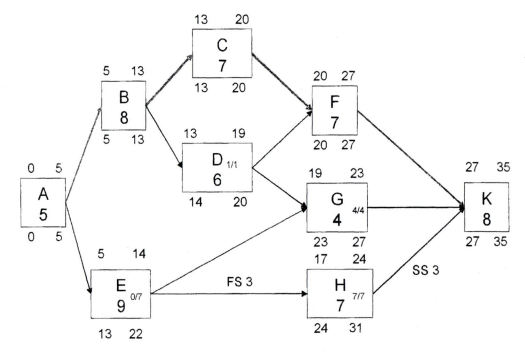

Figure 5.13
Example network for crashing.

Table 5.4 Normal and crash information for example.

Activity	NORMAL Time	NORMAL Cost	CRASH Time	CRASH Cost
A	5	$5,000	5	$5,000
B	8	6,000	3	14,000
C	7	1,000	4	7,000
D	6	5,000	2	11,000
E	9	3,000	6	7,400
F	7	18,000	5	24,000
G	4	1,000	3	4,000
H	7	2,000	5	10,000
K	8	15,000	8	15,000
Total		$56,000		

Table 5.5 Modified Siemens' algorithm.

	ITERATION									
Activity	Paths Requiring Reduction			Cost Slope ($/Day)	Time Reduction Available (Days)	Iteration			
	ABCFK	ABDFK	ABDGK			1	2	3	4
B	1	1	1	1,600	4	533	—————————→		
C	2			2,000	1	2,000	2,000	2,000	——→
D		1	1	1,500	3	750	750	750	750
F	2	2		3,000	0	1,500	1,500	————→	
G				3,000	1	3,000	3,000	3,000	3,000

Initial Path Length	35	34	31	Iteration	Action	Iteration Cost	Cumulative Cost
Remaining Time Reduction Required	5	4	1	0			$56,000
	4	3	0	1	Cut B 1 day	1,600	57,600
	2	1	0	2	Cut F 2 days	6,000	63,600
	0	1	0	3	Cut C 2 days	4,000	67,600
	0	0	−1	4	Cut D 1 day	1,500	69,100

float of the path through activity D is 1 day. Therefore, this path and its path length are listed next (Table 5.5). The total reduction to a duration of 30 days (T_S) is required, so 5 days must be eliminated from the current project duration. Consequently, all paths having a total float of less than 5 days will require reduction. The last path listed (Table 5.5), A-B-D-G-K, is listed because, with a total float of 4 days, its length is currently 31 days, or 1 day longer than the desired project duration. The initial reductions required in each path are listed below the "Initial Path Length" row (Table 5.5). The values 5, 4, and 1 represent the difference between the current path durations and the desired path duration of 30 days and correspond to iteration zero, as does the initial cumulative project cost of $56,000.

The rows under the column "Activity" are filled by all of the activities that appear in at least one of the "Paths Requiring Reduction" These are activities that can be crashed. Notice that activity A is not listed because its normal and crash duration are both 5 days (Table 5.4). Consequently, activity A cannot be crashed. A similar condition is true for activity K. The cells beneath "Paths Requiring Reduction" across from each activity are marked out with X when the activity is not found in the corresponding path. There are no Xs in the row for B, because B is found in all three paths. However, activity G appears in only one path. Thus, the other two cells are filled with Xs. In the begining of the crashing analysis those cells that have not been marked out with Xs are left blank.

The "Time Reduction" column shows how many days the activity in that row can be crashed. In the row for activity B, the time reduction value is first 5 because initially activity B can be crashed from its current 8-day duration to a crash duration of 3 days.

The "Cost Slope" column is filled with the $\Delta C / \Delta T$ for each activity. For activity B, ΔC equals $14,000 minus $6,000, or $8,000, whereas ΔT equals 8 days minus 3 days, or 5 days. Thus, the cost slope equals 8,000/5, or $1,600 per day (Table 5.5). Activities D, F, and G's cost slopes are also recorded in this column in their corresponding row. The effective cost slopes must also be obtained. The effective cost slope for each activity is its cost slope divided by the number of inadequately shortened paths. For activity B, this means the $1,600/day cost slope is divided by the three paths that require shortening. Thus, its effective cost slope is $533/day (Table 5.5). The effective cost slope values are listed for each activity beneath the "Iteration 1" column (Table 5.5).

The cells that have no Xs beneath the paths requiring reduction are filled in with the outcomes of the action steps taken. Begin by selecting the *lowest effective cost slope* activity found in the path requiring the *most* reduction. This is path A-B-C-F-K, the initial critical path, so activities B, C, and F must be considered. Activity B has the lowest effective cost slope at $533/day. Remember, there are rules for breaking ties when they exist. Now shorten activity B as much as possible. Because activity B is in all three columns, which represent additional paths, these other paths must be tested for the smallest time reduction demand. Path A-B-D-G-K needs only 1 day, and activity B has 5 days that it can be crashed. The rule says to take the minimum; thus, activity B is crashed 1 day. The cost slope (not the effective cost slope) multiplied by the number of days crashed gives the increase in cost. The cost for reducing activity B's duration 1 day, is $1,600, and each path that activity B appears in is reduced 1 day for iteration 1. The "Time Reduction Available" for B has been reduced by 1, and A 1 is now placed in the B row of the previously blank columns under "Paths Requiring

Reduction" (Table 5.5). The total in the "Paths Requiring Reduction" columns is subtracted in each iteration from the last "Remaining Time Reduction Required" value.

Path A-B-C-F-K still needs the greatest amount of reduction, 4 days. Activity F has the smallest effective cost slope for this path, $1,500 per day. The minimum reduction required for the two paths activity F affects is 3, but F can only be crashed 2 days; therefore, crash activity F by 2 days. Crashing activity F by 2 days costs $6,000 and reduces each of the two paths F appears in by 2 days. Two days now also appear in the previously blank columns of the F row under "Paths Requiring Reduction." Just as activity B would not be used again after iteration 1, now activity F cannot be used again. A horizontal line is drawn through future potential iterations (Table 5.5).

Two days must still be removed from the A-B-C-F-K path (see Table 5.5 data in cells to left of cut F 2 days). Only activity C can be reduced, and its effective cost slope is $2,000. As activity C can be crashed up to 3 days, crash it 2 days, at a cost of $4,000 for iteration 3. After this iteration, the A-B-D-F-K path must still be reduced 1 day. The only activity that has not been crashed and is contained in this path is activity D. The effective cost slope is $750, whereas its cost slope is $1,500. Activity D can be crashed up to 4 days, but only 1 day is needed. Crashing D by 1 day gives a −1 in the A-B-D-G-K path. When there are negative numbers in one or more paths, activities should be elongated to reduce the project cost (step 6) in the Modified Siemens' Method. However, the only activity in this path involves activity G, and it has not been crashed. Thus, the result of this process is to put 1 day of float back into the A-B-D-G-K path and arrive at a final cost of $69,100 for a 30-day project.

Project Costs

When the direct cost and indirect cost curves are combined, a total cost curve is derived. Figure 5.14 demonstrates the derivation of the total cost curve from these curves. Direct costs are those costs that can be assigned to individual bid items or activities, whereas indirect costs are those project costs that account for labor, materials, and equipment that are of general use to the project and cannot be assigned discretely to bid items or activities. Also included in direct cost is all of the job overhead, such as job office salaries, supplies, utilities, engineering, consultants, and the debt service or finance charges on job borrowing. Indirect costs are often modeled as a linear curve increasing with time. John Fondahl[5] created what is termed an *envelope of project costs*. Two curves are generated for the total project cost. One is a minimum much like the total cost curve shown in Figure 5.14, whereas the other is the much less desirable maximum total cost curve. These two curves, together, make up Fondahl's envelope of project costs.

The envelope begins with the minimum total cost curve shown in Figure 5.15; the premise with this curve is that each activity is chosen for least cost at each daily interval. The curve grows steeper until the minimum duration is reached. Thus, the crashed project is the result of crashing all activities that will shorten the project duration. In the case of the minimum cost curve, even though additional activities could be crashed, no further reduction of the project duration occurs.

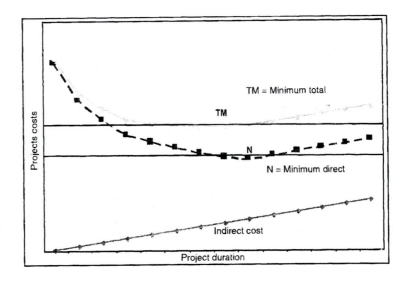

Figure 5.14
All project costs.

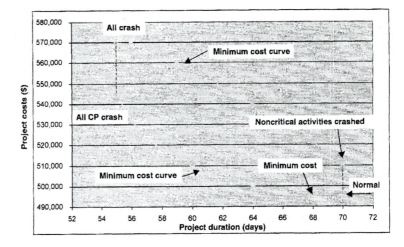

Figure 5.15
Fondahl's envelope of costs.

The maximum cost curve of the envelope is obtained by first crashing all noncritical activities and then crashing the maximum cost activity at each daily interval. The maximum total cost curve tends to flatten as it reaches the point where all activities are crashed. Both the minimum and maximum cost curves are duration cost curves comparing specific project durations with specific project costs.

It is evident from the envelope that a contractor's bid should be above the envelope's maximum curve to prevent potential losses due to crash costs in excess of the minimum. Each company must make its own profit decision based on the anticipated construction costs and potential risks to successful project completion. However, creating an envelope for each project can help a company analyze bids, profits, and final project durations to improve bid performance.

Fondahl's Envelope Example

Using the information from the Modified Siemens' Method example, the minimum and the maximum project time-cost curves will be developed. The network must be crashed to its shortest duration from the original 35-day duration. Table 5.6 is modified from Table 5.4.

Begin with the maximum cost curve. This curve begins at project duration 35 days with all of the noncritical activities crashed to their minimum duration. Therefore, crash activities D, E, G, and H to the maximum cost, minimum duration (Table 5.7).

Table 5.6   Normal and crash information.

		NORMAL		CRASH	
Cost Slope $/day	Activity	Time	Cost	Time	Cost
0	A	5	$ 5,000	5	$ 5,000
1,600	B	8	6,000	3	14,000
2,000	C	7	1,000	4	7,000
1,500	D	6	5,000	2	11,000
1,466.67	E	9	3,000	6	7,400
3,000	F	7	18,000	5	24,000
3,000	G	4	1,000	3	4,000
4,000	H	7	2,000	5	10,000
0	K	8	15,000	8	15,000
	Total		$56,000		

Table 5.7   Crash noncritical activities.

Activity	Crash Days	$/Crash Day	Activity Crash Cost
D	4	1,500	$6,000
E	3	1,466.67	$4,400
G	1	3,000	$3,000
H	2	4,000	$8,000
Total			21,400

Table 5.8 Crash for maximum curve.

Crash Activity	Current–New Duration (days)	Project Duration (days)	Cost ($)	Total Project Cost ($)
				77,400
F	7–6	34	3,000	80,400
F	6–5	33	3,000	83,400
C	7–6	32	2,000	85,400
C	6–5	31	2,000	87,400
C	5–4	30	2,000	89,400
B	8–7	29	1,600	91,000
B	7–6	28	1,600	92,600
B	6–5	27	1,600	94,200
B	5–4	26	1,600	95,800
B	4–3	25	1,600	97,400

Table 5.9 Crash information for minimum curve.

Iteration	Possible Crash Activity	Available Crash Duration	Crash Cost ($/Day)	Project Duration (days)	Total Project Cost ($)	Comment
0				35	56,000	
1	B	5–4	1,600	34	57,600	
2	B	4–3	1,600	33	59,200	
3	B	3–2	1,600	32	60,800	
4	B	2–1	1,600	31	62,400	
5	B	1–0	1,600	30	64,000	
6	C	3–2	2,000	29	66,000	D critical
7	C and D	2–1, 4–3	3,500			H and E
	F	2–1	3,000	28	69,000	critical
8	C , D, and E	2–1, 4–3	4,966.67			
	F and E	1–0, 3–2	4,466.67	27	73,466.67	
9	C , D, and E	2–1, 4–3, 2–1	4,966.67	26	78,433.34	
10	C , D, and E	1–0, 3–2, 1–0	4,966.67	25	83,400.00	B, C, E, and F all crashed to minimum duration

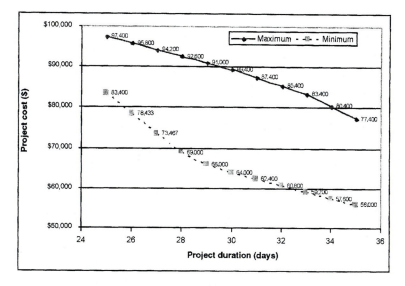

Figure 5.16
Fondahl's envelope of costs example.

The maximum cost curve begins at day 35 with a cost of $56,000 + $21,400 (non-critical in crash cost) = $77,400. The remaining points on the maximum curve are found by crashing the most expensive activity for each day of schedule reduction—Table 5.8 shows each iteration.

The minimum cost curve begins by crashing the least-cost activity first, and proceeding one day at a time in like manner (Table 5.9). As new paths become critical, they must be crashed in concert with the original critical path. Days are crashed one at a time until one of the critical paths has no more crash days available—this is the minimum duration and should match the 25 days on the maximum cost curve. The resulting envelope (cost-duration curves) is shown in Figure 5.16.

Problems and/or Questions

1. What resources are most critical in the current local construction market? Support your answer with data and describe how you would incorporate this information into the schedule.

2. Develop a cost slope matrix for the graph of activity G, on the next page.

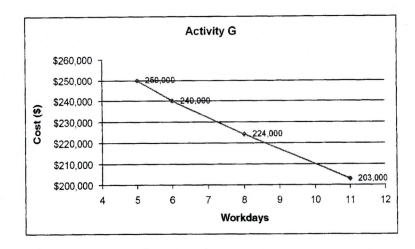

3. From the following time cost data,

    a. Draw the precedence diagram.

    b. From the precedence network with a normal duration of 34 days, compress the network from its normal duration to its expedited duration of 27 days. List those activities that were expedited and the cost associated with each compression.

    c. Plot the minimum duration cost curve.

No.	Activity	Preceding Activity	NORMAL		CRASH	
			Time	Cost	Time	Cost
5	A	———	5	$ 5,000	5	$ 5,000
10	B	5	8	6,000	3	18,000
15	E	5	6	3,000	5	4,500
20	C	10	2	1,000	2	1,000
25	D	10	6	5,000	2	9,000
30	H	15	5	2,000	4	3,000
35	F	20,25	7	18,000	3	20,000
40	G	15,25	5	1,000	3	4,000
45	K	30,35,40	8	15,000	8	15,000

4. Complete the matrix for activity B according to its duration-cost graph. The normal duration for activity B is 7 days.

From \ To		C	Pt1	Pt2	N
		3	5	6	7
C	3				
Pt1	5				
Pt2	6				
N	7				

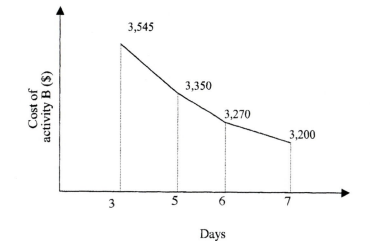

5. From the following information, determine the least expensive way to shorten the project 3 days.

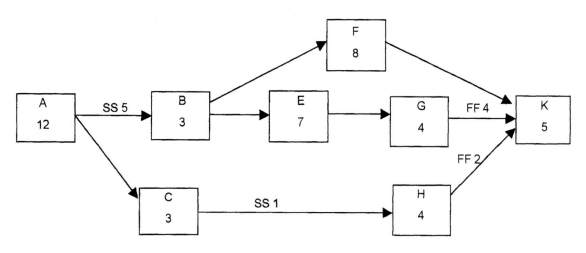

First, calculate the network, including dates and floats.

Cost Curve
Activity A

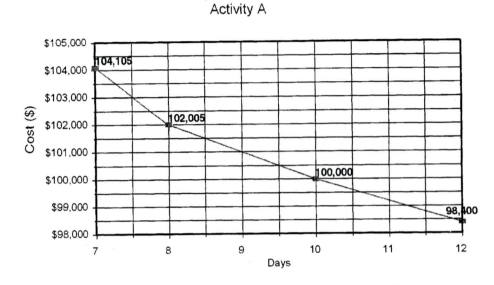

Second, create a cost slope matrix from the graph for activity A. Use an empty matrix similar to the one shown for problem 4.

Third, using these cost slope matrices, determine the least expensive way to shorten the network 3 days. Show all steps and trials, as well as the solution.

Activity A

To	C	Pt1	Pt2	N
From	7	8	10	12
C 7				
P1 8				
P2 10				
N 12				

Activity E

To	C	Pt1	Pt2	N
From	5	6	7	9
C 5	0	-795	-723	-761
P1 6	795	0	-650	-750
P2 7	723	650	0	-800
N 9	761	750	800	0

Activity K

To	C	Pt1	Pt2	N
From	3	4	5	7
C 3	0	-1,000	-1,500	-938
P1 4	1,000	0	-2,000	-917
P2 5	1,500	2,000	0	-375
N 7	938	917	375	0

Be careful; not all current activity durations are equal to N.

Activity G

To	C	Pt1	N
From	3	4	5
C 3	0	-3,000	-3,525
P1 4	3,000	0	-4,050
N 5	3,525	4,050	0

Activity F

To	C	Pt1	Pt2	N
From	5	7	8	10
C 5	0	-375	-417	-300
P1 7	375	0	-500	-250
P2 8	417	500	0	-125
N 10	300	250	125	0

Activity H

To	C	Pt1	N
From	3	4	6
C 3	0	-4,000	-2,667
P1 4	4,000	0	-2,000
N 6	2,667	2,000	0

6. Use the Modified Siemens' Method to crash the network given in problem 3 to its crash duration of 27 days. Use the tabular format shown in the chapter to develop your solution based on the problem 3 cost data.

7. Use the Modified Siemens' Method to crash the following network to its minimum duration at the cheapest cost. Show your results in the tabular format shown in the chapter.

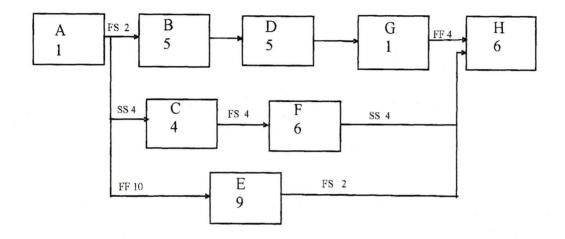

Activity	Total Cost $	Activity	Total Cost $
A	5,000	E	18,000
B	12,500	F	18,000
C	8,000	G	3,000
D	15,000	H	15,000

Activity	Minimum Duration (days)	Crash Cost per Day ($/day)	Activity	Minimum Duration (days)	Crash Cost per Day ($/day)
A	1	——	E	5	2,900
B	3	4,500	F	4	4,250
C	3	3,750	G	1	——
D	3	4,250	H	3	2,700

8. From the data in problem 3, plot the Fondahl's envelope of costs.

9. From the data in problem 5, plot the Fondahl's envelope of costs.

Notes

1. Joseph J. Moder, Cecil R. Phillips, and Edward W. Davis, *Project Management with CPM, PERT, and Precedence Diagramming,* 3rd ed. New York: Van Nostrand Reinhold Co. 1983.
2. Ibid., p. 245.
3. Ibid., p. 247.
4. Ibid.
5. Robert B. Harris, *Precedence and Arrow Networking Techniques for Construction.* New York: Wiley, 1978, p. 12.

CHAPTER 6

Leveling and Constraining

Goal

Demonstrate computerized resource reallocation.

Objectives

- Describe the difference between leveling and constraining.
- Describe and demonstrate the traditional, or conventional, method of resource leveling.
- Describe and demonstrate the traditional, or conventional, method of resource constraining.
- Provide examples of resource leveling and resource constraining.

Introduction

Leveling and constraining are two methods the manager has to investigate resource distributions in light of resource limits. The premise behind both methods (leveling and constraining) is that, by using the available total float, activities can be moved to create a more uniform resource distribution and, therefore, a better resource profile. If the average resource use (resource/day) could be applied on each day, the result would be a uniform distribution or a rectangle of resource that has the same value on day 1 as on the last day of the project (Figure 6.1). The resulting cumulative, or s-curve (Figure 6.1), would not be an "s" shape but, rather, a line that increases linearly as the project progresses from day 1 to the end of the project.

Leveling

Figure 6.2 shows a nonuniform resource profile. The histogram is shown on a daily basis, so that resource requirements are not hidden by aggregation. *Leveling* suggests that resources can be better allocated than the peaks and valleys shown in Figure 6.2, while staying within the limits of each activity's total float. Therefore, no extension of project duration is expected with leveling. When the project is to be held to a planned duration, peaks can exceed the desired level, and/or all activities can be pushed to their late start and finish dates. When activities move to their late dates, a buildup of resource use occurs toward the end of the project. A buildup of resource requirements late in the project is often more objectionable to managers than the peaks and valleys.

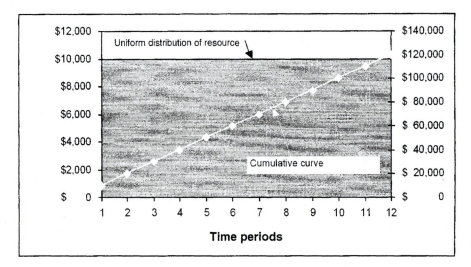

Figure 6.1
Uniform period resource distribution and s-curve.

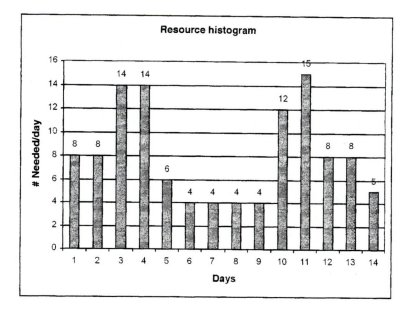

Figure 6.2
Sample leveling and constraining histogram.

Conventional, or Traditional, Resource Leveling

There are several approaches to resource leveling, including the conventional, or traditional, method; the minimum moment method; and the Modified Siemens' Method. The minimum moment method is discussed in Chapter 17 and the Modified Siemens' Method was discussed in Chapter 5. The conventional, or traditional, method is discussed in this chapter.

The leveling process is conducted by investigating resource use and the *desired level* on each day, using a day-by-day approach, beginning on the first day of the project and working toward the end. This is the forward leveling process. Each day that the resource use exceeds the desired level, an *algorithm* is used to determine which activities should be scheduled and which should be postponed or pushed. The algorithm may require that the activity with the least total float be scheduled first or the one with the most total float delayed. Other algorithms can compare late finish dates, free float, or other activity attributes. Moder, Phillips, and Davis[1] suggest that the result of any of the algorithms for the forward leveling process provides as good a revised resource profile as any other algorithm, including a random selection process. Other authors propose the use of the minimum moment algorithm, which takes two passes through the network, one from back to front and the subsequent one from front to back. The last pass in this algorithm calculates a "resource improvement coefficient," which must reach a certain level before an activity is moved. In other words, the profile must improve or the change is not made. This tends to improve the potential buildup of resources toward the end of the project. However, the minimum moment method is not

Activity Information				Workdays														
I.D.	Desc	Dur	Total Resource	1	2	3	4	5	6	7	8	9	10	11	12	13	14
10	A	4	32	8	8	8	8										
20	B	3	6			2	2	2				→					
30	C	7	28			4	4	4	4	4	4	4					
40	D	2	14										7	7			→
50	E	5	25										5	5	5	5	5
60	F	3	9											3	3	3	→
Sum			114														
Period Sum (Early Start)				8	8	14	14	6	4	4	4	4	12	15	8	8	5
Cumulative Sum				8	16	30	44	50	54	58	62	66	78	93	101	109	114

Figure 6.3
Bar chart supporting the Figure 6.2 histogram.

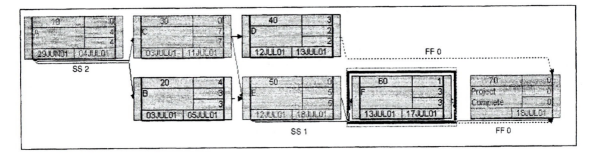

Figure 6.4
Network diagram underlying Figures 6.2 and 6.3.

designed to be used efficiently when doing calculations manually. Thus, to demonstrate the leveling process, a more traditional, forward leveling method is discussed here.

Figure 6.3 is the bar chart that supports the histogram in Figure 6.2, and Figure 6.4 shows the underlying network.

It is often helpful to show critical path resources separately from noncritical path resource contributions. Figures 6.5 and 6.6 show the bar chart and the histogram with the critical path isolated.

Selecting the Trial Resource Level

When leveling manually or with computer software, one of the first tasks is to determine an appropriate resource level to attempt to achieve. Recall that the uniform rectangular distribution (the ideal) is created from the average usage. The average for the example

I.D.	Desc	Dur	Total Resource	1	2	3	4	5	6	7	8	9	10	11	12	13	14
	Activity Information									**Workdays**							
10	A	4	32	8	8	8	8										
20	B	3	6			2	2	2	→								
30	C	7	28			4	4	4	4	4	4	4					
40	D	2	14										7	7	→		
50	E	5	25										5	5	5	5	5
60	F	3	9											3	3	3	→
	Sum		114														
Period Sum Critical Path				8	8	12	12	4	4	4	4	4	5	5	5	5	5
Period Sum Noncritical				0	0	2	2	2	0	0	0	0	7	12	3	3	0

Figure 6.5
Tabulated critical path and noncritical path resources.

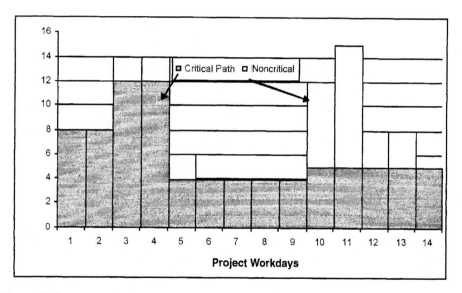

Figure 6.6
Resource histogram separated, showing critical path.

network is 114 / 14 = 8.14 resources per day. It is evident that no network can achieve a level lower than the maximum of the critical path activities. The example shows that activity A contributes eight resources per day, and this is the highest critical path contribution. However, activities A and C overlap one another and together contribute twelve resources per day, or the maximum resource contribution on the critical path.

The average can also be modified by deleting the critical path activity durations and their resource contributions that are not overlapped by noncritical activities from the average calculation. This solution assumes that all relationships will remain constant. In the example, the first 2 days of activity A are not overlapped. Thus, the modified average is

$(114 - 2*(8)) / (14 - 2) = 98 / 12 = 8.16$. All three resulting numbers (8.14, 12, 8.16) need to be compared, and the number that makes the most sense needs to be selected. Here, the best choice is to select a level of 12 or higher, as 12 is the highest of the maximum values on the critical path, and it is higher than the average and the modified average.

Moving Activities

From the histogram in Figure 6.2 or the period sum row on the bar chart in Figure 6.3, and using 12 as the level, the first day that 12 is exceeded is day 3. The daily resource contribution of 14 is constructed by the contribution from 3 activities. Activity A is in progress, and the premise used in this text is that all activities are continuous. Therefore, activity A cannot be moved or split. Activity C is on the critical path (as is activity A) and cannot be moved unless the duration of the project can be extended. That leaves only activity B for consideration. Moving activity B by 1 day would give the result shown in Figure 6.7.

When activity B is moved 1 day, the period amount for day 3 drops to an acceptable level of 12. Because B does not push or affect any other activity (it has free float), no other activity is affected—this movement does not cause a following activity to move. The next iteration considers day 4. The result is the same as on day 3, and activity B is moved 1 more day because it still has float. The result is shown in Figure 6.8.

The last work day that has a resource requirement exceeding the leveling limit of 12 is day 11. Moving F 1 day results in the bar chart shown in Figure 6.9.

The question the reviewer should ask once leveling is complete is whether the resulting histogram is better than the one prior to leveling. The minimum is still 4; however, the maximum has been reduced. Figure 6.10 shows the before and after histograms side by side. The reviewer must determine if the new profile is (1) achievable and (2) a better distribution of resource usage.

Activity Information				Workdays													
I.D.	Desc	Dur	Total Resource	1	2	3	4	5	6	7	8	9	10	11	12	13	14
10	A	4	32	8	8	8	8										
20	B	3	6				2	2	2	→		▶					
30	C	7	28			4	4	4	4	4	4	4					
40	D	2	14										7	7	→		▶
50	E	5	25										5	5	5	5	5
60	F	3	9											3	3	3	▶
	Sum		114														
Period Sum (Early Start)				8	8	12	14	6	6	4	4	4	12	15	8	8	5
Cumulative Sum				8	16	28	42	48	54	58	62	66	78	93	101	109	114

Figure 6.7
Activity B moved 1 day.

Activity Information				Workdays													
I.D.	Desc	Dur	Total Resource	1	2	3	4	5	6	7	8	9	10	11	12	13	14
10	A	4	32	8	8	8	8										
20	B	3	6					2	2	2	→						
30	C	7	28			4	4	4	4	4	4	4					
40	D	2	14										7	7	→		
50	E	5	25										5	5	5	5	5
60	F	3	9											3	3	3	→
	Sum		114														
Period Sum (Early Start)				8	8	12	12	6	6	6	4	4	12	15	8	8	5
Cumulative Sum				8	16	28	40	46	52	58	62	66	78	93	101	109	114

Figure 6.8
Move B a second day.

Activity Information				Workdays													
I.D.	Desc	Dur	Total Resource	1	2	3	4	5	6	7	8	9	10	11	12	13	14
10	A	4	32	8	8	8	8										
20	B	3	6					2	2	2	→						
30	C	7	28			4	4	4	4	4	4	4					
40	D	2	14										7	7	→		
50	E	5	25										5	5	5	5	5
60	F	3	9											3	3	3	→
	Sum		114														
Period Sum (Early Start)				8	8	12	12	6	6	6	4	4	12	12	8	8	8
Cumulative Sum				8	16	28	40	46	52	58	62	66	78	90	98	106	114

Figure 6.9
All period amounts less than or equal to 12.

Constraining

Using the same example as used for the leveling discussion, consider the elements of *constraining*. When resources have a definite limit, holding to that limit can cause the project duration to be extended. Constraining the network indicates a limit on one or more resources. The resource limit is so stringent that increasing the project duration is preferable to obtaining additional resources, or the additional resources may simply not be available. Assume that the network shown in Figures 6.2 and 6.3 has a resource limit of ten. What is the resulting increase in project duration if this limit is fixed? Figure 6.3 suggests that activity C must be moved 2 days. When C is moved, D and E

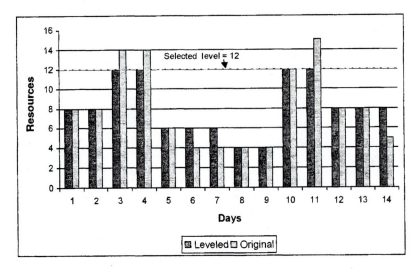

Figure 6.10
Comparison of original and leveled histogram.

Activity Information				Work Days																
ID	Desc	Dur	Total Resource	1	2	3	4	5	6	7	8	9	10	11	12	13	14	15	16	17
10	A	4	32	8	8	8	8													
20	B	3	6			2	2	2	→											
30	C	7	28			X	X	4	4	4	4	4	4	4						
40	D	2	14													7	7			
50	E	5	25										X	X	5	5	5	5	5	
60	F	3	9													3	3	3		
	Sum		114																	
Period Sum (Early Start)				8	8	10	10	6	4	4	4	4	4	4	12	15		8	5	
Cumulative Sum				8	16	26	36	42	46	50	54	58	62	66	78	93	101	109	114	

Figure 6.11
Moving activities C, D, E, and F.

also move because C pushes D and E. Because E moves, so does F. The "Project Duration" is now 16 days, Figure 6.11.

By moving activities C, D, E, and F the project completion is extended 2 days. An excess of ten resources is still apparent on 2 days of the project, days 12 and 13. On day 12, there is a choice as to what to move. Moving either D or E is possible. Activity D still has 3 days of float, but, by inspection, it is obvious that moving D within the limits of E will result in a minimum of twelve resources needed. The manager must decide

I.D.	Desc	Dur	Total Resource	1	2	3	4	5	6	7	8	9	10	11	12	13	14	15	16	17	18
	Activity Information										Workdays										
10	A	4	32	8	8	8	8														
20	B	3	6			2	2	2													
30	C	7	28		X	X	4	4	4	4	4	4	4	4							
40	D	2	14												7	7					
50	E	5	25										X	X	X	X	5	5	5	5	5
60	F	3	9												3	3	3				
	Sum		114																		
	Period Sum (Early Start)			8	8	10	10	6	4	4	4	4	4	4	7	10	8	8	5	5	5
	Cumulative Sum			8	16	26	36	42	46	50	54	58	62	66	73	83	91	99	104	109	114

Figure 6.12
Final constrained bar chart.

whether to move activity D by 5 days or to move activity E by 2 days to resolve the problem. By selecting E, the manager adds 2 more days to the project, for a total of 5 days, or more than a 33% increase in the project duration to achieve a decrease of less than 20% in resource availability.

The final constrained bar chart shows the option of extending activity E by 2 additional days to stay below the resource limit of ten. The final duration is 19 days. It is the manager's duty to compare the cost of this 5-day extension of the project with the cost of the additional resources needed to meet the original project schedule.

Conclusion

The number of resources available each day to use in constructing a project are often less than the number required based on the scheduled work activities for the day. Therefore, activities must be rescheduled, into float whenever possible, to stretch resource use evenly across the time duration of the work. When resource requirements exceed the limited amount available, the manager must resource-constrain the project. In so doing, it is always necessary to constrain in such a manner that there is as little effect of the project duration as possible. Constraining resources, however, implies that the project duration will be extended. Leveling resources has the connotation that the project duration will remain the same.

Problems and/or Questions

1. Using a real project, discuss the daily histogram of its most critical resource. Submit the histogram with the discussion.

2. Using a real project, level the most critical resource for 5 days. Find the appropriate level, showing your work and discussing the discarded values.

3. Consider a common construction resource value, such as one or two crews, that matches assigned resources for your current class project. Show the before and after histograms once the network has been constrained to the common level. Discuss each step in the constraining process.

4. Using the network below and indicated budgeted resource requirements (shown in the table) that follow, find the most appropriate resource level to use and then level the network.

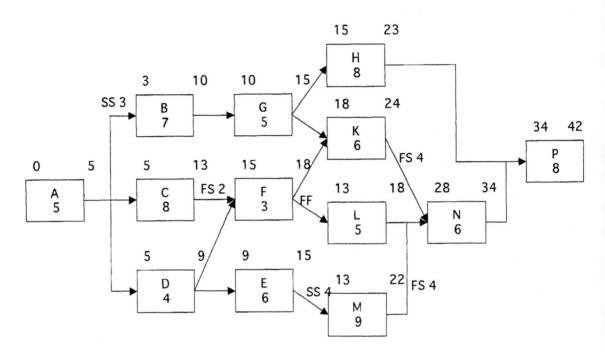

Activity	Resource	Activity	Resource
A	15,000	H	6,000
B	14,700	K	3,000
C	12,000	L	2,500
D	4,000	M	13,500
E	12,000	N	4,200
F	6,000	P	4,000
G	7,500		

5. Using the following network and the resources from problem 4, select a trial level and then level the network. Include a histogram with your solution, showing the critical path resources separated from the noncritical path resources, as well as a bar chart.

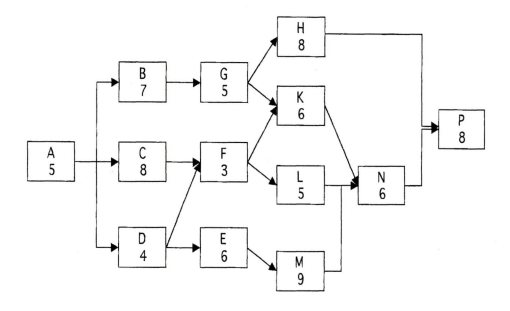

6. Using the network and resources that follow, level the network, showing each step such that the final profile matches the table that follows.

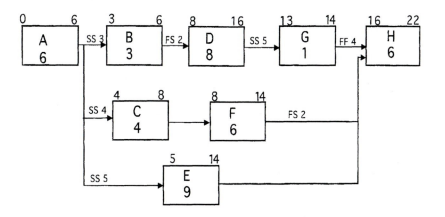

Desired final profile:

Activity	Resource Rate/Day	Day(s)	Rate
A	8	1–4	8
B	16	5–6	18
C	10	7	26
D	12	8	38
E	12	9	37
F	9	10–12	21
G	7	13-14	33
H	4	15–16	24
		17	16
		18	23
		19–20	16
		21–22	4

7. Level the network that follows, showing each step to the final profile that most closely matches the table that follows.

Activity	Duration	Depends On	Resource Rate
A	4	———	100
B	6	A	50
C	5	A (FS 2)	200
D	3	A (FF 2)	150
F	2	B	100
G	4	C	75
H	3	C (FS 0), D (FS 2)	125
J	3	F, G	200
K	7	H, G	100
L	4	J, K	100

Preferred Histogram

Day	Daily Res. Sum	Day	Daily Res. Sum
1	100	14	250
2	100	15	175
3	100	16	200
4	100	17	300
5	150	18	300
6	150	19	300
7	350	20	100
8	200	21	100
9	250	22	100
10	250	23	100
11	250	24	100
12	250	25	100
13	250	26	100

8. From the network and resources provided, find the three potential levels, tell the level to select, and determine the first day an activity must be moved based on the level you have selected. Supply a bar chart and an early start histogram with your solution.

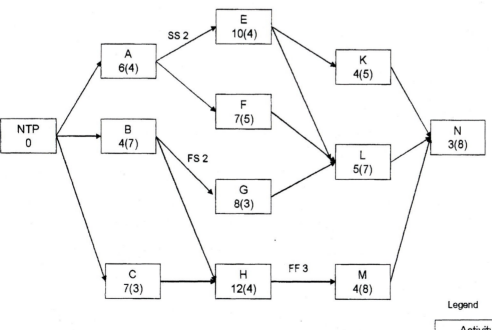

Notes

1. J. J. Moder, C. R. Phillips, and E. W. Davis, *Project Management with CPM, PERT, and Precedence Diagramming*, 3rd ed. New York: Van Nostrand Reinhold, 1983.

SECTION THREE

SCHEDULE CONTROL, MONITORING, AND MANAGEMENT

CHAPTER 7

Constraints

Goal

Present the motivation for the use of schedule constraints and the mechanics of their use.

Objectives

- Describe and demonstrate conditional constraints:
  - Scheduled early start
  - Scheduled late finish
- Describe and demonstrate mandatory constraints.
- Discuss constraints versus relationships.
- Discuss zero floats.

Introduction

There are essentially two types of constraints: the conditional constraint and the mandatory constraint. Both types of constraints can be applied to the start or the finish of an activity and, usually, to the early and late times, too. Some constraints, found in certain scheduling application programs, can be applied to activities to constrain both total and free floats.

The purpose of a constraint is to limit when an activity can start or finish. Milestones, crucial material deliveries, and subcontractor scheduling can create the need for constrained activity starts and finishes. Early and late constraints that are conditional and those that are mandatory are discussed in the following sections.

Start Constraint—Scheduled Early Start

When the constructor receives information that the delivery of materials, the ability of subcontractors, or other resources will not be available until a certain date, the *start no earlier than*—or scheduled early start (SES)—constraint is often used to delay earlier calculated start times (Figures 7.1 and 7.2).

When the early start constraint is earlier than the calculated date (Figure 7.1, 45 before 49) the calculated date (day 49) is what is used in calculating the schedule. However, when the early start constraint (Figure 7.2, 45 after 40) is later than the calculated date (day 40), the constraint date is used in calculating the schedule.

$$ES_{\text{SES Constrained Activity}} = MAX \text{ (Calculated ES or SES)} \qquad (7\text{-}1)$$

Note that even though activities G and K in Figure 7.2 are sequential, their total float will be different. Activity G will have 5 more days of total float than activity K. Activity G will also have 5 days of free float, even though it is the only predecessor of activity K. These float values can change as the network is updated.

Figure 7.3 shows how the result of the constraint on activity K affects the floats on both activities. Notice that the total float on activities G and K are now different, even though they appear to be a virtual activity. *The rules about float no longer apply when constraints are used.*

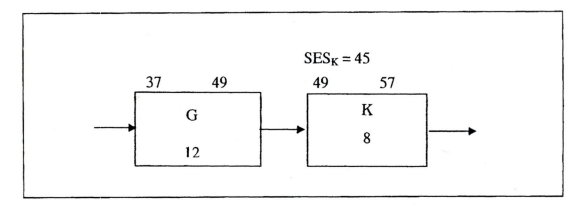

Figure 7.1
Calculated date greater than scheduled date.

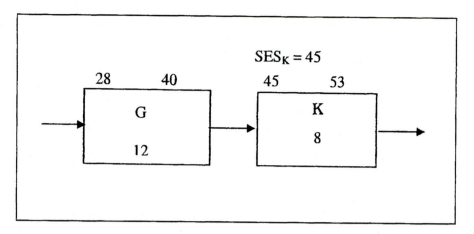

Figure 7.2
Scheduled early start (SES) overrides calculated date.

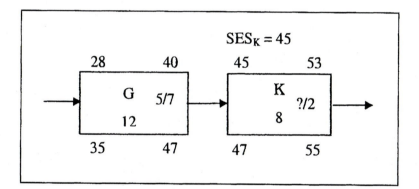

Figure 7.3
Floats resulting from constraints. The "?" indicates that free float cannot be determined.

Finish Constraints—Scheduled Late Finish

Figure 7.4 shows the effect of attaching a "finish no later than" or *scheduled late finish* (SLF) to activity G that is earlier than the calculated late finish (50). The SLF is used in the calculation when it is earlier than the calculated date.

$$LF_{SLF\ Constrained\ Activity} = MIN\ (Calculated\ LF\ or\ SLF) \qquad (7\text{-}2)$$

Using the Constraints Window in Primavera®, the user can apply a start constraint—Early, Start, or Start On selections. In MS Project®, the user can introduce constraints in the Task Detail Form from Start As Soon As Possible to Start No Earlier Than. By

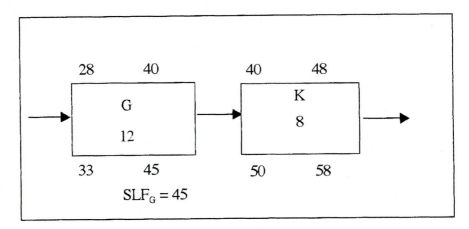

Figure 7.4
Scheduled late finish (SLF).

attaching one of these constraints to an activity, the user can limit the start to the indicated date or later. Similar constraints exist for activity finishes.

Mandatory Constraints

When an activity *must* start or finish on a specific date, the mandatory constraint is used. Mandatory constraints operate differently than early start/finish or late start/finish constraints. No matter what the calculated date is, the mandatory constraint *is recognized and used in both the forward and backward pass calculations.* Figure 7.4 shows how the mandatory constraint is used for a start—must start on (MSO) or schedule must start (SMS).

The total float of activity G is −2, as is its free float. The total float on activity K is 0 and will always be 0 until the activity is complete. However, its free float is 9, which invalidates the original rule that TF is always greater than or equal to free float. The total float on activity Z is 10. Activities G and K should follow the rules for a virtual chain, but they fail to do so due to the use of the constraint.

Because scheduled dates, whether starts, finishes, or mandatory constraints, are the only way of creating *negative float,* special attention should be given to the application of constraints and to the network analysis when constraints are used. Mandatory constraints do not allow float to pass them.

Figure 7.5 is a partial network for *soldier-pile and tremie concrete (SPTC)* foundation walls. The figure shows the actual application of a mandatory constraint applied to a pile driving activity. Notice that the preceding activities are not critical. The must start was 3 days later than the calculated date. Therefore, the activities that had been on the critical path prior to the must start constraint and terminating in the pile driving activity now have a plus 3 days of total float. The project is also 3 days longer than before, because the pile driving activity was on the critical path before the application of the must start. The early and late dates on the pile driving activity are the same.

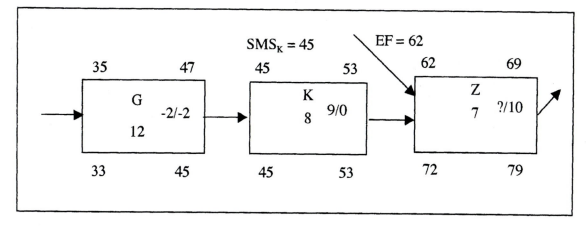

Figure 7.5
Using the mandatory constraint.

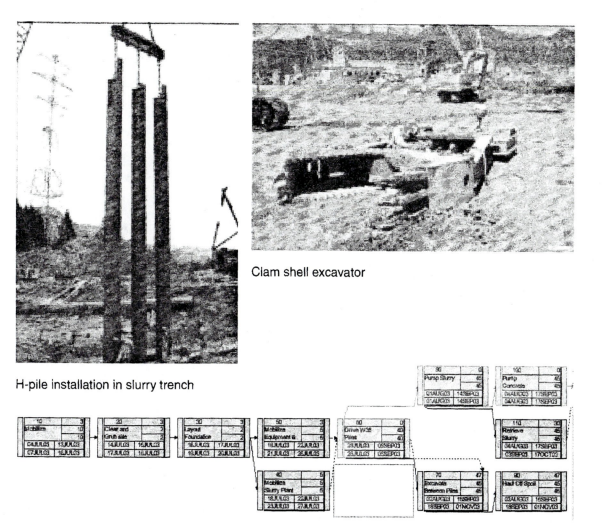

Clam shell excavator

H-pile installation in slurry trench

The effect of a must start constraint

The critical path now begins with the pile driving activity and continues to the end of the network. Constraints such as the one shown in Figure 7.5 can change the original definition of the critical path as being the longest path through the network.

Constraints versus Relationships with Lag Values

Moving activities later in time with constraints is not the only way to impose a delay. Relationships with lag values can achieve the same result. However, the result is often temporary and may require significantly more resources to monitor and control. Figures 7.6 and 7.7 illustrate this point.

Figure 7.6 illustrates that both the constraint (upper part of figure) and the relationship with a lag value (lower part of figure) can cause activity K to begin on workday 45. The early finish (EF) of the unidentified activity preceding activity K (not G) is shown to be workday 32. Neither activity G nor the activity with the EF = 32 is forcing the start of activity K when the constraint is in place; however, activity K is being pushed by activity G when the FS 6 relationship is in place. This can become a problem when the duration of activity G changes or when the path leading to activity G is elongated. Figure 7.7 shows the result of a change in the beginning of activity G.

In Figure 7.7, the original intent of the start constraint is lost when the lag is used. To limit the start of activity K to day 45 or later prevails with the use of the constraint. The calculated date, 52, is larger than the constraint date of workday 45. However, when the relationship and lag are used, the start of activity K is delayed an additional 6 days past when the activity could have started. At worst, this delay in the start of activity K is misleading if it is unchanged during the updating process. If the lag is to be

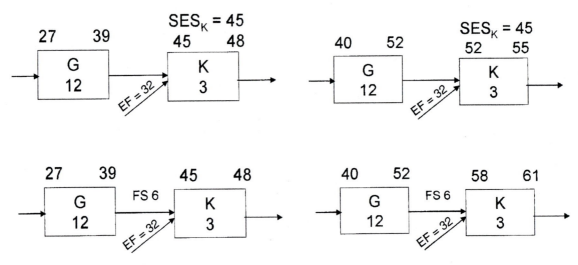

Figure 7.6
SES constraint versus relationship and lag value.

Figure 7.7
Activity G is delayed.

changed, then there is the additional work necessary of identifying the problem and correcting it when the effectiveness of the network is measured.

Creation of Zero Total Float and Zero Free Float

There are times when activities need to be linked together, such as the notification of a subcontractor 30 days prior to the subcontractor's beginning work. A way to link these two activities so that the notification activity always begins 30 days prior to the subcontractor's work activity is to use a constraint that creates zero free float. In Figure 7.8, the scenario is illustrated with the addition of a pushing activity for the subcontractor's work, "Subcontractor work area available," and a predecessor to "Subcontractor notification."

There are multiple activities intervening between "Site preparation" and "Subcontractor work area available." If there were no constraint on "Subcontractor notification," this activity would be allowed to begin just after notice to proceed (NTP), and it would have 121 days of free float (FF = 151 − 30 = 121). At each update, the notification would likely have not started (occurred) and would be scheduled to begin on the data date, moving forward in time at each update interval. It would be better if "Subcontractor notification" moved in unison with "Subcontractor work" and had zero free float. With "Subcontractor work" occurring as shown, the start of "Subcontractor notification" would begin on day 121. Placing an SES of workday 121 on this activity would help until the activity "Subcontractor work" moved in time. Should this happen, notification would no longer begin just 30 days before the work. Consequently, a new kind of constraint is needed to link the two activities such that notification has zero free

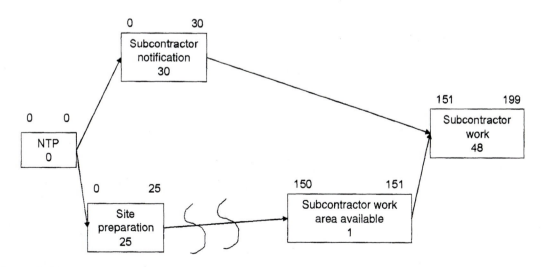

Figure 7.8
Example partial network.

float. Both P3® and SureTrak® provide this type of constraint in addition to those already described.

There may be similar reasons to make an activity have zero total float—make it appear to be critical—when the traditional calculation logic would not create this condition. The zero total float constraint in SureTrak® and P3® can accomplish this goal.

Sometimes, extraordinary network manipulations with regard to constraints can create more problems than they fix, especially when the manipulations are undertaken by a novice. Exercise care when using zero float constraints and mandatory constraints because they may create unexpected float conditions on linked activities.

Conclusion

The use of constraints helps the manager include owner-imposed schedule dates and the limits imposed by material deliveries, subcontractor availability, and weather-related conditions in the schedule. The effect of using constraints is that the relationships originally presented between total and free float no longer apply. Also, the definition of the critical path can be changed when constraints are imposed on a network. With a constraint in the network there may be more than one critical path that does not emanate from the first activity and terminate at the last activity. Instead, paths without total float or with negative total float may begin and end anywhere within the network, based on the type and location of the applied constraints.

Problems and/or Questions

1. Use the network in Figure 7.6. Give activity K an SES of 25, activity G an SLF of 19, and activity H an SMS of 22. Recalculate the network, showing the new dates and floats.

2. In the network described in problem 5, Chapter 5, what is the difference between the original network and one with a SMF on activity K of day 36?

3. Answer the following questions from the diagram that follows:

   a. What is the early finish of activity F?

   b. What is the late start of activity W?

   c. What is the early finish of activity K?

   d. What is the late start of activity K?

   e. What are the FF and TF on activity W?

   f. What is the FF on activity E?

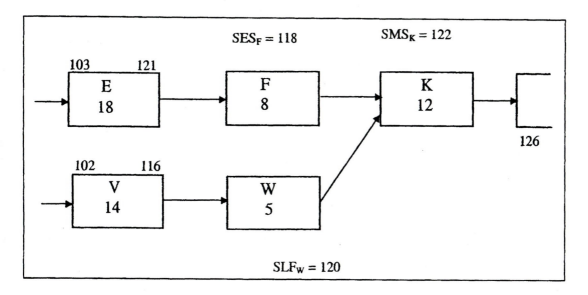

4. Use the following diagram to calculate the dates (early and late) and the total and free floats. The relationship between activity F and activity L is finish-to-finish zero.

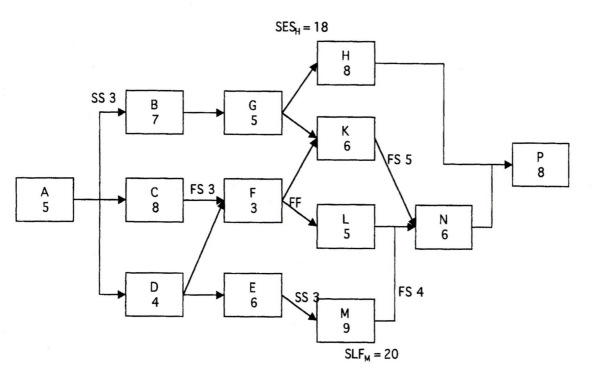

5. Use the diagram from problem 6, Chapter 6. Compare and contrast the effects of using a zero free float constraint on activity G with a finish-to-finish 8 relationship between activities G and H or with an SES on activity G of workday 17 if the duration of activity F became 12 days instead of the 6 days now scheduled.

CHAPTER 8

Updating

Goal

Point out the importance of schedule updates and describe and demonstrate their use.

Objectives

- Describe and demonstrate monitoring and recording progress as they relate to the data date.
- Describe and demonstrate how resources are updated.
- Describe other types of network changes during the update period.
- Describe and demonstrate the analysis of updated schedules.
- Identify problem resolution techniques.
- Describe update reporting and its importance.

Introduction

Updating a network has two specific components, *monitoring project progress* and *making changes* such as logic and duration adjustments to the network to better reflect project expectations. To function efficiently as management tools, networks must be updated. The current job status and the predicted effects of progress on downstream activities afford project management the opportunity to assess the risk of outcomes, to evaluate potential changes, and to make informed decisions.

One important outcome of the update is the ability to compare the current project status with the anticipated progress as represented by the original schedule and budget. Capturing the schedule, prior to any progress reporting, and storing it as a *baseline* is essential for this type of comparison. Some scheduling programs call this baseline a *target* schedule. Some scheduling programs keep more than one baseline, or target, schedule.

Monitoring Schedule Progress

Once a baseline schedule has been saved for comparison purposes, the project progress can be recorded. This means that a *data date,* or progress status date, should be selected. Data collected until this date is actual and known. Information about future events is conjecture. These estimates about future events may be based on experience, like the information in the original schedule. Once the data date is selected, the actual starts and finishes for each activity occurring prior to this date must be collected.

Actual starts, actual finishes, and *remaining durations* are the data elements needed for *statusing,* or monitoring, project progress. An actual start date identifies when an activity actually began. It is clear that actual starts should not be identified unless they occur prior to the data date. If the activity finishes prior to the data date, an actual finish date is needed for the activity. However, if the activity has started but will not finish prior to the data date, a remaining duration is needed. The remaining duration is an estimate of the amount of time, in worktime units (days, hours), needed to complete the activity. The calculated early finish of an activity that is in progress is found in equation 8-1.

$$EF_{calculated} = Data\ Date\ +\ Remaining\ Duration \qquad (8\text{-}1)$$

Although scheduling programs have the option of allowing the user to report the actual start dates and finish dates and/or remaining durations, they also generally allow the user to assign a percent complete to the activity. The user should be cautious when using percent complete, as the program's calculated results may not match the user's expectations.

Consider the baseline network in Figure 8.1. The forward pass calculation is done and activities A-C-H-M-N form the critical path. If the data date for the network's first update is workday 15, denoted by the dashed line, which activities have begun, which ones have finished, and which are in progress?

From the Figure 8.1 baseline schedule it appears that activities A, C, and D should be complete by workday 15 and that activities B, E, G, and H should be in progress, based on the original network calculations. However, the scheduler must rely on personal observation or reports from the field to know the actual project status. Once the progress has been included in the network, the project status must be analyzed. Management personnel must be satisfied that the schedule that is submitted describes the project accurately and that any uncompensated time extensions have been reviewed and adjusted if needed. The following is the update information for the project shown in Figure 8.1:

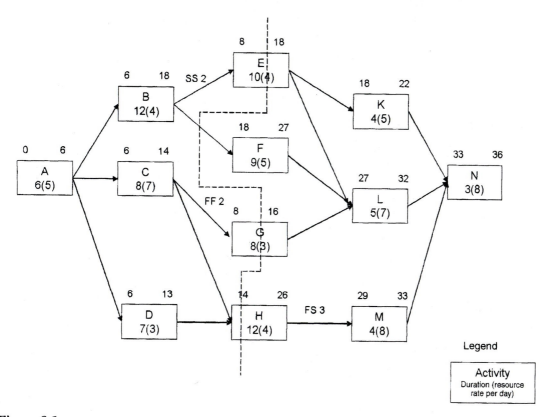

Figure 8.1
Example network for update.

Data Date: Workday 15

From the field—

- Activity A began as planned but took 2 days longer than originally planned, due to inclement weather.
- Activities B, C, and D all began as soon as possible, when activity A was complete.
- Anticipated productivity improvements over projections are expected to be responsible for activity B's reduction in duration from 12 days to 10 days.
- Activity C is expected to require its original duration.
- Activity D has 1 day of remaining duration.
- Activity E began as soon as allowed by its predecessor and is expected to be complete within its original 10-day duration.

Although the field scheduler was contacted, no other progress data available. There were, however, changes to the baseline network:

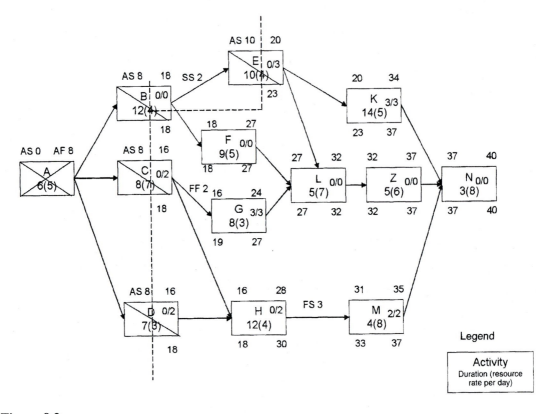

Figure 8.2
Updated network diagram.

- The original duration of activity K was entered improperly and should have been 14 days.
- Another activity must be entered between L and N. Activity Z has a 5-day duration and uses six resources per day.

Figure 8.2 shows the result of updating the network with the information provided. The activities that are complete have "Xs" through their boxes, whereas those that are in progress have a slash mark. These symbols help identify an activity's status quickly. Activities that are complete have actual start (AS) and finish (AF) dates and no late dates or floats. Activities that are in progress have actual starts, early and late finish dates, and total and free floats. All relationships seem to be holding until the C-G relationship is investigated. The only predecessor to activity G is activity C, with a finish-to-finish 2 relationship. Activity C is scheduled to finish tomorrow (workday 16). The relationship would suggest that activity G should finish on day 18. Consequently, it should have started on day 10. In consultation with the field personnel, no progress was reported for activity G. Some computer programs use the morning of a day to describe the start of an activity, whereas others use the evening of the day prior. The hand calculations done thus far have used day 0 as the start of the first activity, which is the end of the day prior—the first activity actually begins on day 1. Therefore, the soonest G could start is the day after the data date, day 16 (15 + 1). The calculation for activity G begins on day 16, and it is not in progress.

The project duration has increased 4 days and the critical path has changed (now B, F, L, Z, and N). Project personnel must now analyze the updated schedule and decide if 40 days' duration is too long and will cost more in liquidated damages than crashing the network the required number of days. They must also decide on the appropriateness of the activities on the critical path and possibly make some decisions regarding activities and relationships.

Updating Resources and Costs

Figures 8.3, 8.4, and 8.5 show a network diagram, a bar chart, and a histogram of a baseline schedule. A list of progress statistics is also provided. Use these diagrams as practice to find the pre- and post-update histogram and network diagram with calculations. A solution, along with an analysis of the results of the changes, is shown in Appendix A.

The update information provided includes

- Data date is workday 14.
- Activity A was extended 2 days, due to an equipment breakdown, and the cost increased by $200.
- Activity B did not start until day 5 but was completed in its original duration.
- Activity E began as soon as its predecessor was complete and has a remaining duration of 1 day.
- Activity C is 67% complete.
- A new activity, L, with a duration of 2 workdays, follows activity F and precedes activity K. Its cost is $300/day.
- All other activity dependencies remain the same, and no other information is available at this time.

The actual resource use to date for an activity or the total resource use when an activity is completed should be documented during each update. This updated information enables management to accurately compare the current project condition with the baseline or originally estimated condition. One method of making this comparison is to use an *earned value analysis* (Chapter 9). When using a computerized scheduling program, such as Primavera®, resources update automatically, relying on the calculated percent

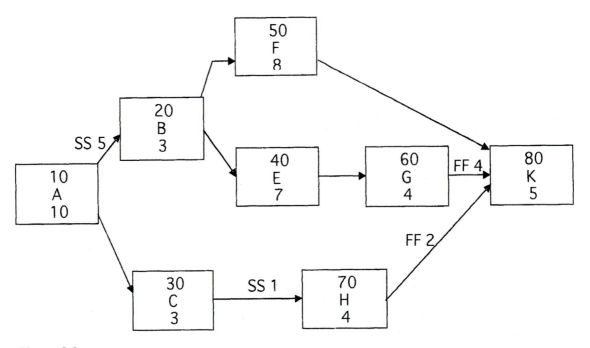

Figure 8.3
Network diagram.

ID	Activity	Dur	Resource Rate ($/day)	1	2	3	4	5	6	7	8	9	10	11	12	13	14	15	16	17	18	19	20	21	22	23
10	A	10	100	100	100	100	100	100	100	100	100	100	100													
20	B	3	200						200	200	200															
40	E	7	125									125	125	125	125	125	125	125								
50	F	8	200									200	200	200	200	200	200	200	200	→						
30	C	3	150											150	150	150					→					
70	H	4	220											220	220	220	220					→				
60	G	4	350																350	350	350	350				
80	K	5	450																			450	450	450	450	450
Period Totals				100	100	100	100	100	300	300	300	425	425	475	695	695	545	545	550	350	350	800	450	450	450	450

——→ Total float   ▓▓▓ Critical activities

Figure 8.4
Bar chart of Figure 8.3.

complete of each updated activity. Though in reality, resource use is not usually uniformly distributed throughout the activity's duration, this is the default and most common method of allocation by scheduling programs. Therefore, when the manager relies on a computer scheduling program to calculate resource use to date based on percent complete, an inaccurate picture of resource use frequently emerges. When using the construction schedule to manage and improve construction sequencing and productiv-

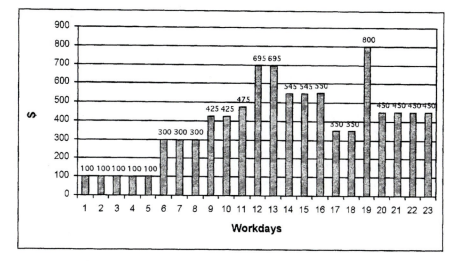

Figure 8.5
Original network histogram (from Figure 8.1 network).

ity projections in the future, or when relying on these documents for change orders or claims, *accuracy is essential.* Therefore, actual usage and the best possible projection of the final resource total should be policy. This requires careful examination of the up-dated schedule and not blind acceptance of what a software program produces.

Changes to Network Components

When other changes are required to make the network more descriptive or to correct errors, changes to durations, descriptions, constraints, and resources may be required. When these changes are made, the scheduler must review the resulting schedule to en-sure that the specification-related constraints are still met. The best example of this checking that the contract-required completion date is still met—the schedule should not exceed the specified duration.

How Scheduling Programs Assign Dates

Once a network has been updated, the revised project duration can be identified and compared with the target schedule to determine if the completion date is acceptable. Changes to the end date must be analyzed to determine their impact with respect to specified project requirements. If the project has been extended past its specified completion date, changes may be required in activity duration, by crashing, or in activity relationships. Replanning should also be done to determine if additional crews or equipment could bring the schedule into alignment. Choices regarding the cost trade-offs of double shifting or increased resources (crashing) should be weighed against the cost of delays, such as liquidated damages and increased *overhead.*

Computerized scheduling programs do not always assign actual dates to activities when the data date is changed. Instead, they rely on the project professional to note real progress dates. This practice is preferred because it makes the to-date and final as-built record reflect real progress and real dates, so that the schedule is an effective historical record that can be used in court, if needed, and so that update reports highlight problems early, while there is ample time to correct them. If an activity was supposed to have started or to have been completed during the current update period, but there was no progress reported, the program will likely make assumptions. If no start is reported, it is likely that the program will give the activity a calculated start on the data date or the day after, depending on how dates are viewed programmatically. Similarly, if an actual start has been assigned to an activity, but no remaining duration has been given, the program will again assign the data date or day after as the closest day to a remaining duration of zero. The schedule can therefore be adversely affected by errors and omissions in progress reporting—the program will make fictitious assumptions when data is lacking.

Correcting Problems

What type of change is most effective? Changes to scheduled duration mean changing productivity estimates. This is accomplished in the field by increasing the crew size, employing more productive workers (more journeymen and fewer apprentices), or scheduling more work time for each day worked (e.g., 10-hour shifts or two shifts instead on a normal 8-hour work day). Another alternative is to change the work calendar from a 5-day workweek to a 6- or 7-day workweek. It is critical that changes be made to the longest path (critical path) through the network. Shortening the duration of a noncritical activity only increases its float (see Chapter 5). Shortening noncritical activity durations does not shorten the network duration, although it can shorten a path duration if a milestone date is exceeded.

Logic can also be changed to shorten paths. Alternate construction methods may be needed to change logic relationships. Care should be taken when making previously serial activity strings into more parallel formations. Remember that logic constraints are often resource-dependent. Be sure that resources are available or can be made available more quickly than originally planned when logic is changed.

Reporting

As previously mentioned, the narrative report is generally required with the update submittal. The narrative gives a complete account of what has occurred on the project since the last update or, if no other update has been performed, since the project start. It highlights the progress that has been made in the intervening period, notes any difficulties and the proposed or actual solutions, explains implemented changes in sequencing, and notes any changes to the planned project completion. Appendix B provides a sample narrative report.

In addition to the narrative, specifications often require a request for payment. For hard money projects the information in the request for payment can be supported by an earned value report if activities are resource-loaded with prices that reflect the bid total. The earned value report requires a target schedule to be effective. Although the report may not be one the company would like to submit to the owner because it compares actual with budget and it compares planned with budget, it does provide a resource percent complete and to-date values that can be compared update to update. The percent complete or the compared to-date values can be used to support a request for payment. Many requests for payment require a total of all work done to date less what has been previously paid to determine the current amount due to the constructor. Many contracts also require the deduction of a fixed percentage (5 to 10%) as retained earnings to be paid the constructor when the project is finally accepted. Some samples of "Request for Payment" forms are available in Appendix C.

Conclusion

Once prepared, the schedule must be updated regularly through a well-defined procedure. The update should be prepared with input from the project team—those intimately familiar with the work. During this process, the integrity of the schedule must not be compromised by changes in logic or changes in the constraint dates. The updated schedule should indicate the percentage of an activity that is complete and its remaining duration.

During the updating process schedule discrepancies can be created when actual construction progress data is not supplied and the scheduling software makes fictitious assumptions. Therefore, a validity or reality check of the schedule must always be made before an updated schedule is accepted.

Accurate and detailed reports such as those generated when a schedule is updated provide the critical information for tracking and controlling the numerous activities of a construction project. The updated schedule is an effective instrument for assessing the project progress and for determining the impact of delay on all subsequent activities. Together the updated schedule and the baseline schedule provide the necessary understanding of project delays that help management develop courses of action to eliminate or reduce the impact of such delays. When both the owner and the contractor are following a common baseline schedule, time-related changes that arise during the course of the project and that are depicted by the updated schedule can be clearly understood and resolved.

Problems and/or Questions

1. Use the information that follows to construct the pre-updated network and calculate the activity dates and floats. Then apply the update information and determine the changes that have occurred.

Activity	Duration	Successor	Lag Type	Lag Value
A	7	B	FS	0
		C	SS	2
		E	FS	0
B	12	K	FS	3
C	8	F	FS	0
E	3	F	FS	0
		G	FS	5
F	6	K	FS	0
		H	FS	0
G	5	H	FS	0
		L	SF	10
K	4	M	FS	0
H	5	M	FS	0
		N	FF	4
L	3	N	FS	0
M	2	P	FS	0
N	5	P	FS	0
P	6	—		

- Data date = day 12.
- Activity A began as planned but was delayed, due to subcontractor productivity. Activity A finished on day 9.
- Activities B and E started when activity A was complete. Activity E has a 1-day remaining duration, whereas activity B's remaining duration is 8.
- Activity G began as planned and finished on day 8.
- Activity K's duration is expected to be 7 days, due to anticipated union wage-renegotiation delays.
- The SF 10 relationship between activities G and L was input incorrectly. The correct relationship is FS 5.
- A new activity, J, is added between activities K and M. Its duration is 3 days.

2. List the reports that should be submitted to the project manager so that he or she can best determine the status of the project. Describe why each report is appropriate and why the number of reports you have selected is appropriate.

3. Review the reports in Appendix D. Write a narrative that describes the current status of the project.

4. Analyze the reports in Appendix D and suggest how 3 days could be taken out of the schedule. Support your contentions.

5. Data for a small project follow. The initial starting date, or base date, is zero and the data date is workday 15. All activities started as planned prior to the data date, unless otherwise specified. All activities except D, F, G, H, K, and L have been completed. Activity D has 5 days' remaining duration. Activity H is also no longer preceded by activity G. Activity L has been reduced by 1 day, and activity K remains unchanged.

   a. Construct the original scheduled precedence network.

   b. Update the project and determine the new total and free floats, the project duration, and the new critical path. Construct a new histogram for the resources.

Activity	Duration	Depends On
A	7	——
B	5	A
C	2	A
D	7	B
E	1	B, D
F	8	B, D
G	6	B, C, D
H	6	E, G
K	3	E, G, F
L	3	H, K

6. Update the following network. The information for the update is as follows:

   a. Data date = workday 12.

   b. Activities A and E were completed in their original durations.

   c. Activity B began as planned but took 1 additional day to complete.

   d. Activity C took 2 additional days to complete after starting on day 0.

   e. Activity D began on day 9 and has 2 days remaining.

   f. Activity H began when activity E was completed but has 7 days remaining.

   g. There is now an SMS date on activity K of day 25.

Prior to updating the network, calculate the early and late dates and the free and total floats and identify the critical path. Incorporate the update data into the network. After updating the network, recalculate the early and late dates, find the floats, and label the critical path.

Activity	Duration	Depends On
A	3	———
B	7	———
C	6	———
D (SES 10)	5	A, B (FF 4)
E	1	B
F	4	C
G	4	D
H (SLF = 17)	3	E, C
I	7	F, G, H
J	6	G (FS 4)
K	3	J (SS 2), I

CHAPTER 9

Earned Value

Goal

Present earned value as a method of measuring schedule and resource achievement.

Objectives

- Describe and discuss the three earned value measures:
  - Budgeted cost of work performed
  - Actual cost of work performed
  - Budgeted cost of work scheduled
- Demonstrate the use of earned value reporting and its use in management by exception.

Introduction

Earned value analysis was developed by the U.S. Department of Defense (DoD) as the Cost/Schedule Control System Criteria (C/SCSC) to help DoD decision makers improve the performance of their projects. Earned value reporting requires a budgeted resource and an updated resource value, as well as a baseline, or target, schedule with corresponding resource values for appropriate comparison. The earned value can be established for any resource: money, material, equipment, or labor. This chapter will use the money and manpower resources for discussion and description.

Earned Value Calculations and Reporting

Earned value reporting relies on three measures of performance: the *budgeted cost of work performed (BCWP)*, or *the earned value;* the *actual cost of work performed (ACWP);* and the *budgeted cost of work scheduled (BCWS)*. Each of these measures comes from one of the schedule components previously mentioned.

The budgeted cost of work performed can be found for an activity or the project. For the project, it is a summation of the budgeted values for the prescribed resource for work completed to date. Figure 9.1 shows how the BCWP, or earned value, is calculated for a sample project.

The data date shown in Figure 9.1 is workday 6, and the earned value of activity A is 32; of activity B, 4; and, of activity C, 12. Thus, the earned value for the project up to the data date is 48. The earned value, or BCWP, gives little information unless it is compared with another measure. Figure 9.2 shows the actual resource-use bar chart for the same network.

Data date is day 6.

I.D.	Desc	Dur	Total Resource	1	2	3	4	5	6	7	8	9	10	11	12	13	14	15
10	A	4	32	8	8	8	8											
20	B	3	6					2	2	2		→						
30	C	7	28				4	4	4	4	4	4	4					
40	D	2	14											7	7		→	
50	E	5	25											5	5	5	5	5
60	F	3	9													3	3	3
Sum			114															
Period Sum (Early Start)				8	8	8	12	6	6	6	4	4	4	12	12	8	8	8
Cumulative Sum				8	16	24	36	42	48	54	58	62	66	78	90	98	106	114

Figure 9.1
Earned value bar chart.

Data date is day 6.

I.D.	Desc	Dur	Total Resource	1	2	3	4	5	6	7	8	9	10	11	12	13	14	15
10	A	4	35	7	9	9	10											
20	B	3	8					3	3	2		→						.
30	C	7	34				5	5	5	5	6	4	4					
40	D	2	14											7	7		→	
50	E	5	25											5	5	5	5	5
60	F	3	9													3	3	3
Sum			125															
Period Sum (Early Start)				7	9	9	15	8	8	7	6	4	4	12	12	8	8	8
Cumulative Sum				7	16	25	40	48	56	63	69	73	77	89	101	109	117	125

Figure 9.2
Actual cost updated bar chart.

Activity Information				Workdays														
I.D.	Desc	Dur	Total Resource	1	2	3	4	5	6	7	8	9	10	11	12	13	14
10	A	4	32	8	8	8	8										
20	B	3	6			2	2	2									
30	C	7	28			4	4	4	4	4	4	4					
40	D	2	14										7	7			
50	E	5	25										5	5	5	5	5
60	F	3	9										3	3	3		
Sum			114														
Period Sum (Early Start)				8	8	14	14	6	4	4	4	4	12	15	8	8	5
Cumulative Sum				8	16	30	44	50	54	58	62	66	78	93	101	109	114

Figure 9.3
Baseline bar chart.

The actual cost of work performed (ACWP) is not the same as the BCWP for the project. The ACWP for activity A is 35; for B, 6; and for C, 15. Thus, the project ACWP, as of the data date, is 56.

The budgeted cost of work scheduled (BCWS) is derived from the baseline, or target, schedule for the network. It is the "cost" of the activities that were supposed to be completed by the data date. Figure 9.3 shows the baseline bar chart for the Figure 9.1 network used in this example.

On the data date, day 6, activity A should have contributed thirty-two resources; activity B, six resources; and, activity C, sixteen resources. Thus, the project BWCS should be 32 + 6 + 16 = 54.

Measures of Performance

There are two primary methods of comparing BCWP with ACWP. One method calculates what is known as the cost performance index (CPI) but can refer to the "cost" of any resource. For example, if the values of BCWP and ACWP were work hours, this calculation would still be termed the cost performance index.

$$Cost\ Performance\ Index = \frac{BCWP}{ACWP} \qquad (9\text{-}1)$$

The cost performance index for the project shown in Figures 9.1 and 9.2 is

$$CPI = \frac{48}{56} = 0.86$$

It is quite clear that a cost performance index of less than 1.0 indicates a project that is *over budget,* because the actual cost is greater than the budgeted cost. A CPI can be calculated for the project or for each activity. Once the manager identifies a project requiring attention due to a CPI of less than 1.0, individual activity CPI values can be used to determine which activities are most responsible for the overall poor project performance.

The cost variance, the other method of cost comparison, is the difference between the BCWP and ACWP:

$$Cost\ Variance = BCWP - ACWP \qquad (9\text{-}2)$$

The cost variance for the example project is –8. A negative variance indicates an *over budget* condition, whereas a positive variance indicates an *under budget* condition. Just as with the CPI, the cost variance can be also be calculated for each activity. Identifying the activities with the largest negative variance can help the manager quickly isolate troubled activities—reducing the number of activities that need detailed scrutiny enables the manager to *manage by exception* those conditions that are the exception instead of the rule.

The schedule performance may also be evaluated using an index or a variance. The schedule performance index (SPI) is calculated using the following formula:

$$Schedule\ Performance\ Index = \frac{BCWP}{BCWS} \qquad (9\text{-}3)$$

$$SPI = \frac{48}{54} = 0.89$$

Just as with the CPI, an SPI value that is less than 1.0 is undesirable. Values such as 0.89 indicate that the project is *behind schedule*. Values over 1.0 indicate a project that is ahead of schedule. When the SPI is 1.0, the project is considered to be on schedule.

The schedule variance is the difference between the BCWP and BCWS:

$$Schedule\ Variance = BCWP - BCWS \qquad (9\text{-}4)$$

The schedule variance for the example project is –6. Negative variances indicate behind-schedule conditions, whereas positive variances indicate ahead of schedule conditions. Just as with the SPI, the schedule variance can be calculated for each activity as well as for the project.

Another method of comparison is to plot the CPI and SPI on the axes of a graph like that shown in Figure 9.4.

The Figure 9.4 diagram shows the cost performance index on the vertical scale (ordinate) and the schedule performance index on the horizontal scale (abscissa). These axes could be reversed, with corresponding changes to the quadrant descriptions.

Each quadrant in the diagram shown in Figure 9.4 relates to a composite of the project's performance. Quadrant 1 is the most preferable project condition, ahead of schedule and under budget, whereas quadrant 3 is the least preferable.

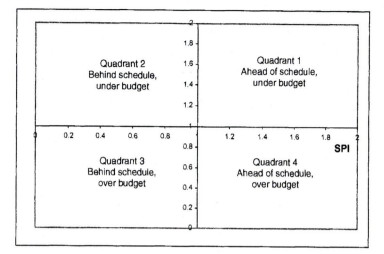

Figure 9.4
CPI/SPI comparison.

Managers should use variances and performance indices with care. Recall that the default in some computerized scheduling programs, and the most common method of resource distribution, is uniform, with equal resource measures being allocated to each workday of an activity's duration. Consider what the outcome might be if the baseline and current budget had resources distributed uniformly but in reality the activity had 80% of its cost in the first 20% of the time (perhaps this is due to a large equipment purchase expense) and distributed uniformly thereafter for the remainder of the project duration. Assume that the duration of the activity is 10 days and the cost is $10,000. Figure 9.5 shows how the resource might actually be distributed, as compared with how it is assigned by the program's default uniform distribution. If the data date cut the sample activity at its 50% complete mark, or workday 5, and no dates had slipped, the result would be

$$\text{Cost Variance} = \text{BCWP} - \text{ACWP} = \$5,000 - \$8,750 = -\$3,750$$
$$\text{CPI} = \text{BCWP/ACWP} = 5,000/8,750 = 0.57$$
$$\text{Schedule Variance} = \text{BCWP} - \text{BCWS} = \$5,000 - \$5,000 = 0$$
$$\text{SPI} = \text{BCWP/BCWS} = 1.0$$

The manager would correctly conclude that this activity was on schedule. However, the conclusion might be tempered by the fact that the activity appears to be over budget. This conclusion might be in error and the result of an inaccurate or inappropriate allocation of resources throughout the duration of the activity. Thus, the manager must be cognizant of resource-use requirements and allocation schemes before drawing conclusions based on earned value reporting when all activity resources are allocated in a uniform manner.

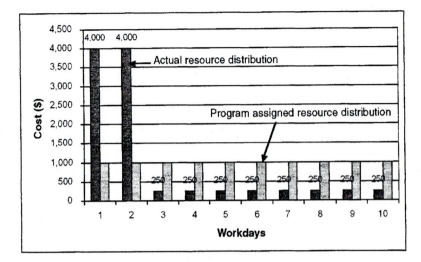

Figure 9.5
Sample resource distribution histogram.

ACTIVITY ID	PCT CMP	ACTUAL	CUMULATIVE TO DATE EARNED	PLANNED	VARIANCE COST	SCHEDULE	AT COMPLETION BUDGET	ESTIMATE
- Project Executive								
D1010	100.0	111.00	100.00	100.00	-11.00	.00	100.00	111.00
D1025	100.0	.00	.00	.00	.00	.00	.00	.00
D1070	20.0	45.00	11.20	33.60	-33.80	-22.40	56.00	56.00
D2010	100.0	80.00	80.00	80.00	.00	.00	80.00	80.00
D2025	100.0	40.00	40.00	40.00	.00	.00	40.00	40.00
D2070	80.0	32.00	32.00	28.00	.00	4.00	40.00	40.00
D1020	100.0	.00	.00	.00	.00	.00	.00	.00
D2020	100.0	.00	.00	.00	.00	.00	.00	.00
D1140	.0	.00	.00	.00	.00	.00	32.00	32.00
D2140	.0	.00	.00	.00	.00	.00	32.00	32.00
D1990	.0	.00	.00	.00	.00	.00	8.00	8.00
D2990	.0	.00	.00	.00	.00	.00	8.00	8.00
TOTAL	66.5	308.00	263.20	281.60	-44.80	-18.40	396.00	407.00

Figure 9.6
P3® earned value report.

Figure 9.6 shows a P3®-generated project earned value report. Notice that the report shows variance directly but does not calculate indices or show graphs. Although two of the beginning columns and the title lines have been excluded, Figure 9.6 shows the heart of the earned value report. Under the heading "Cumulative to Date," the reviewer will find the ACWP (actual), BCWP (earned), and BCWS (planned), in that order. The variances are shown so that it is apparent that the cost variance in D1010 is equal to BCWP – ACWP = 100.0 – 111.0 = –11.0, or over budget by 11.0 units. The schedule variance for activity D2070 is equal to BCWP – BCWS = 32.0 – 28.0 = 4.0 and means that this activity is ahead of schedule. The negative totals in both the cost and schedule variances for this project indicate that the project as a whole is over budget and behind schedule. It is also apparent that the problems are only in two activities, D1010 and D1070. Since activity D1010 is complete, changes will not help. However, the manager could focus attention and invest time in activity D1070, which is only 20% complete by resource. The *management by exception* principle is effectively demonstrated in Figure 9.6. Even though there are few activities shown in the project, it is clear where problems exist. Imagine the time savings that could be achieved if this were a project with more than 1,000 activities.

Figure 9.7 shows the way MS Project® handles earned value analysis, with column headings for each of the three primary earned value reporting measures and both the cost and schedule variance.

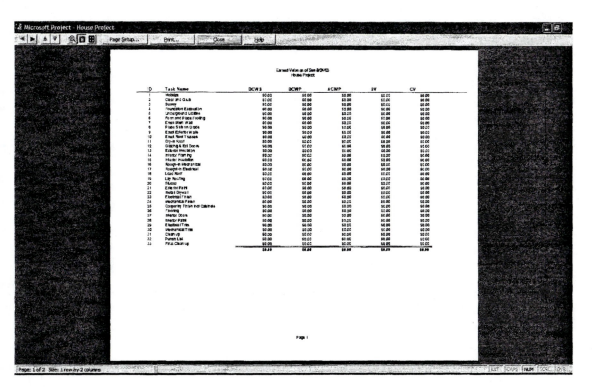

Figure 9.7
An earned value report from MS Project®.

Other Resource Allocation Schemes

Of the three programs mentioned in this text, P3®, MS Project®, and SureTrak®, only P3® allows other resource allocation schemes over the entire duration of the activity. Figures 9.8, 9.9, and 9.10 show three of P3®'s predefined allocation schemes. P3® also lets the user create other, nonstandard allocations.

Each of the three curves shown in Figures 9.8, 9.9, and 9.10 demonstrates an alternate way of distributing resources over the duration of an activity. Notice that, in each case, the duration is divided into ten segments, and the total of the percentages in each of these segments is 100%. Thus, when the P3® user opts to create a nonstandard distribution, the same attributes apply.

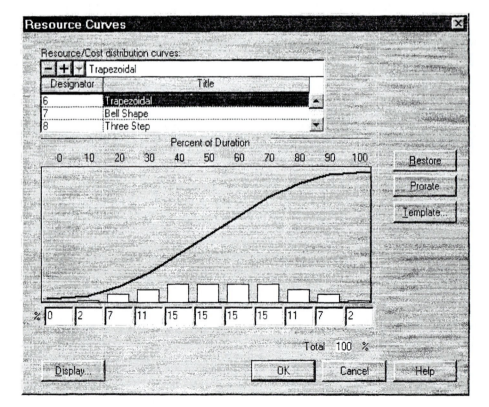

Figure 9.8
P3® curve 6, trapezoidal distribution.

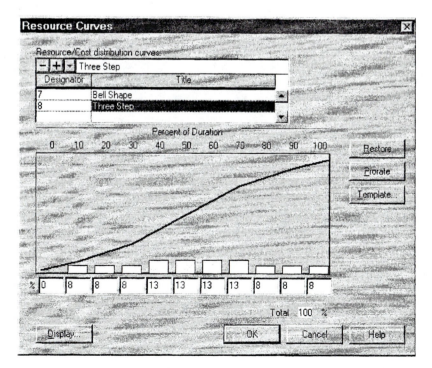

Figure 9.9
P3® curve 7, bell-shaped.

Figure 9.10
P3® curve 8, three-step.

Conclusion

Earned value is a quantitative management tool for tracking information about project status. It provides numerical measurements for reviewing project progress. Comparing planned (BCWS), earned (BCWP) and actual (ACWP) value for the project or for a project task provides an indication of cost and schedule performance. Indexes and variances of these values can provide management with early insight into problem areas. Earned value analysis consists of comparing the estimated versus actual resource expenditure.

The earned value management is the process of representing physical progress achieved on the project in terms of a cost/resource-based measure. Cash measures of cost or quantity measures of progress can be misleading and serious distortions can arise if physical progress is not related to resource expenditure in earned value terms. Scheduling programs use various rules and techniques to allocate the value of work performed to date as a proportion of the total activity value. These techniques must match the actual expenditure rate to avoid distortion of the earned values indexes and variances.

Problems and/or Questions

1. Describe how a project's earned value can be used to better manage projects.

2. Show a complete earned value analysis for a recent or current resource-loaded schedule. Describe the significance of all variances. Describe each resources allocation scheme used in the project.

3. There are blanked-out numbers in the earned value report that follows. Answer the questions that follow the report.

    a. What should the total resource percent complete be for this report?

    b. What is the cost variance for activity 213?

    c. What is the schedule variance for activity 308?

    d. What is the cost variance for activity 306?

    e. What is the budget at completion for 213?

    f. Is the project ahead or behind schedule, over or under budget?

Acme Motors

PRIMAVERA PROJECT PLANNER

Plant Expansion and Modernization

REPORT DATE 10APR00 RUN NO. 7
            20:44

EARNED VALUE REPORT - QUANTITY

START DATE 19JUL93   FIN DATE 13FEB95

Earned Value Report - Units

DATA DATE 27SEP93   PAGE NO. 1

ACTIVITY	RESOURCE	PCT CMP	.......CUMULATIVE TO DATE.......			......VARIANCE......		......AT COMPLETION......	
			ACWP	BCWP	BCWS	COST	SCHEDULE	BUDGET	ESTIMATE

ELECTRCN - Electrician

ACTIVITY	RESOURCE	PCT CMP	ACWP	BCWP	BCWS	COST	SCHEDULE	BUDGET	ESTIMATE
213	L ELECTRCN AS105	23.0	2850.00	2576.00	3248.00	?	?	?	11200.00
214	L ELECTRCN AS315	100.0	8385.00	8385.00	8385.00	.00	.00	8385.00	8385.00
216	L ELECTRCN BA670	100.0	7200.00	7200.00	7200.00	.00	.00	7200.00	7200.00
306	L ELECTRCN BA710	100.0	22500.00	20000.00		?	?	20000.00	22500.00
308	L ELECTRCN BA712	.0	.00	.00	800.00	?	?	1400.00	1400.00
310	L ELECTRCN BA730	.0	.00	.00	.00	.00	.00	1500.00	1500.00
312	L ELECTRCN BA731	.0	.00	.00	.00	.00	.00	10000.00	10000.00
416	L ELECTRCN BA860	.0	.00	.00	.00	.00	.00	72000.00	72000.00
418	L ELECTRCN BA913	.0	.00	.00	.00	.00	.00	9600.00	9600.00
436	L ELECTRCN BA850	.0	.00	.00	.00	.00	.00	6000.00	6000.00
516	L ELECTRCN BA750	.0	.00	.00	.00	.00	.00	2800.00	2800.00
526	L ELECTRCN BA780	.0	.00	.00	.00	.00	.00	1000.00	1000.00
626	L ELECTRCN BA901	.0	.00	.00	.00	.00	.00	9600.00	9600.00
	TOTAL	?	40935.00	38161.00	19633.00				163185.00

		ACWP	BCWP	BCWS				ESTIMATE
REPORT	TOTALS	40935.00	38161.00	19633.00				163185.00

141

4. Discuss the purpose of the "Estimate at Completion" column in the earned value report in problem 3. How do you see managers using the information it provides?

5. Discuss the difference between percent complete measured by resource and that measured by time. Use an example to illustrate your contentions.

6. Following is a simple project of four activities. The project is represented here as a bar chart. The sum of the amounts for the activities in the schedule of values approximates the originally anticipated cost of the project. Project duration is 5½ months.

- Schedule of values:

   A—$1,000   B—$3,000   C—$2,000   D— $2,000

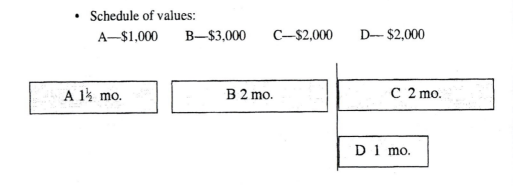

After 3 months, the following has been accomplished:
- Activity A: 100% complete, total cost $900
- Activity B: 60% complete, cost to date $1,600
- Activity C: 50% complete, cost to date $1,000

With the given information, determine the schedule of variance and the cost variance. State if the project is over or under budget and if the project is ahead of or behind schedule.

CHAPTER 10

Reporting

Goal

Present reporting requirements and how programs can be used to meet specified reporting requirements.

Objectives

- Describe and demonstrate report preparation techniques:
  - Matching report output to recipient
  - Determining report content
  - Sorting report content
  - Limiting reports through selection criteria
- Describe and demonstrate report interpretation:
  - The narrative
  - The request for payment
  - The historical value of the schedule
- Gain knowledge about reporting requirements and programmatic response.

Introduction

Reports are the bridge between what the schedule creator envisions and what the report readers understand. Knowing who will be reading the report will help the report creator choose how the report is ordered, what it contains, and how the information is displayed. Remembering that project reports are intended to be true representations of the status of a project, a specific snapshot in time that may become evidence to support claims, should impel the scheduler to make every effort to keep the record accurate and complete. Report interpretation is the key to knowing what is being communicated to management, prime contractors, owners, or other reviewers. Reports presented to the company by subcontractors and others must also be interpreted and analyzed.

Report Preparation

The Narrative

The purpose of the narrative is to tell the story of the schedule documents and, therefore, the project's progress in words. A good narrative is concise, complete, accurate, and informative. The total picture of the job's progress since the last update, or the project start, should be presented. It is often easiest to group the information by work breakdown structure (WBS) elements or subsystems, such as earthwork and concrete. The status of recently completed activities and those in progress should be presented in the narrative. Activity and project difficulties should be noted, along with their anticipated remedies, pending change orders, and/or expected outcomes. Details of construction errors not directly affecting the schedule or the owner should be omitted. Take the most positive stand possible while reporting candidly on project events. As this document is a part of the schedule submittal, it, too, may become a part of the ongoing project record, which may be used as evidence in project-related litigation. The narrative is the written evaluation of the many reports making up the schedule submittal. Therefore, the scheduler must first read and interpret the schedule reports before writing the narrative.

Although all of the information about the project is detailed in the schedule, a narrative report describing the project's progress, obstacles, and problem resolutions should accompany schedule submittals. Owners often require such a narrative from the prime contractor. Care should be taken in constructing the original network, and when updating it, to ensure that the network accurately reflects the facts. The original schedule, along with schedule updates, can become a legal record of performance. Although the narrative is not printed output from the scheduling program, it is a synopsis of what the reports contain. Professional language and thought are essential to the preparation and submission of an effective report. A sample narrative report is included in Appendix B.

The Recipients

When subcontractors report work to a prime contractor, they must clarify what has been accomplished and when, along with what is planned for the future. Additionally, deviations from the original plan should be noted and the results of these changes detailed.

- The owner, through the specifications, may require specific reports listing the activities by their early start dates or by their total float. The contractor should know how to prepare these reports for the owner.
- The construction company may have its own schedule reporting requirements as a part of a standard operating procedure or for inclusion in its master schedule.
- The prime contractor often has specified schedule submission requirements to which all subcontractors must conform.
- Lenders may require the contractor to supply project-processed monetary cash flows based on accomplishment of schedule activities.

Each report recipient may require a different level of detail or different organizational schemes for the reports received. Level of detail is often the key to whether the schedule reports are read and understood or filed without review. The construction company president may want a status overview of all the company's projects without any detail unless specifically requested. The project manager may want to know only about the *outliers* (exceptions), those activities on the project that have performed extremely well or extremely badly. The manager often chooses to ignore all of the other details. The project engineer, conversely, may want all of the project detail, and the concrete superintendent may want to see only the details of concrete-related activities.

The result of this need for varying levels of detail is that the individual responsible for the schedule must be capable of creating and delivering a variable set of documents that serve many different users. This may appear on the surface to be quite simple but generally it turns out to be the biggest challenge after the initial schedule is prepared.

The Scheduling Program Default Report Content

What is contained in the written report is crucial; too much information can be detrimental and daunting, whereas too little information can be mystifying. Most scheduling programs have some sort of default report content. For P3®, the default is the activity code line, which contains the activity identification number and its description, duration, early and late calendar dates, and total float, along with any activity codes that have been assigned. SureTrak® uses what is displayed on the screen to fashion its reports, thus WYSIWYG (what you see is what you get). MS Project® allows the user to print both a report and a view. Its reports are primarily predefined and span the gambit from tabular schedule reports to resource reports and graphics.

Report Sorting

The order in which the content of a report generated by a scheduling program is shown can be assigned by the scheduler. Typical sorting options include early start, total float, and activity identification. A report that is sorted by early start dates has activities arranged in ascending order, with activities occurring the earliest listed first. The last activity to occur is shown at the end of the list. The early start sort is useful when the order in which activities occur is most beneficial to the decision maker, as when what is happening in the next several weeks is the important information.

A report sorted by total float begins with the critical path and ends with the activity with the largest amount of float. The total float sort is useful for ensuring that the critical path activities are on the critical path and for determining near-critical activities and the activities with the largest floats.

When the report is sorted by activity identification, the numeric identifications precede the alpha identification and are used when the floats and dates for the activities of interest are unknown, as with a relationship report. The relationship report that details the predecessors and successors of each activity can help the reviewer follow paths of float, so that errors can be traced easily. The reviewer must know what the components of the path are and follow them—this is done best when activities are ordered by the identification numbers.

Some reports require nested sorting criteria, such as a report sorted first by total float and then by early start. The resulting report has activities primarily ordered by float. Then within each float category the activities are ordered by their early start dates. With such a report the critical path logic can almost be identified without any other information.

Figure 10.1 shows the P3® sort options on the report format screen. To obtain a report sorted first by total float and then by early start, a P3® user inputs those criteria, in order. The report that is produced looks like the one found in Figure 10.2. Note that the data date for the Figure 10.2 report is 15 May 03, so completed activities (at the top of the report) do not have total float data presented.

Not only tabular reports but also graphic data can be sorted in this way. Figure 10.3, using the Figure 10.2 data, shows a SureTrak® bar chart sorted by total float and then early start. Figure 10.4 shows an MS Project® Gantt chart sorted first by total float (the critical path appears first) and then by early start, so all of the activities flow from left to right across the bar chart.

Reports can also be sorted by activity codes, creating a report resulting, for example, in carpenters' being separated from pipe fitters or subcontractor "A" being separated from subcontractor "B." Activity codes are often used to create sorting and selection options that match different facets of the project. Activity codes can be used to indicate the project's *work breakdown structure (WBS)*. The WBS is a representation of successive layers of detail within the project. Figure 10.5 shows a typical project WBS; but many others can be developed.

Activity codes frequently relate to the person or group responsible for the work (e.g., superintendent or subcontractor), the location (e.g., building, column line, or

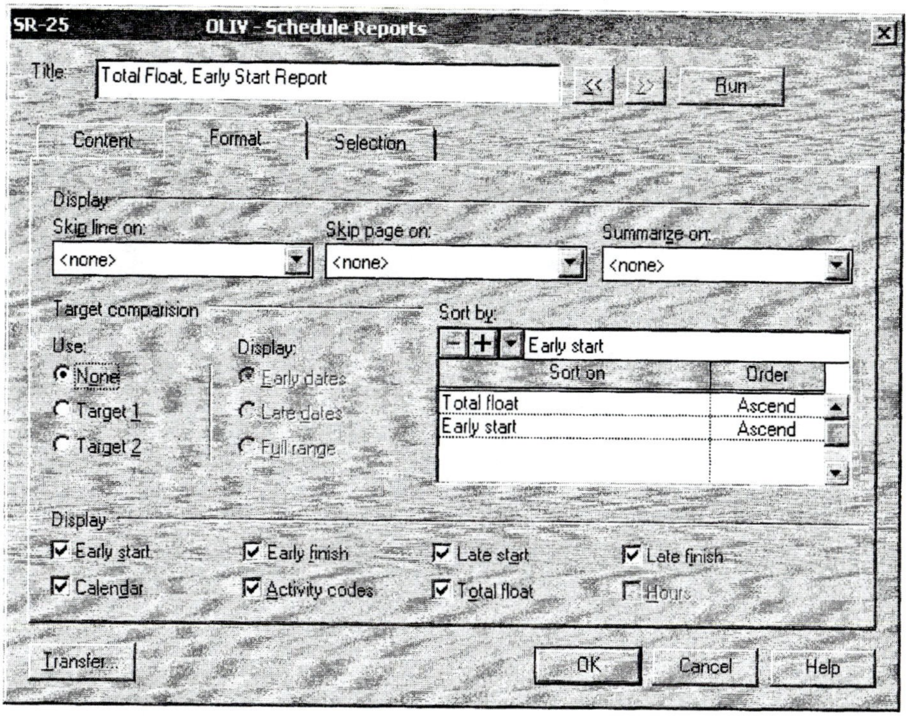

Figure 10.1
P3® schedule report format screen.

floor), the discipline or system (e.g., civil or mechanical), the type of work (e.g., concrete or pipe), and to project phases. A typical work breakdown structure as it relates to Figure 10.5 would have the first level equal to the company and level 1.3 equal to project 3, whereas level 1.3.3 would pertain to the mechanical work on project 3. This scheme continues to the last item at the lowest level. Most often, the lowest level is the activity level. Many contractors use activities codes in lieu of WBS designations.

Report Selection Criteria

To create a report that is limited to subcontractor 1 or just the activities on the critical path, the scheduler needs to use selection criteria. Activity codes, such as those identifying individual subcontractors, can be used to establish some of the limitation criteria. Other criteria are similar to those used for sorting or ordering the report. For example, reports can be limited by float, by dates or date ranges, by identification, and even by words in the activity description. Resource reports can have activities selected by a specific resource or by a range of resources.

```
Student Construction                    PRIMAVERA PROJEC T PLANNER          Camelback Country Club
REPORT DATE 10SEP03  RUN NO.   39                                          START DATE  9APR03  FIN DATE 15A UG03
           11:23
Total Float, Early Start Report                                            DATA DATE  15MAY03  PAGE NO.    1
```

ACTIVITY ID	ORIG DUR	REM DUR	%	CODE	ACTIVITY DESCRIPTION	EARLY START	EARLY FINISH	LATE START	LATE FINISH	TOTAL FLOAT
10	3	0	100		Clearing	9APR03A	14APR03A			
20	2	0	100		Surveying	15APR03A	17APR03A			
40	5	0	100		Fencing	15APR03A	22APR03A			
30	1	0	100		Locate Utilities	18APR03A	21APR03A			
50	3	0	100		Excavation and Shoring	22APR03A	25APR03A			
60	2	0	100		Fire Lines	28APR03A	30APR03A			
70	2	0	100		Rough Utilities	1MAY03A	5MAY03A			
80	2	0	100		Grade	6MAY03A	8MAY03A			
90	1	0	100		Temporary Fence	9MAY03A	12MAY03A			
100	1	1	0		Building Layout	13MAY03A	15MAY03		15MAY03	0
110	1	1	0		Termite Treatment	15MAY03	15MAY03	15MAY03	15MAY03	0
130	2	2	0		Dig Footings	16MAY03	19MAY03	16MAY03	19MAY03	0
140	3	3	0		Rebar /Forms	20MAY03	22MAY03	20MAY03	22MAY03	0
150	1	1	0		Pour Footings	23MAY03	23MAY03	23MAY03	23MAY03	0
160	1	1	0		Rebar / Forms	26MAY03	26MAY03	26MAY03	26MAY03	0
170	1	1	0		Pour Sidewalks	27MAY03	27MAY03	27MAY03	27MAY03	0
180	3	3	0		Asphalt	28MAY03*	30MAY03	28MAY03	30MAY03	0
190	1	1	0		Striping	28MAY03	28MAY03	28MAY03	28MAY03	0
200	3	3	0		Masonry Site Walls	29MAY03	2JUN03	29MAY03	2JUN03	0
210	2	2	0		Grout Walls	3JUN03	4JUN03	3JUN03	4JUN03	0
220	5	5	0		Rough Frame	5JUN03	11JUN03	5JUN03	11JUN03	0
230	5	5	0		Roof	12JUN03	18JUN03	12JUN03	18JUN03	0
240	2	2	0		Windows / Doors	19JUN03	20JUN03	19JUN03	20JUN03	0
250	4	4	0		Fire Caulk / Sprinkler s	23JUN03*	26JUN03	23JUN03	26JUN03	0
270	2	2	0		Insulate Roof Deck and Walls	26JUN03	27JUN03	26JUN03	27JUN03	0
280	3	3	0		Track and Studs	30JUN03	2JUL03	30JUN03	2JUL03	0
290	1	1	0		Insulate	3JUL03	3JUL03	3JUL03	3JUL03	0
300	2	2	0		Drywall	4JUL03	7JUL03	4JU L03	7JUL03	0
310	2	2	0		Screws	8JUL03	9JUL03	8JUL03	9JUL03	0
320	3	3	0		Tape and Texture	10JUL03	14JUL03	10JUL03	14JUL03	0
330	2	2	0		Interior Doors and Win dows	15JUL03	16JUL03	15JUL03	16JUL03	0
340	3	3	0		Paint	17JUL03	21JUL03	17JUL03	21JUL03	0
350	3	3	0		Ceiling Grid and Tiles	22JUL03	24JUL03	22JUL03	24JUL03	0
370	4	4	0		Trim HVAC -Electrical-Plumbing	25JUL03	30JUL03	25JUL03	30JUL03	0
380	1	1	0		Millwork	31JUL03	31JUL03	31JUL03	31JUL03	0
390	1	1	0		? frp	1AUG03	1AUG03	1AUG03	1AUG03	0
400	3	3	0		Install Flooring	4AUG03	6AUG03	4AUG03	6AUG03	0
410	1	1	0		Accesories Installed	7AUG03	7AUG03	7AUG03	7AUG03	0
420	1	1	0		Final Walk Thorugh	8AUG03	8AUG03	8AUG03	8AUG03	0
430	3	3	0		Final Clean up	11AUG03	13AUG03	11AUG03	13AUG03	0
440	2	2	0		Punchlist	14AUG03	15AUG03	14AUG03	15AUG03	0
120	1	1	0		Deliver All Materials	15MAY03	15MAY03	19MAY03	19MAY03	2
260	2	2	0		Rough In Utilities	19JUN03	20JUN03	24JUN03	25JUN03	3

Figure 10.2
Sample total float, early start report.

Report Interpretation

Red Flags

Red flags go up when the report reviewer sees evidence of inaccurate or inappropriate scheduling practices. This is because small errors may indicate significant problems. Typical red flags are:

- Negative floats
- Negative lag values
- Activity buildup on the data date

Act ID	Description	Orig Dur	Remaining Duration	Percent Complete	Early Start	Early Finish	Late Start	Late Finish	Total Float
10	Clearing	3	0	100	09APR03 A	14APR03 A	09APR03 A	14APR03 A	
20	Surveying	2	0	100	15APR03 A	17APR03 A	15APR03 A	17APR03 A	
40	Fencing	5	0	100	15APR03 A	22APR03 A	15APR03 A	22APR03 A	
30	Locate Utilities	1	0	100	18APR03 A	21APR03 A	18APR03 A	21APR03 A	
50	Excavation and Shoring	3	0	100	22APR03 A	25APR03 A	22APR03 A	25APR03 A	
60	Fire Lines	2	0	100	28APR03 A	30APR03 A	28APR03 A	30APR03 A	
70	Rough Utilities	2	0	100	01MAY03	05MAY03	01MAY03	05MAY03	
80	Grade	2	0	100	06MAY03	08MAY03	06MAY03	08MAY03	
90	Temporary Fence	1	0	100	09MAY03	12MAY03	09MAY03	12MAY03	
100	Building Layout	1	1	0	13MAY03	15MAY03	13MAY03	15MAY03	0
110	Termite Treatment	1	1	0	15MAY03	15MAY03	15MAY03	15MAY03	0
130	Dig Footings	2	2	0	16MAY03	19MAY03	16MAY03	19MAY03	0
140	Rebar /Forms	3	3	0	20MAY03	22MAY03	20MAY03	22MAY03	0
150	Pour Footings	1	1	0	23MAY03	23MAY03	23MAY03	23MAY03	0
160	Rebar / Forms	1	1	0	26MAY03	26MAY03	26MAY03	26MAY03	0
170	Pour Sidewalks	1	1	0	27MAY03	27MAY03	27MAY03	27MAY03	0
180	Asphalt	3	3	0	28MAY03 *	30MAY03	28MAY03	30MAY03	0
190	Striping	1	1	0	28MAY03	28MAY03	28MAY03	28MAY03	0
200	Masonry Site Walls	3	3	0	29MAY03	02JUN03	29MAY03	02JUN03	0
210	Grout Walls	2	2	0	03JUN03	04JUN03	03JUN03	04JUN03	0
220	Rough Frame	5	5	0	05JUN03	11JUN03	05JUN03	11JUN03	0
230	Roof	5	5	0	12JUN03	18JUN03	12JUN03	18JUN03	0
240	Windows / Doors	2	2	0	19JUN03	20JUN03	19JUN03	20JUN03	0
250	Fire Caulk / Sprinklers	4	4	0	23JUN03 *	26JUN03	23JUN03	26JUN03	0
270	Insulate Roof Deck and Walls	2	2	0	26JUN03	27JUN03	26JUN03	27JUN03	0
280	Track and Studs	3	3	0	30JUN03	02JUL03	30JUN03	02JUL03	0
290	Insulate	1	1	0	03JUL03	03JUL03	03JUL03	03JUL03	0
300	Drywall	2	2	0	04JUL03	07JUL03	04JUL03	07JUL03	0
310	Screws	2	2	0	08JUL03	09JUL03	08JUL03	09JUL03	0
320	Tape and Texture	3	3	0	10JUL03	14JUL03	10JUL03	14JUL03	0
330	Interior Doors and Windows	2	2	0	15JUL03	16JUL03	15JUL03	16JUL03	0
340	Paint	3	3	0	17JUL03	21JUL03	17JUL03	21JUL03	0
350	Ceiling Grid and Tiles	3	3	0	22JUL03	24JUL03	22JUL03	24JUL03	0
370	Trim HVAC-Electrical-Plumbing	4	4	0	25JUL03	30JUL03	25JUL03	30JUL03	0

Figure 10.3
SureTrak® bar chart descriptive columns sorted by TF and then ES.

- Slipped project duration, milestones, and changes in the level of detail depicted
- Calendars

Negative float can appear only when constraints are used and their imposed dates exceeded. Negative floats indicate that an owner- or constructor-imposed constraint has been violated. Sometimes, the constraint is inadvertently added to the project by establishing a "project must finish by" criterion when setting up the schedule initially. The project personnel responsible for preparing and updating the schedule must be

ID	Task Name	Duration	Total Slack	Start
1	Mobilize	3 days	0 days	Thu 7/24/03
2	Clear and Grub	1 day	0 days	Tue 7/29/03
3	Survey	1 day	0 days	Wed 7/30/03
4	Foundation Excavation	1 day	0 days	Thu 7/31/03
5	Underground Utilities	1 day	0 days	Thu 7/31/03
6	Form and Place Footing	3 days	0 days	Fri 8/1/03
7	Erect Stem Wall	2 days	0 days	Fri 8/8/03
8	Place Slab on Grade	1 day	0 days	Tue 8/12/03
9	Erect Exterior Walls	2 days	0 days	Thu 8/14/03
10	Erect Roof Trusses	1 day	0 days	Mon 8/18/03
11	Dry-in Roof	1 day	0 days	Tue 8/19/03
14	Interior Framing	8 days	0 days	Wed 8/20/03
17	Rough-in Electrical	3 days	0 days	Mon 9/1/03
15	Interior Insulation	2 days	0 days	Thu 9/4/03
22	Install Drywall	5 days	0 days	Mon 9/8/03
23	Electrical Finish	3 days	0 days	Mon 9/15/03
25	Carpentry Finish incl Cabinets	5 days	0 days	Thu 9/18/03
26	Interior Paint	7 days	0 days	Thu 9/25/03
29	Flooring	3 days	0 days	Mon 10/6/03
31	Clean up	1 day	0 days	Thu 10/9/03
32	Punch List	4 days	0 days	Fri 10/10/03
33	Final Clean up	1 day	0 days	Thu 10/16/03
16	Rough-in Mechanical	2 days	1 day	Mon 9/1/03
24	Mechanical Finish	2 days	1 day	Mon 9/15/03
27	Interior Doors	1 day	2 days	Mon 10/6/03
28	Electrical Trim	1 day	2 days	Mon 10/6/03
30	Mechanical Trim	1 day	2 days	Mon 10/6/03
12	Glazing & Ext Doors	2 days	27 days	Tue 8/19/03
18	Load Roof	1 day	27 days	Wed 8/20/03
13	Exterior Insulation	2 days	27 days	Thu 8/21/03
19	Lay Roofing	2 days	27 days	Thu 8/21/03
20	Stucco	4 days	27 days	Mon 8/25/03
21	Exterior Paint	2 days	27 days	Fri 8/29/03

Figure 10.4
MS Project® bar chart sorted by total float and then early start.

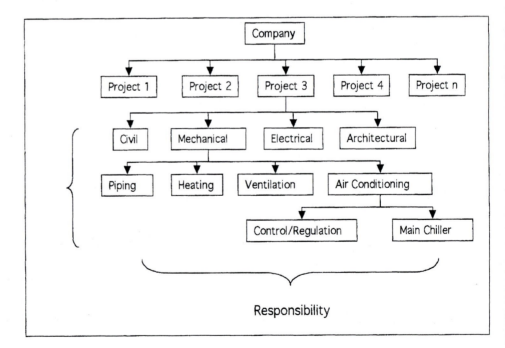

Figure 10.5
WBS.

skilled enough to identify negative floats, understand their cause, and either modify the schedule to remove them or explain their cause and present a proposed cure to management in the narrative report.

Although negative lag values are allowed by many scheduling programs, they tend to make the reviewer ask the company submitting the schedule for justification. As discussed elsewhere in the text, it is often difficult to justify the use of negative lag values. A finish-to-start -5 between a 10-day duration activity and its follower may well mean that the activities are related start-to-start 5 days. Justification is the key to using all relationships and lag values, but it is essential with negative lag values.

When activities have large floats and go unstarted at each update period, their updated start appears on the data date or the day after, depending on the program. This may not be inconsistent with project planning. However, when activities should have started and their floats are small or they join or create a new critical path, the reviewer is wise to question the resulting schedule submittal. Reducing the overall project float profile, especially on those activities that have a limited amount of float, can increase the likelihood that the project completion date will be delayed.

Once the initial project schedule is accepted and/or approved, the owner and the contractor agree as to the anticipated project duration. Even when the project duration is established in the specifications and the submitted schedule uses less than what is allowed, delays can be contested by the owner. Requests for additional time may be denied, and this may become the basis of costly claims. Reviewers and project managers must closely review the schedule when the end date has slipped. One or more possible solutions should be identified and tested for feasibility and cost, using the what-if capability of the computerized scheduling program. The cost of liquidated damages must be compared with the cost of crashing the schedule to meet project duration expectations.

Milestones and Level of Detail

When zero duration milestones become time-consuming activities or when the number of activities greatly increases or greatly decreases, the flags are flying. Milestones should not become activities. They are simply markers that indicate when major events have occurred. Large decreases in the number of project activities can mean that the contractor is trying to merge activities and hide problems in the aggregation of previous tasks. Justification should be required if this happens. If the schedule grows dramatically, the reviewer must determine the cause. Sometimes, the growth is the result of the availability of more information. In cases such as this, the reviewer must be sure that the additional activities correctly represent the expected logic and time estimates.

Calendars

Last, the use of multiple calendars may be a cause for further scrutiny. Projects usually have a common workweek calendar of 5 or 6 days per week. The calendar usually applies to about 90% of the activities in the schedule. Sometimes, an additional calendar is needed for activities working all 7 days per week, such as concrete curing, or a 7-day calendar may be used for comparing workdays to calendar days. When a 7-day calendar is used for comparison, it is not necessarily assigned to activities. A special calendar may be created to show projected winter shutdowns of outdoor work planned for inhospitable climates. However, there should be adequate justification when three or more calendars appear in one schedule.

Example Reports

The report sorted by total float and then early start is an effective way of seeing both those activities with negative float and those with large, positive float values. Figure 10.6 presents portions of a report showing both negative and excessive positive floats. Negative floats of over 100 days and positive floats of over 300 days on this report should be immediate indicators of project performance problems.

The early start report is often scanned for the number of activities and the condition of the activities appearing to start on the data date. Figure 10.7 shows a portion of an early start report noting only the activities found on the data date 1 Mar 00. It is interesting that, on this report, there are activities that have large, positive total float values as well as some with negative float. The large float values indicate that these activities will continue to appear on the data date on all future reports until project conditions dictate that their start or their float diminishes significantly. The activities with negative float are already behind schedule, and the failure to start them before the next update will only increase their negative float values.

```
Sample Constructors                    PRIMAVERA PROJECT PLANNER            Crystal Treatment

REPORT DATE 13SEP00  RUN NO. 1                                 START DATE          FIN DATE
             11:58
Special Total Float Early Start Report                         DATA DATE           PAGE NO.    1
```

ACTIVITY ID	ORIG DUR	REM DUR	CAL	%	ACTIVITY DESCRIPTION	EARLY START	EARLY FINISH	LATE START	LATE FINISH	TOTAL FLOAT
1050	0	0	2	0	START SYSTEM PERFORMANCE & OPERATIONAL TESTING	22AUGC0		6MAY00*		-108
1065	58	58	2	0	PLANT COMMISIONING	25OCT00	21DEC00	10JUL00	5SEP00	-107
1070	10	10	2	0	WEATHER DELAYS	22DEC00	31DEC00	6SEP00	15SEP00	-107
1080	0	0	2	0	SUBSTANTIAL COMPLETION		31DEC00		15SEP00	-107
1090	0	0	2	0	FINAL COMPLETION		29APR00		16JAN00*	-104
3650	40	40	2	0	Air Compressor Proc/Del.	1MAR00	9APR00	14DEC00	22JAN00	-77
4980	15	15	2	0	Electric Heat Tracer Tape Review	7MAR00	21MAR00	17NOV00	1DEC00	255
1600	50	20	2	60	Structural Metals Proc/Del	25NOV00A	20MAR00		2DEC00	257
2600	15	15	2	0	Carpet-Glue Down Review	7MAR00	21MAR00	25NOV00	9DEC00	263
2870	15	15	2	0	Metal Lockers & Shelving Review	7MAR00	21MAR00	28NOV00	12DEC00	266
4710	120	16	2	87	Full Port Ball Valves Proc/Del.	7NOV00A	16MAR00		20DEC00	279
1710	150	38	2	75	CAST IN PLACE CONC. PROC/DEL	26AUG00A	7APR00		16JAN01	284
2720	15	15	2	0	Markerboard Review	7MAR00	21MAR00	18DEC00	1JAN01	286
2900	15	15	2	0	Fire Extinguishers Review	7MAR00	21MAR00	18DEC00	1JAN01	286
2780	15	15	2	0	ID Devices Review	7MAR00	21MAR00	20DEC00	3JAN01	288
2810	15	15	2	0	Wall & Door Signs Review	7MAR00	21MAR00	20DEC00	3JAN01	288
2840	15	15	2	0	Warning Signs Review	7MAR00	21MAR00	20DEC00	3JAN01	288
2750	15	13	2	0	Wall & Corner Guards Review	7MAR00	21MAR00	28DEC00	11JAN01	296
4890	1	1	2	0	MEMBRANE SERVICE CONTRACT	1MAR00	1MAR00	16JAN01	16JAN01	321
4920	1	1	2	0	MEMBRANE REPLACEMENT CONTRACT	1MAR00	1MAR00	16JAN01	16JAN01	321
1000	0	0	2	0	FORCE ACCOUNT WORK	1MAR00	28FEB00	17JAN01	16JAN01	322

Figure 10.6
Total float report.

```
--------------------------------------------------------------------------------
Sample Constructors                 PRIMAVERA PROJECT PLANNER        Crystal Treatment

REPORT DATE 13SEP00  RUN NO. 2                              START DATE        FIN DATE
            12:33
Special Early Start Report                                 DATA DATE  1MAR 00  PAGE NO.    1

----- -----  ---- ---- - ---  -----------  --------------------------  -------- -------- -------- -------- -----
ACTIVITY     ORIG REM                                                  EARLY    EARLY    LATE     LATE     TOTAL
  ID         DUR  DUR CAL  %          ACTIVITY DESCRIPTION             START    FINISH   START    FINISH   FLOAT
----- -----  ---- ---- - ---  -----------  --------------------------  -------- -------- -------- -------- -----
   1000         0   0 2   0    FORCE ACCOUNT WORK                      1MAR00   28FEB00  17JAN01  16JAN01   322
   1310        10  10 2   0    Paving Proc/Del                         1MAR00   10MAR00  3OCT00   12OCT00   216
   1335        15  15 2   0    Irrigation System Proc/Del              1MAR00   15MAR00  4NOV00   19NOV00   248
   1630        60  60 2   0    Steel Joists Proc/Del                   1MAR00   29APR00  1MAR00   29APR00     0
   1660        21  21 2   0    Steel Roof Deck Proc/Del                1MAR00   21MAR00  16APR00  6MAY00     46
   1730        15  15 2   0    Fixed Alum. Access Ladder Review        1MAR00   15MAR00  23SEP00  7OCT00    206
   1770        32  32 2   0    Handrailing Proc/Del.                   1MAR00   1APR00   24MAY00  24JUN00    84
   2080        10  10 2   0    Firestopping Proc/Del.                  1MAR00   10MAR00  19JUN00  28JUN00   110
   2110        15  15 2   0    Conventional Roofing Proc/Del.          1MAR00   15MAR00  15OCT00  29OCT00   228
   2170        10  10 2   0    Sealants Proc/Del.                      1MAR00   10MAR00  14JUN00  23JUN00   105
   2220        60  60 2   0    Int. Alum. Doors & Wndws Proc/Del.      1MAR00   29APR00  19JAN00  19MAR00   -41
   2250        30  30 2   0    Coiling Doors & Grills Proc/Del.        1MAR00   30MAR00  20OCT00  18NOV00   233
   2280        60  60 2   0    Aluminum Storefront Proc/Del.           1MAR00   29APR00  19JAN00  19MAR00   -41
   3105        42  42 2   0    Self Cont. Alum Gts Embed Proc/Del.     1MAR00   11APR00  4FEB00   17MAR00   -25
   3350        10  10 2   0    VFD Non Clog Cent Pmps Proc/Del.        1MAR00   10MAR00  16JAN00  25JAN00   -44
```

Figure 10.7
Early start report.

The earned value report is also useful in identifying anomalies from expected project condition. Figure 10.8 shows an earned value report. The cost and schedule variances provide ample evidence for identifying activities that are not performing to expectation. Additionally, the reviewer can determine the effort the report preparer has made in resource control. The "Budget at Completion" column should reflect the project's initial budget, whereas the "Estimate at Completion" column should include actual or expected changes to the budget. For example, activity 6020 in Figure 10.8 is 25.9% complete and has used 55.02 of its planned 60 resources, yet the "Estimate at Completion" still indicates that the activity will use only a total of 60 resources. This is unlikely and should alert the reviewer to the possibility of other, similar errors in the schedule and prompt questions to those responsible for updating the values shown in this report.

Each report prepared and submitted or requested should help illuminate a portion of the project's progress. However, it is the narrative report that presents the complete picture. This written report requires all of the analytical abilities of the report preparer. A sample appears in Appendix B.

Request for Payment Based on Schedule

Many reports can be used to substantiate requests for progress payment. The percent complete of each activity forms the basis of one such claim. Cost-loaded schedules can produce histograms and s-curves. The cash flow report provides anticipated cash outflows for each time period (e.g., week). However, when the project is updated, the curve and cash flow may change. Providing the updated cash flow report can help the contractor substantiate payment requests when cash represents cost plus profit and overhead. Some large contracts and government contracts require earned value reporting. This is another means of providing support for payment requests. In addition to the

COST ACCOUNT	RESOURCE	ACTIVITY ID	PCT CMP	CUMULATIVE TO DATE			VARIANCE		AT COMPLETION	
				ACTUAL	EARNED	PLANNED	COST	SCHEDULE	BUDGET	ESTIMATE
XX1030		6170	.0	.00	.00	28.00	.00	-28.00	60.00	60.00
XX1030		6230	.0	.00	.00	28.00	.00	-28.00	60.00	60.00
XX1030		6260	.0	.00	.00	28.00	.00	-28.00	60.00	60.00
XX1030		6290	.0	.00	.00	28.00	.00	-28.00	60.00	60.00
XX1030		6320	.0	.00	.00	60.00	.00	-60.00	60.00	60.00
XX1030		6350	.0	.00	.00	28.00	.00	-28.00	60.00	60.00
XX1030		6380	.0	.00	.00	28.00	.00	-28.00	60.00	60.00
XX1030		6410	.0	.00	.00	28.00	.00	-28.00	60.00	60.00
XX1030		5520	.0	.00	.00	7.00	.00	-7.00	30.00	30.00
XX1030		5550	100.0	10.00	10.00	10.00	.00	.00	10.00	10.00
XX1030		5580	100.0	30.00	30.00	30.00	.00	.00	30.00	30.00
XX1030		5610	.0	.00	.00	.00	.00	.00	60.00	60.00
XX1030		5640	.0	.00	.00	7.00	.00	-7.00	30.00	30.00
XX1030		5670	.0	.00	.00	7.00	.00	-7.00	60.00	60.00
XX1030		5700	.0	.00	.00	28.00	.00	-28.00	60.00	60.00
XX1030		5750	100.0	30.00	30.00	30.00	.00	.00	30.00	30.00
XX1030		5780	15.0	9.00	9.00	48.40	.00	-39.40	60.00	60.00
XX1030		5810	15.0	4.50	4.50	30.00	.00	-25.50	30.00	30.00
XX1030		5840	15.0	9.00	9.00	51.38	.00	-42.38	60.00	60.00
XX1030		5900	15.0	9.00	9.00	51.79	.00	-42.79	60.00	60.00
XX1030		5930	.0	.00	.00	20.00	.00	-20.00	60.00	60.00
XX1030		5960	.0	.00	.00	20.00	.00	-20.00	30.00	30.00
XX1030		5990	.0	.00	.00	20.00	.00	-20.00	30.00	30.00
XX1030		6020	25.9	55.02	15.54	15.56	-39.48	-.02	60.00	60.00
XX1030		6050	41.0	24.60	24.60	52.75	.00	-28.15	60.00	60.00
XX1030		6080	.0	.00	.00	7.00	.00	-7.00	30.00	30.00
XX1030		6110	.0	.00	.00	7.00	.00	-7.00	30.00	30.00
XX1030		6140	.0	.00	.00	28.00	.00	-28.00	60.00	60.00
XX1030		6170	.0	.00	.00	28.00	.00	-28.00	60.00	60.00
XX1030		6200	100.0	30.00	30.00	30.00	.00	.00	30.00	30.00
XX1030		6230	.0	.00	.00	28.00	.00	-28.00	60.00	60.00
XX1030		6260	.0	.00	.00	28.00	.00	-28.00	60.00	60.00
XX1030		6290	.0	.00	.00	28.00	.00	-28.00	60.00	60.00
XX1030		6320	.0	.00	.00	60.00	.00	-60.00	60.00	60.00
XX1030		6350	.0	.00	.00	28.00	.00	-28.00	60.00	60.00
XX1030		6380	.0	.00	.00	28.00	.00	-28.00	60.00	60.00
XX1030		6410	.0	.00	.00	28.00	.00	-28.00	60.00	60.00
XX1030		5520	.0	.00	.00	7.00	.00	-7.00	30.00	30.00
XX2050		1740	.0	.00	.00	7.00	.00	-7.00	32.00	32.00
XX2050		1770	.0	.00	.00	28.00	.00	-28.00	32.00	32.00
XX2050		1740	.0	.00	.00	7.00	.00	-7.00	32.00	32.00
XX2050		1770	.0	.00	.00	28.00	.00	-28.00	32.00	32.00
XX2050		1830	100.0	60.00	60.00	28.00	.00	32.00	60.00	60.00
		TOTAL	21.6	724.22	684.74	1909.18	-39.48	-1224.44	3284.00	3284.00

Figure 10.8
Earned value report.

use of an earned value report or cash flow s-curve, the specifications may require that the entire monthly schedule be submitted on time and approved prior to a progress payment. Sample requests for payment can be found in Appendix C.

Value of Historical Schedule Information

Historical schedules can help estimators revamp and update their productivity estimates for certain crew configurations and geographic locations. Sometimes, estimates are prepared without all of the detailed information available, as with a design-build project or conceptual estimates and schedules. The updated schedule can help provide needed information in these instances. In addition, the as-built schedule, when compared with the baseline schedule, provides a clear picture of the proposed and actual construction methods. Not only is this useful for the full-time estimator, but it also provides a basis for supporting claims.

Specification Ordered—Reporting Requirements

Sometimes, the specifications are very specific about the content, order, timing, and number of copies of the reports and graphics needed for each submittal. At other times, the specifications require very little, perhaps only a bar chart or a list of the activities needed to complete the work. Some general contractors pass along detailed owner-provided schedule requirements to their subcontractors, whereas others impose schedule constraints of their own on subcontractors.

James Zack[1] published an article describing some schedule "games" contractors play, especially in the public construction sector. He has suggested some changes in specifications that can be used to circumvent the wily contractor. These changes include prescribed maximum activity durations, joint ownership of float, and linking schedule submittals to progress payments. Although Zack's is only one point of view, there is value in reviewing his thoughts and witnessing the result of his suggestions in the specifications used each day.

Conclusion

Once prepared the project schedule must be updated regularly. By the use of detailed reports generated, each time the schedule is updated, management gains the ability to better control the work. The reporting of project progress—schedule updating—should follow a well-defined procedure established and agreed upon by both the owner and the contractor. The generated reports are tailored to the recipient's needs; therefore reports become more detailed at lower levels of management.

One of the most important parts of schedule reporting is the narrative, which details, at a minimum, the critical path, activities started, in progress and completed, along with a description of logic changes from the previous update. The narrative must discuss current problems and potential problem solutions.

Problems and/or Questions

1. Using the schedule information in Appendix D, create five new reports that could help you better manage this and future projects. Tell how each new report can help.

2. Using the same project from the reports in Appendix D, and the specifications in Appendix E, create the required reports for the project shown in Appendix E. Describe why the owner might benefit from these reports.

3. Read Zack's article and compare and contrast it with the specifications in Appendix E.

4. Show how float can be "sequestered," as suggested by Zack. Explain why this is inappropriate.

5. Provide examples from two specifications of constraints on activity duration.

Notes

1. James G. Zack, "Schedule 'Games' People Play and Some Suggested 'Remedies.'" *Journal of Management in Engineering* 8(2), (1992): 138–52.

CHAPTER 11

Computer Applications

Goal

Provide a discussion of the differences and similarities among many of the commonly used scheduling software packages.

Objectives

- Discuss computerized scheduling tools.
- Explain the data used by scheduling programs.
- Explain common scheduling program features.
- Explain the output available from scheduling programs.

Introduction

Although manual methods of scheduling are effective for small projects, the power of the computer is quickly evident once a project network of any size is planned. There are many commercially available computer programs for scheduling; some are specifically intended for use in construction. The sophistication of each computerized scheduling application is reflected in its price.

Computerized Scheduling Tools

More than a dozen computerized construction scheduling programs have been developed internationally. Some are stand-alone products to do just scheduling, whereas others are integrated with other useful tools, such as estimating, financing, or project management (tracking purchase orders, change orders, submittals, subcontract management, and the like). Some are offered online for collaboration among project participants. Online offerings may be purchased or rented or leased by the month and by the number of users.

Most computerized scheduling programs are based on the precedence critical path method (CPM) scheduling method. In general, the programs can be separated by price and corresponding capabilities. They are found in essentially one of three price ranges. The lowest level, ranging to about $500, provides basic services for smaller contractors or those needing less resource and reporting flexibility. Some programs in this price range provide an instantaneous picture of changes made to the schedule, so that, as new activities are added and linked to their predecessors and successors, their position with respect to all of the other activities and the project calendar is shown immediately. SureTrak® is one of the programs in this price range.

The next price plateau is at about $1,000. Some programs in this price range also provide an instantaneous picture of changes made to the schedule. The schedule is automatically updated with new information. Programs in the $500 to $1,000 price range generally have a way of turning off this automatic calculation facility, so that when schedules get large there is no delay each time a new activity is entered. MS Project® is one of the programs in this price range.

The final price range plateaus at about $6,000. Programs in this price range are usually very sophisticated and may have exceptional graphics. Programs in this group are often enterprise solutions that enable multiple user input, multiple schedules, and input via the Internet and PDAs. Resource and reporting flexibility are key for these products. All of these products are built using sophisticated databases and are often the outgrowth of older, mainframe (large computer) programs. Primavera Project Planner® is a member of this group.

An online review of the tools that each program has, along with a comparison of the firm's current and anticipated needs, is a good place to start in making selection decisions. Many programs provide free or low-cost demonstration versions. Many of these demonstration versions are fully functional but limit the user to a specified time of use, limit the number of activities that can be entered, or limit the user's ability to save work or print output reports. Some software purchases are driven by specification requirements. When considering a program to respond to specifications, be sure that the estimated cost of this item includes training.

Transitioning to Computer Scheduling

Using the computer to do scheduling is extremely beneficial if the computer user is already familiar with the computer and is doing either a large or complex construction project or many smaller construction projects. The computer makes schedule evaluation and manipulation far easier than when these tasks are done by hand. There are only three tasks needed when using computerized scheduling: data input, scheduling and leveling, and data or information output. Although this sounds simple, some of the tasks can be complex because they take thought and planning by the scheduler.

Input

Data entry, or input, is a relatively clerical function once the data to be entered are laid out in a logical order. The data for entry, at a minimum, include the activity descriptions, durations, and relationships. Additional data can be included, such as activity identifications, codes for sorting and selecting, notes, and help, constraints, resources and costs, to name a few.

Activity Descriptions

When creating an activity description for a computerized scheduling program, the user should adhere to the basics; the activity type should be acknowledged. The activity can be a task representing procurement, production, or management, or it can be a milestone representing a beginning or an ending event.

Procurement activities may begin with words such as *fabricate (fab), order,* or *deliver* or a combination of those words that make sense in identifying the activity. The description should continue with the item descriptions, such as turbine shaft, 10,000 BTU chiller, or 28-cubic foot refrigerator. If there are multiples of an item, numbers, phases, or locations should be added to the description to distinguish one item from another. The same rules apply to production activities, except that, instead of *fab, order,* and *deliver,* an action verb should be used, such as *install, erect, place, lay,* or one of the many others that apply to construction. Management activities are generally unique and have descriptions that are equally unique. Some scheduling programs have a limit to the number of characters that will fit in the description field (the limit for P3® and SureTrak® is 48; MS Project® has a default of 24 but can exceed 100). For convenience, just as with hand-generated activity descriptions, the user is advised to use common abbreviations when needed.

Milestone activities have no duration and merely mark the beginning or ending of a work sequence. Often, they are owner-directed in the specifications. An example of a start milestone is "Detour Open to Traffic," whereas an example of a finish milestone is "Building Enclosed."

Activity Durations

Durations are generally entered in scheduling programs in whole days. However, some programs allow the user to enter activity durations in minutes, hours, days, weeks, or months. The user of the scheduling program should begin by assigning durations in a consistent set of units, such as all whole days. Mixing units or using more than one calendar should be reserved for the experienced program user.

Relationships

The relationships between activities must also be input to form a complete network with only one start and one finish. The most frequently used personal computer programs are based on the precedence, or activity on node, scheduling technique and use the critical path method. Each of these programs allows all four types of links between activities (finish-to-start, start-to-start, finish-to-finish, and start-to-finish) and all lag values, including negative lags. Some programs require that the predecessor relationship(s) be entered, whereas others allow either predecessors or successors to be entered. Knowing how the program expects the relationship to be reported is important to good data entry. If a program requires the user to input only activity descriptions, durations, and relationships, a simple list can be made that resembles an activity list with these three columns. Once all of the data are recorded, the clerical role of data entry can be easily accomplished. Once the data are input, and assuming that the network logic is being updated with each new activity entry, the user should check the following:

- Is there only one start and one finish (with no other open ends)?
- Are there loops?
- Is the critical path where it was expected?
- Does the project finish on time?
- Does the logic make sense?
- Are the simple things, such as spelling and punctuation, correct?

If any of these problems appear, they should be corrected and the results rechecked. Once the user is satisfied with the network, reports can be generated, or what-if scenarios can be applied and tested.

This is the simplest part of data entry. Thinking is required to identify the activities, to determine their durations, and to link them to their predecessors and successors. These tasks are often left up to the estimator or the project manager when the project network is created initially—both of these individuals are familiar with the project details.

Activity Identifications

Activity identification codes (activity I.D.s) can be strictly numerical and just serve as a counter. Some programs assign activity I.D.s automatically, beginning at 1 and incrementing by 1, whereas others increment by 10. Some programs allow for alphanumeric activity I.D.s. This tends to increase the usefulness of the I.D. in providing information to the schedule reviewer. Chapter 2 discusses how the activity I.D. can be segmented and how each element can represent a portion of the activity description—it can tell where the work is to be done, what type of work it is, and what subelement of the work is involved. For example, 21DCONC31 might represent the intersection of column lines 21 and D and concrete work (CONC), with the next number, 3, representing structural concrete and the last number, 1, representing lift (layer of concrete) one.

Some programs allow up to ten alphanumeric characters for the I.D., whereas others count by one up to six characters, or 999,999. The activity I.D. scheme can be simple or sophisticated, whichever works best for the schedule reviewers.

Codes for Sorting and Selecting

The work breakdown structure (WBS) is a common way of identifying activities in their hierarchical structure. The company may be the top of the hierarchical pyramid (level 1), and below it is each of the company's projects (level 2), see Figure 10.5. Each project may be further divided into disciplines, such as the 16 Construction Specifications Institute (CSI) codes (general requirements, site construction, concrete, masonry, etc.). This would act as level 3. Beneath the CSI codes or divisions may be the details, such as concrete walls, columns, beams or girders, slabs, and architectural elements (level 4). Level 5 may further disaggregate level 4, so that slabs may be slab-on-grade (SOG) or elevated slabs. The final level in this example WBS, level 6, would identify the activities or tasks, such that each SOG and each elevated slab would be distinguished by location and/or size. There may be a final, seventh level that distinguishes one activity from another. A resulting 6-level WBS might read 1.3.3.4.1.5, or company 1, project 3, concrete, slab, slab-on-grade, in the fifth location.

With a WBS-type system, reports can be produced that are for only the concrete work. A report limited to only the concrete might be suitable for the person scheduling the concrete deliveries, the concrete superintendent, or the concrete subcontractor. A WBS does not need as many levels as has been shown. Levels 3 to 6 may be all that are needed for most companies and projects.

Activity codes are similar to the WBS, but they eliminate the need for the hierarchical structure. There can be one code that identifies the person or company that is responsible for the activity, such as the prime contractor or subcontractor A, or the responsible field engineer. There can be another code that distinguishes the type of work, such as concrete or concrete walls, and another code used to identify a location on the project site, such as building 1, column line A, or subproject 4. Activity codes offer the same flexibility as the WBS but they lack the rigid structure.

Whether a WBS or an activity code is used, the purpose of its inclusion with each activity's data is to provide a consistent means of sorting or selecting limited portions of the network's activities to appear in reports and graphics. The schedule developer should keep this feature in mind when creating a schedule. It cannot be duplicated easily by hand.

Constraints

Constraints are a scheduling technique to hold or move activities in time without using relationships. As an example, consider special gold-plated bathroom fixtures that are being imported from Mexico. The supplier notifies the contractor that, due to high order volume, the order cannot be filled until a certain future date. The best way to keep the installation of these fixtures held to that future date is to use a constraint. (See Chapter 7 for a discussion of relationships versus constraints.) Of the three most commonly used constraints, the "start no earlier than" constraint is best used in this example situation.

Although constraints are easily incorporated into hand-generated schedules, they are equally easily added to computerized schedules. Many programs have early start and finish constraints and late start and finish constraints, which hold these dates in time unless the calculated date overrides the constraint date. Many programs also have mandatory start and finish dates, which hold the activity's dates in time, no matter the logic imposed. The only thing that overrides a mandatory date is an actual date. Some programs have additional constraint types that can zero out free or total float. Others have "as late as possible" or "as early as possible" constraints, which function somewhat similarly as limited float constraints.

Usually, assigning constraints in computer programs is a matter of entering a date next to the appropriate constraint description for the affected activity. Remember, the computer is best used for large or complex schedules or for many small, repetitive ones. Using constraints can help with managing subcontractors and suppliers, and it can be an effective tool in helping manage resources.

Resources and Costs

Resources include labor, materials, subcontracts, and money. Money can be represented as cost (direct cost, field cost, or total cost) or earnings. Some computer applications handle cost (cost or earnings) separate from other resources. Although most applications will allow the user to treat costs or earnings as a resource, they do require that the amount of resource (or cost) be specified either as the total (total number of work hours) or as a daily rate. A daily rate for a crew of four working an 8-hour day would be 32 work hours per day. Less expensive programs often have a very specific way of entering resources. These may require that the user show the number of units per hour—for a crew of four, four units per hour. Other programs want a percentage. For programs like this, percentages can be greater than 100%, showing more than one resource unit. For example, 1,500 tons of steel would be 150,000%. More sophisticated programs allow the user to designate the units and the units of measure for each resource. In programs such as these, the user can specify hours of crane use, dollars of direct cost, and tons of steel directly.

Many programs allow the user to attach costs to resources, so that the user may say each ton of steel costs $85.00. The program then assigns a cost for an activity based on the sum of the costs for each of its resources. This, in turn, means that the user must either assign all resources to each activity, pricing the pieces equivalently with the bid price, or include all costs with one or two assigned resources. In many cases, it is easier for the user to have a resource called *cost* and include the activity equivalent cost.

Recall that one of the attributes that distinguishes more expensive programs from less expensive ones is the way in which resources are handled. The flexibility of resource assignment is one of those subattributes. Another is whether the user has control over how the resource is used in connection with the activity's duration. Some programs view the available resource and the activity's need for the resource and determine an activity's duration. Thus, unless the user is comfortable with the way the program operates, some resource conversions may be needed when resource data are entered.

In most programs, resource calendars can be assigned to tell the program on which days a particular resource may be assigned to work. If activity resources include people, such as a designer, their vacations can be input into the resource calendar. These calendars can then be used to determine the duration of the activities using each resource. Both resource calendars and resource-determined activity durations are advanced topics for resource allocation. Another advanced topic is the nonuniform distribution of resources over an activity's duration.

Although most programs default to the uniform allocation of resources over each day of an activity's duration (10 days, $1,000, or $100/day), some programs also have a method of applying resources for only a portion of the activity's duration. For example, an activity for form, rebar, and place concrete that has a concrete resource would not want that resource divided up over the entire activity duration. Instead, the placement of concrete will likely take place on the last day or two of the activity. This method of allocation produces a much more accurate resource distribution profile.

Notes

Many of the major programs available for construction scheduling have one or more areas where notes can be attached to activities. These notes can aid in recalling important information in support of change orders or claims when more than one individual works on the project or when there has been a time delay between the occurrence of the noted information and the need for that information. Some notes areas are free-form, like a word processor, whereas others are structured into lines of text that can be displayed or hidden in reports typically showing notes.

Help

All reasonable computerized scheduling programs have help functions that explain programmatic elements, such as what each constraint type is and how it works. The better and more explanatory the help function is, the better the program is generally. Company marketing programs that have a large number of users receive lots of feedback from their clients on how the programs can be improved. These companies want to keep their customers happy and encourage new ones; thus they are responsive to customer-requested program changes.

Some help functions resemble Microsoft® applications help, whereas others are both contextual (F1 while in an input area) and general (go to help on the task bar). Again, generally the better programs have better help functions.

Once the input phase is complete the network may need to be scheduled (run) to identify the start and finish dates of each activity, the project finish date and duration, and the location of the critical path.

Scheduling and Leveling

As previously mentioned, some programs automatically update the logic and placement of new activities as they are tied or related to existing activities. These programs lay out the activities in relation to each other and time. It was also noted earlier that the automatic update provision of these programs can be disabled to speed the data entry process. When this function is disabled or when the program always requires calculation intervention, the next step after data input is to calculate the network.

Schedule Calculations

Performance of schedule calculations is usually as simple as pushing a button or selecting a function from a menu. The program then checks for loops and open ends. Barring any fatal logic errors, the program then assigns start and finish dates and floats to each activity, based on the network logic, activity durations, and constraints. The user should always carefully review the produced schedule, checking for loops and the validity of the logic.

If no specific resource requirements must be met, the user can proceed to the output section. However, if resource considerations are important, the user may want to level or constrain the schedule.

Leveling and Constraining

Computerized scheduling is the only reasonable way to level or constrain a schedule of over fifty activities. Leveling allows the scheduler to use the total float within the network to reorganize activities so that resources will be more uniformly distributed. When a network is leveled, fewer peaks and valleys should be evident in the resource distribution. The leveling process requires that the user estimate a maximum resource level. The process works day by day (when the durations are in days) to try to keep the daily resource total below this level. If there is not enough total float, resource peaks exceeding the desired level will be allowed. Thus, the project duration is not extended.

Constraining the schedule works similarly to leveling, except that the desired level may never be exceeded. When the total float is exhausted while constraining, the project duration is extended to keep the daily resource allocation below the desired level. (Additional information on leveling and constraining appears in Chapter 6.)

As both leveling and constraining are day-by-day processes, networks for projects that are large (have many activities), complex, or extend over a long duration, as well as those for which more than one resource requires leveling or constraining, should only be tackled with the computer. Once resources are assigned to activities and a resource limit is input, all that is left for the user to do is to initiate the process and review the results.

Output

Output can be categorized as written reports, graphic reports, and input to other programs. Output is essential because it is how the schedule's information is communicated to the company, subcontractors, the owner, and any other interested party.

Written Reports

Many computer scheduling programs have a variety of standard reports that users can initiate to evaluate their current network. Other programs provide reports based on how the screen appears (what you see is what you get—WYSIWYG). For these programs, the screen representation becomes the foundation for both the input and the output. Other programs provide maximum flexibility by allowing the user to determine the following:

- Report content
  - Fields to be shown (dates, float, workday numbers, notes, and others)
  - Line spacing
- Report format
  - Page and line breaks
  - Summarization
  - Target and current schedule
  - Sorting information
- Activity selection criteria
  - Limit by date
  - Limit by float
  - Limit by code

Written reports are not a part of the hand-processed network environment unless the user prepares them based on the manual calculations and graphics. Reports can only be generated automatically within the confines of the computer scheduling programs. When deciding what report to generate, the user should ask the following questions:

1. What level of detail does the report reviewer need or want?
2. What is the purpose of the report?
3. What information must be displayed and what information should be displayed?
4. Is this report a part of a series of reports?
5. Are resource reports required?

The report level of detail should match the schedule reviewer, so that the company owner gets a summary level of detail compared to that delivered to the project manager. When preparing a report for the project owner, the scheduler should be aware of any requirements for schedule reporting present in the contract documents. For some companies, the same level of detail applies to all schedule recipients.

The purpose of a report may be to describe float or to show how activities are related to one another. The purpose may be to show only the activities occurring during the next 14 days. These criteria are addressed by the sorting and/or selecting abilities of the computer program. If the user is interested in showing a report sorted by total float, activities are grouped by float amount, beginning with the least and ending with the most. If the user wants to show only those activities with zero total float, then the selection criteria limiting the report to these activities are used.

Some programs have the ability to limit, select, or organize the columns present in the report. It may be effective to limit a report for a subcontractor or supplier, so that it shows only the early dates for each activity. Some programs can also include rows of information such as resources, notes, or workday numbers, in addition to the traditional activity I.D. and description, duration, dates, and float that are frequently the default.

Resource reports that are not graphic may include the earned value report or the resource-loaded report. Like other written reports, these resource reports can be sorted and limited. The caveat is that the user should always consider the audience and the picture that should be painted.

Often, companies or projects require a regular list of reports with each monthly update. Once reports are identified in the computer program, often for the network, they can be used repeatedly to obtain the appropriate project information. Some programs also allow reports to be grouped together for what was once known as batch processing—all reports are produced, one after another, until they are all complete.

No matter the number or type of reports needed, computerized output is generated easily once the network information has been input and the schedule calculated. Graphics can be produced similarly.

Graphic Reports

Graphic reports are of two types: those that represent the network and those that represent the network's resources. The network graphics are separated into network diagrams and bar charts. Many programs rely on the bar chart as the default, or primary, means of viewing the network. This graphic becomes the primary source of output. Network diagrams typically resemble precedence network diagrams done by hand. Activities appear as rectangular boxes linked by arrows. Some programs depict the arrows so that they represent the relationship type. Thus, a start-to-start relationship would have the arrow coming from the start of the predecessor and terminating in the start of the successor. Other programs make all arrows from the finish of the predecessor to the start of the successor. However, when activity relationships are depicted in this way, the relationship type and lag value are recorded near the arrow. Some programs have diagrams that appear as linked bars, as in a bar chart with relationships.

Bar charts may look just like the screen representation, or they may be slightly different, depending on the software program selected. Bar charts need enough room to show data to the left of the calendar-bar area on the right. If data are used on the left, very few dates may be displayed on the right, and many pages may be needed to show the entire bar chart.

A user wanting to print the network diagram or bar chart graphic report should bear in mind that, if printing is done on a normal desktop printer, the output may take several pages. Even small, sixty-activity networks can take up to 6 or 8, 8½" × 11" pages to display. Larger plotting devices should be considered for the scheduling user expecting to generate these kinds of graphic reports for large projects.

The other types of graphic reports are based on the network's resources. Both histograms (daily resource distribution) and cumulative or s-curves are graphic reports linked to the network and the activity-assigned resources. These reports are often required by owners to help them understand their periodic financial obligations. The contractor often uses these reports to identify time periods requiring resource leveling. The reports also identify times when the leveling has been effective and times when it has not.

Input to Other Programs

Many programs have methods of importing or exporting data from other programs or from other devices, such as e-mail, PDAs, or the Internet. Some programs link to database files and spreadsheet files. Each of these options offers the user additional flexibility for collaboration with other project participants and other formats for viewing the data. Data export is often helpful in making mass changes to a network and in establishing the required import and export format. The required steps needed to export data are often limited to determining what data to export and what format to save them in. Importing is sometimes harder because the user may need to know the exact data field name and characteristics, such as length and whether the field is numeric or alpha.

Conclusion

Overall, computerized construction scheduling is a means of structuring the input and output of precedence schedules. It enables the user to create repeatable chunks of the network that can be used over and over again. By computerizing, the user can produce default or customized reports, tailor reports to schedule reviewers' needs, and analyze the project's time performance. Computerization reduces the time needed to develop and modify the network and helps ensure that the user will make fewer mistakes because the program highlights mistakes. Networks of any size (more than fifty activities) should be tracked in a computer program.

Computerization's disadvantages are often limited to learning the program, so that input and output are easily accomplished. Most programs can be learned by doing, but it is often advantageous to have some professional instruction. Most computer program providers supply training for a fee. Also, a number of consultants are available for hire. Ten to 20 hours of training are often enough to make the user proficient with the fundamentals of a program, assuming that the computer user is familiar with scheduling and familiar with other computer applications.

Problems and/or Questions

1. Input the following network into a computerized scheduling program. Determine the project duration, critical path, and maximum float. Develop reports that will show these project characteristics. Check your results with a hand-drawn and hand-calculated precedence network. Assume all relationships

are FS 0. What advantages and disadvantages do you find for each method? Use all appropriate diagramming techniques.

Activity (Dur)	Depends On	Activity (Dur)	Depends On
A (5)	-	M (6)	A and B
B (7)	-	N (10)	M and P
C (8)	-	P (6)	A, B, L
E (3)	-	Q (8)	P
F (12)	-	R (10)	G
G (4)	E	S (3)	K, Q, W
H (3)	C	T (2)	K, Q, W
K (4)	H and F	W (6)	G
L (7)	C		

2. Review two computerized scheduling programs and compare and contrast their features and cost.

3. Describe the user flexibility displayed in one program—pick from P3®, MS Project®, or Sure Trak®.

4. Input the following network and resources in a computerized scheduling program. Display the output in written reports and graphic reports.

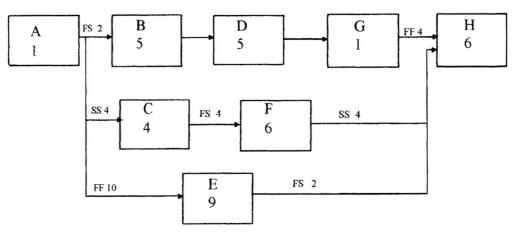

Activity	Total Cost	Activity	Total Cost
A	$5,000	E	$18,000
B	$12,000	F	$18,000
C	$8,000	G	$ 3,000
D	$15,000	H	$15,000

CHAPTER 12

Change Orders and Claims

Goal

Present the use of schedules in the preparation and support of change orders and claims.

Objectives

- Describe and demonstrate the use of the schedule to aid change order preparation.
- Describe and demonstrate the use of the schedule in claims.
- Describe the shared nature of float.

Introduction

King County in Washington State defines a change order as "a legal document used to modify a CONSTRUCTION SERVICES CONTRACT. Multiple change proposals and/or REQUEST FOR CHANGE ORDERS may be contained in a single CHANGE ORDER."[1] Change orders are the result of ambiguities in the contract language and/or design, differing site conditions, design incompatibilities with *constructability,* and owner-requested additions or modifications. The causes of change orders—in addition to project problems and owner-requested modification to the work—often include poor resource planning and management, inadequate subcontract performance, and adverse weather conditions. The result of any of these is schedule delay and increased cost.

Change orders are unresolved when the contractor and owner disagree on cause and effect; the result may be legal claims for time and/or monetary compensation. Many dispute resolution strategies, including mediation, arbitration, and partnering, have been used to keep change requests from escalating to claims.

Use of a Schedule to Aid in Change Order Preparation

The "but-for," or "what if," schedule compares the as-built schedule, minus contractor-caused delays, to the baseline, or proposed, schedule. The resulting delays are suspected to be outside of the contractor's control and potentially created by the owner. The schedule plays a critical role in obtaining this valuable information. It is the contractor's duty to create the initial schedule with his or her highest level of skill, to save it, and to update it with actual event (activity) data. Notes attached to altered activities explaining changes are valuable information. Candor, skill, and consistency are needed to create useful documents in support of change orders and claims. Sometimes, the task of preparing and updating the construction schedule is given to the junior field engineer, or it is made a small part of the project engineer's larger responsibilities. When too little attention is given to the schedule, it will not support project planning or the as-built schedule's after-project role in estimate review and change order or claim preparation and defense.

Development of a Schedule to Support Potential Claims

When a project begins, there is usually consensus that certain aspects of the project contain the most risk. These are the areas that require the most diligent planning and conscientious review, as well as the most thorough scheduling effort. Creating work-consistent activity relationships and durations and appropriate task detail and aligning activity resources and costs are key to an appropriate beginning. Arranging the activities in a work breakdown structure (WBS) or another job-related structure will help the scheduler better monitor ongoing events and locate problems. Frequent and truthful updates keep the schedule current. Notes attached to altered activities are beneficial, especially when projects are long and post-project debriefing reports are rare.

There are books available on the causes, avoidance, preparation, and outcomes of claims. The best way for a contractor to prepare for a claim, however, is to work to avoid it through partnering, honest communication, and quality workmanship. Avoiding claims is also important to owners. In an online white paper, lawyer Andrew D. Ness describes some claims-avoidance techniques that owners can use.[2] He recommends that there be an outside, independent review of all contract documents. "A good scheduling specification should include a combination of provisions addressing all elements in the development, review, approval and monitoring of a schedule."[3]

- The owner should provide major project milestones.
- Specifications should state the frequency of schedule updating.
- Specifications should tie progress payments to the schedule.

Ness goes on to say "Managing a dispute-free project also requires, to the extent possible, that all change orders are prepared, evaluated and executed in a timely fashion. . . . The direct costs of performing the changed work and the potential impact the change may have on the project schedule should be promptly analyzed. . . . The owner could encounter schedule delays if the contract does not explicitly provide for the performance of a change order pending final agreement on its pricing."[4]

The Role of Float and the Meaning of Criticality

It has already been mentioned that total float is the most commonly used float in construction contracts. It identifies the maneuverability of activities within the network because it is defined as the amount of time an activity can be delayed without delaying project completion. Thus, activities with no total float are considered critical. Any delay in the progress of critical activities will delay the project completion, whether the delay is due to an activity's starting later than expected or due to an increase in the activity's duration. Many owners are primarily concerned with on-time completion of the project, and may have no regard for delays experienced in intermediate, noncritical activities. The owner's value of the on-time completion is frequently evidenced in contractually established liquidated damages. The higher the damages, the more critical on-time completion is to the owner. If intermediate progress is also important, the contract may establish milestone dates for crucial activities and may tie bonuses or penalties to their completion dates. The message is that critical activities, those with no total float, must be tracked carefully and should meet expected productivity estimates. Sometimes, for large projects with long durations, critical activities may be described as those having 5 days or less of total float.

Manipulating float requires careful attention to the total schedule and to the contractual definition of float ownership. Float is usually shared between the owner and the contractor by contract specification. Consequently, rain delays or owner-furnished equipment delays in noncritical activities are usually compensated by float claimed by the owner. If contractor-caused delays later in the same activities create a delay in the project completion, the shared nature of the float may be questioned. Float should be monitored effectively and used wisely. The use of total float can help smooth peak resource demands, including the orderly transition of crews from one location to another. Float is usually contained within chains and is, therefore, shared among all the activities in the chain. A delay in one activity in a chain will reduce the float in all of the activities in the chain. Thus, five activities, all with 9 days of total float, may not have all of their durations increased by 9 days. Instead, the total of their duration increases may total only 9 days.

During the schedule evaluation, erosion in float should be noted. If float is nearing a critical level, the management team may elect to make sequence or duration changes by making crew or work hour changes to reduce the chance of missing the scheduled project completion date.

Change Orders

A *change order* is a legal document used to modify a construction contract. Either the owner or the contractor may initiate change proposals or requests for a change order. Contract provisions usually include provisions so that owners can make adjustments to the plans and specifications or incorporate contractor suggestions for changes or value engineering. The contract also provides a framework for submitting claims for additional compensation as well as a process for the escalation of disputes between the contractor and the owner. When reviewing the contract specifications, the contractor should pay special attention to change clauses to determine if changes must be within the scope of the original contract and if changes must be in writing. It is also important to note who may initiate the change request and if there are limits on its purpose. The constructor should note the terms of the escalation process and the time frame for each step in the process. Change orders are often thought of as requests made by the contractor for changes in cost and/or project duration to compensate for the work related to changed project conditions. However, unresolved disputes between the owner and the contractor over the facts, the cause and effect of a changed condition, or the compensation requested in the change request can also result in claims.

The resolution of claims may be specified and may require that the parties engage in either mediation or arbitration. When mediation, arbitration, or partnering is unsuccessful or is not used, the last course of action for claim resolution may be in the courts.

Change orders can result from any number of differences between what was expected and described in the contract documents and what was found in the field, or they can come from owner-requested changes that are within the scope of the original contract. The value of a change order that modifies or adds to the contract should include *all* costs plus a reasonable profit. Additional work should not be done for the cost of time and materials only. Time extensions will also incur additional overhead costs. In some cases, change orders result from an owner deleting or reducing work from a contract.

The request for a time extension resulting from a change must be based on fact, with supporting documentation. The construction schedule, when required by the contract, is submitted, received, and approved by the owner or the owner's representative. If the project has had each successive schedule approved, the effects of a change can be easily shown. The effects of a change come with the weight of an approved history to support a claim for a time extension and/or the monetary impact. Through the construction schedule, the contractor must faithfully represent the expected work sequence and duration, record progress on a regular basis, and estimate new activities and the costs resulting from each change.

Change orders arise from any number of issues: owner directives, delays caused by owner's agents—architects or designers, subcontractor delays, weather conditions, and unforeseen site conditions, just to mention a few. The reasons for change orders create delays, which often adversely impact the project completion date. These delays can be placed in one of three categories: *compensable, excusable,* and *noncompensable.* Sometimes, delays are divided into the categories nonexcusable, excusable but not compensable, and excusable and compensable. Noncompensable or nonexcusable delays are due to contractor negligence or poor management practices and receive neither a time extension nor any monetary compensation. Examples of noncompensable delays include inadequate or improper planning and/or scheduling, safety violations/accidents, a lack of qualified or trained craft workers, and defective work.

Some delays are merely excusable. These delays include those "caused by factors beyond the control and without fault or negligence of a contractor. Examples of excusable delays are design problems, owner-initiated changes, unusually severe weather, fire and natural disasters. Excusable delays justify an extension of a contract's deadline."[5] Excusable delays are eligible for time extensions, but no money damages. Examples of excusable delays include some weather delays, unusable material delivery or transportation delays (southern U.S. steel delivery delayed by hurricane), or unexpected labor disputes (strikes).

Compensable delays are typically caused by the owner or the owner's representative, such as the architect or designer. Common compensable delays include unforeseen site conditions, delays in the availability of work areas (other contractors not finished on time), delays in the review and approval process, and errors or omissions in the contract documents. When a compensable delay is acknowledged, the contractor is awarded a time extension and monetary compensation. Depending on the limits in the contract language, weather delays may be either compensable or *excusable*. "Acts of God" usually fall into one of these categories.

Many claims arise during multiple construction phases and, due to time constraints, are not easily decided or immediately approved. However, when changes are directed by the owner or the architect, the contractor is generally contractually obligated to proceed with the work, as long as it is within the context or scope of the original contract. Both the American Institute of Architects (AIA) and the Engineers Joint Contract Documents Committee (EJCDC) include language to this effect in the general conditions of their standard contract document forms. One must recognize that the vast majority of claims arising during construction will be handled in a manner convenient to the owner and the procedure is usually specified in the contract documents. Nevertheless, the schedule can provide strong evidentiary material and afford significant leverage in claims negotiations. There need not be an adversarial atmosphere between the owner and the contractor based on false beliefs. The owner and his or her agents will view a schedule favorably when it is well prepared and documented. Poor communication and lack of planning are often the foundation of disputed issues. The following section illustrates two methods for handling claims and changes within the confines of the schedule.

Schedule Documentation

Richard H. Clough has detailed a method for demonstrating the impact of a change that relies on the precedence network. Once the network is fully calculated, examine the unimpacted critical path completion date. Next, add the delaying event to the schedule. In order to accomplish this, it may be necessary to add new activities or to modify the durations of the existing activities. Then, recalculate the schedule. This gives the reviewer the opportunity to visualize the impact of a single change. A change order may then be issued and executed by the owner. The revised schedule now shows the full impact of the change.

Another example of using the schedule for documenting delays revolves around owner/designer delays. Suppose that a request for information (RFI) is sent to the engineer/designer for a substitution or clarification. Further, suppose that days go by without a response. This would be an appropriate time to add a new activity to the schedule designated as "engineer response delay." Each recalculation of the schedule will show the escalating impact on the schedule for every day the engineer fails to respond. Although 1-day delays may appear to have limited merit and may seem trivial, delays are cumulative and costly, even for just 1 day. Clough states that, "when delay decisions are deferred, memories fade, project personnel change, and the dispute is personalized. In the end, the dispute is adjudicated, attorneys are involved, and the cost of the claim increases dramatically."[6]

However, there may be times when a full analysis cannot be undertaken or the facts surrounding the issues are vague. In cases such as these, the scheduler must, after the fact, use analytical scheduling techniques to re-create the project. Impacted baseline and collapsed as-built schedules are two of the most common techniques for re-creating schedules.

In order to better understand these two methods, an example is helpful. Imagine that the contractor for a highway bridge project receives a change order from the owner addressing the rustication detail (see Fig. 12.1) specified for the bridge. The rustication manufacturer was just preparing the machinery to produce the needed panels. The owner authorizes a price adjustment indicated by the change in material that he has requested. The manufacturer begins to manufacture the special panel sections with the new details for the bridge; however, before all of the panel details can be completed, the owner changes her mind once again. The owner decides that the original design is

Figure 12.1
Bridge rustication panel.

the best choice and directs the contractor to use this rustication. When the contractor tells the panel manufacturer of the owner's latest request, the manufacturer tells the contractor to find another supplier. The ensuing delays take the contractor through a winter shutdown of concrete activities. Due to the rustication changes, many other activities are also delayed until after the winter. The project completion, which had been scheduled for the following fall, is now delayed for another 6 months. The total impact of this change cannot be determined until the project is completed that spring. There are far too many unknown variables to quantify the total impact to the downstream, remaining trades and to the prime contractor. A full analysis will have to be completed once the project is finished. However, the owner must be notified of the intent to file a claim for the impact of the changed work.

The impacted baseline schedule requires that the scheduler apply the added days from the delay to the baseline schedule to illustrate and quantify their effect. The collapsed as-built schedule would remove the disruptions from the as-built schedule to illustrate what would have happened without the delays. This "collapsed as-built" schedule is similar to the "but-for" schedule.

Impacted Baseline Schedule

Recall from (Chapters 6 and 8) that a baseline schedule is used as a foundation for comparison. To determine the impact of a delay or series of delays, insert the delays as they occurred, breaking previous logical links from each of the activities interrupted or delayed. Continue this process through the entire network until all delays are accounted for and the new project duration can be determined. This method takes into account both owner and contractor delays. The impacted baseline schedule allows for the analysis of delays caused by both parties, highlighting the causes for delays, enabling the assignment of responsibility, and providing for the determination of the time impact and the associated cost/benefit analysis. Recognize that contractor delays are exposed as well as those of the owner when the impacted baseline schedule is used to illustrate delays. The result of owner scrutiny of the schedule may be to instruct the contractor to accelerate the schedule without compensation.

Two potential drawbacks arise from the use of the impacted baseline method. First, the initial owner review and approval of the baseline schedule may have simply been a minor review, checking to see that the project would complete as scheduled and that the submittal complied with the scheduling specifications. Second, because the means and methods of construction are the contractor's responsibilities, owners distance themselves from accountability. They may claim that the schedule was always unachievable.[7]

From a contractor's viewpoint, however, creating an impacted baseline schedule is a simple, streamlined approach to detailing the impact of delays. This method appears to be cost-effective and unsophisticated. The impacted baseline technique is an effective tool for large projects in which the baseline schedule is an accepted management report and few changes have occurred. This method is less effective in an environment where changes and delays are common because both sides will attempt to shift the blame.[8]

But-for, or Collapsed as-Built, Schedule

The schedule is an integral support document if a change order escalates to a claim. The but-for, or collapsed as-built, schedule takes the baseline schedule and adds the contractor-imposed changes (e.g., increases in duration) to provide the expected project duration. By comparing this but-for schedule to the current schedule, owner-imposed delays should become apparent. Thus, but for the actions of the owner, the project would be complete by the date shown in this schedule—the original schedule plus the contractor delays.

The but-for schedule can be used during construction and/or as a post-project completion recovery method. This technique is more sophisticated than the impacted baseline schedule and requires more sophistication from the scheduler. This method is less effective if all the accompanying documentation is unfair or unbalanced. Therefore, the scheduler is required to demonstrate the documentation of delays caused by owner and contractor alike.

Working backward from the as-built schedule (the reason the name *collapsed as-built* is sometime used), the scheduler removes all delays caused by the owner or a third party. Delay-created activities are removed until the network contains only those activities and relationships contained in the baseline schedule, plus contractor-caused delays or changes. The result is a schedule with a completion date that would have been achievable but for owner or outside interference. The difference between the finish date of the but-for schedule and that found in the as-built schedule is the amount of time requiring owner compensation. This type of schedule is often used to justify claims that are unresolved at the project's completion.

The person who may ultimately be responsible for preparing the claim should keep a list of all known delays that have occurred during the project. It is critical that this log be maintained rigorously and that it fully documents each actual event, including times, dates, responsible parties, other relevant factors, and accompanying logs, submittals, and other relevant documentation. It is important to record events in an unbiased manner. Delays and the activities involved should be listed chronologically.

Some reviewers suggest that each delay be analyzed individually by removing one delay activity from the network at a time and studying the resulting impact. Although only those activities that are on the critical path need be analyzed, frequently the critical path changes as activities are modified and new ones are added.

As a direct result of a delay, contractors often will suspend parallel operations and paths around the delayed activity. In order to measure the true effect of these delays, the artificially suspended activities must also be reduced to their original duration estimates. Each change to the as-built schedule then becomes an audit trail for the delay analysis.

This type of analysis is best suited for projects in which the logic has been dramatically changed or altered. This approach requires that the scheduler account for each addition, subtraction, extension, or reduction in the number of activities and their associated logic changes. But-for analysis is able to account for a large number of delays and changes that are interdependent and impact the project duration. Clearly, the objective is to follow the critical path backwards step by step until the project completion date can be accounted for with support from the delay log.[9]

The Role of the Schedule in the Construction Process

From a legal standpoint, the schedule is the principal document that communicates constructor intentions during the construction phase. The schedule spells out who will be performing which task, what resources will be used, and the timetable for the accomplishment of the task. The schedule is a forecasting tool and it is vital in project communication. Poor communication, or lack of communication, is the most compelling reason for a change order and intent to file a claim. As stated by Clough and colleagues, "The schedule allows the owner to completely consider contractor issues when project-related decisions are being made, therefore protecting both contractor and the owner."[10]

Change orders and claims are an unavoidable fact of project management. When they are managed successfully and handled ethically, fair compensation can be received for changed conditions and claims.

Conclusion

Despite the best efforts of contractors and project owners, changes to the project often develop. When changes do develop, contractors are entitled to an equitable adjustment to the contract time and price when productivity and cost are impacted by the change. The analysis and equitable resolution as to the time and cost effects of changes are greatly aided by the keeping of a project schedule that documents all events that impacts the order or timing of the work and the durations of project activities.

But-for schedules or collapsed as-built schedules are schedule manipulation techniques used to identify actual delays caused by one of the parties (owner or contractor) or by third parties to a contract. The technique removes the delays from the as-built schedule and collapses the schedule to establish when the project would have been completed except for the delays.

Problems and/or Questions

1. Find a court case that relied on schedule information to support a claim. Review and summarize the case. Include a copy of the case with your comments.

2. Find state statutes that relate to the use of schedules as evidence and present them with your interpretation.

3. Visit the engineer of a public owner, such as the state or a city. Discuss with the engineer how schedules are used to support or deny claims or change orders. Document your interview and describe one of the owner's claims or change orders in detail.

4. Visit a contractor who has used a schedule to support a claim or change order. Write it up as a complete case study.

5. For a recent change order from a local company, describe all of the documentation that was kept or created to support the submitted change order.

Notes

1. *www.metrokc.gov/recelec/archives/policies/con713aep.htm* (last accessed 9/12/2003).
2. Ness, Andrew, D. "Owner's Perspective: A Guide to Avoiding and Responding to Construction Claims." *http://www.constructionweblinks.com/Resources/Industry_Reports_Newsletters/Nov_20_2000/owners_perspective.htm* (last accessed 9/12/2003)
3. Ibid., p. 1.
4. Ibid., p. 2.
5. Stephen M. Phillips, "Legal Corner: When Are You Liable for Delay Damages?" *Professional Roofing* (October 2001): 2.
6. Richard H. Clough, Glenn A. Sears, and S. Keoki Sears, *Construction Project Management.* New York: Wiley, 2000, p. 261.
7. Ibid., p. 263.
8. Ibid., pp. 261–63.
9. Ibid., p. 264.
10. Ibid., p. 268.

CHAPTER 13

Schedule Analysis

Goal

Present the owner, construction manager, or prime contractor with the tools for schedule analysis.

Objectives

- Describe and demonstrate the internal process of schedule analysis.
- Describe and demonstrate the analysis of a subcontract schedule.
- Evaluate projects with a bar chart.
- Evaluate projects with the network.

Introduction

A construction schedule is a very dynamic document. Schedule dates are not fixed; they are estimates of when work will be preformed. Activity durations are also estimates. Unanticipated or unforeseeable events will occur making change the only constant. The schedule, however, allows management to identify and properly respond to changing conditions. Schedule analysis is a tool for determining whether the change that is occurring is an advantage or a disadvantage.

A condition that almost always alerts a schedule reviewer to schedule problems is negative lag. The use of negative lag should always be avoided. Another indication of schedule problems is large lag values. When the schedule is depicted by a bar chart, the reviewer must understand that relationships are not explicitly shown, therefore the order of activities must be carefully examined.

Evaluating the Company's Schedule

Because the schedule is often a contractually required document, it can be used by project owners or construction managers to justify action or inaction. Some constructors have felt that their initial schedule was the one they must adhere to throughout the project duration. However, the initial schedule is merely a starting point that illustrates the constructor's "best guess" at productivity. This schedule is often obsolete shortly after it is produced because construction is *dynamic*. Therefore, the circumstances surrounding the project should be known when evaluating a schedule. It is unlikely, even if the project is progressing as expected, that all of the project activities will be completed within their early start and finish dates. Schedule evaluators should not expect all early dates to be met. Instead, the evaluating process should consider (1) if the schedule appears to faithfully report project sequencing and progress, (2) if there are indications of a reasonable construction methodology, and (3) if the progress to date suggests that the project will finish on time.

Project Sequencing and Methodology

The chief estimator and the project manager have a conceptual image of the way in which the project will be built. When estimating and project management are handled by two different individuals, the schedules that each creates can be significantly different. The schedule used to control the job should reflect the activities and relationships described by the project manager. The activities, durations, and relationships depict the construction methodology—for example, machine versus hand-dug trench excavation. All senior project personnel should buy into the construction methodology and the resulting schedule. Once the activities are selected and linked in the desired sequences, the network should be calculated to determine if the schedule meets company and/or contractual deadlines. Sometimes it is necessary to adjust the sequences or change activity durations, based on changes in crew size or composition, in order to bring the schedule into compliance with required deadlines.

During the evaluation, recall that each activity's duration is a reflection of the expected production quantity (e.g., square feet) and the crew's productivity. Check the activities to be sure these measures have been used when determining activity durations. If resources are used in the schedule, consider what each resource represents. For example, if a resource is used to relate cost to each activity, be sure that it is all of the desired costs. This may mean allocating both direct and indirect costs to this resource; it may also include general and administrative costs and expected profit.

Relationships and lag values must be used correctly to represent expected relationships among activities. Negative lag values should be avoided. They are seldom correct and tend to alert the reviewer to these and other potential scheduling problems.

Progress

The schedule reviewer should determine if schedule-identified project progress is consistent with a field evaluation. Are activities that are reported as complete actually complete? Are those that are in progress expected to finish when the schedule indicates their finish? The reviewer must also consider the current finish date and determine if it is consistent with the specification requirement. Changes to network logic or activity duration used to correct completion date overruns should be achievable. The schedule is a record of what was accomplished when and, as such, should be truthful. The record of progress contained in the schedule can be used to support change orders and claims and to aid in fine-tuning estimating procedures. Progress is discussed in more detail in Chapter 8.

Evaluating a Subcontractor's Schedule

Several conditions alert the reviewer to potential problems or a lack of skilled scheduling practice. One of these conditions is the presence of negative lag values. Seldom is a negative lag appropriate. Consider Figure 13.1, in which the negative lag between activity 65 and activity 75 indicates that 5 days before activity 65 finishes, activity 75 may start. Is the finish of activity 65 controlling the start of activity 75? If the answer to this question is no, then the relationship is incorrect. More likely, the relationship should be an SS 7. This would result in the same calculated dates. The relationship between activity 82 and activity 65 truly suggests that activity 82 is the predecessor of activity 65, not its follower. A logic change is required to correct this negative lag value.

Large lag values are also often inappropriate. Finish-to-start relationships with lag values of more than 10 days should be scrutinized, as the lag values often represent a resource constraint. If such a constraint is not apparent, question the relationship and

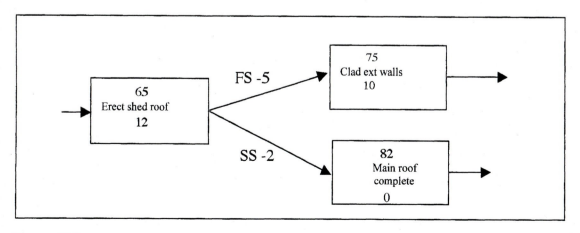

Figure 13.1
Negative lag values.

lag value. Sometimes, inflated lag values are used incorrectly to hide float. Both the contractor and the subcontractor should avoid this practice. It devalues the schedule and, when found, degrades trust.

Updated schedule reviews should include an investigation of the activities occurring on the data date (see Chapter 8). These activities have often been delayed and are unstarted. Prior schedules may have suggested that these activities should have occurred earlier. Although the early start date of activities should not be considered frozen because of the dynamic nature of the schedule, these slipped activities may be the only indication of a project that is behind schedule. Check for changes in the logic of downstream activities—these can go unnoticed.

All of the evaluative concern the constructor gives to the subcontractor will likely be given to the constructor by the owner. Evaluations of the company schedule submittals for these flags are essential to maintaining a healthy level of trust with the owner or the owner's representative.

Evaluating the Project with the Bar Chart

Bar charts are the most universally understood scheduling graphics. It is easy for the bar chart reviewer to see when each activity is scheduled to occur. However, noncomputerized bar charts seldom show relationships or float. Thus, the only evaluative elements are the implied logic, the activity durations, and activity timing.

Implied Logic

The reviewer should be able to determine if the order of the activities is reasonable. Does the roof follow the erection of the exterior walls and precede the interior wall erection? Although the logic among the activities is unidentified, the location and consequent timing of the activities should reflect the selected construction method.

Activity Durations

Durations should be consistent with the work quantity and anticipated productivity. Duration should not merely be a factor of a 5-day week (e.g., 10, 15, or 20 days). Instead, each duration requires a thoughtful determination.

Activity Timing

Activities done without enclosure should not normally be scheduled during anticipated periods of inclement weather. If such activities must be scheduled during these times, their durations should be extended to reduce the risk of delays, or the calendar should anticipate weather days. For example, concrete placement during freezing temperatures or excessive heat is less than desirable and can require extraordinary measures and additional time. This means increased cost, too. Similarly, landscaping may be washed away if scheduled for planting during the heavy rains anticipated in spring.

Evaluating the Project with the Network

Networks have explicit logic, lag values, and floats to help identify problems during project evaluation. Therefore, in addition to the evaluation conditions noted for the bar chart, these additional criteria should also be reviewed for possible logic errors, information conflicts, and construction impossibilities.

Review the relationships among the activities to ensure that they are accurate and that they faithfully represent the construction method. Look for reasonable lag values. Give special attention to lag values that are excessively large or negative. Total float requires similar consideration. Large float values often indicate activities that have not been properly linked and constrained. Negative float is a red flag that signifies that the project or an important date is not being met. Negative float is the result of imposed constraint dates. Review the dates for accuracy before attempting to make logic or duration changes to bring the project back to anticipated deadlines.

Conclusion

The primary tool used to regularly assess project status is the construction schedule. When the schedule has been created with insufficient effort and attention to detail it will not be useful as a tool for managing the project. It is therefore necessary to carefully analyze the sequencing and duration of individual schedule activities in order to assess the feasibility of performing the work in the field. While there are many analytical methods for analyzing a schedule, a simple review that checks lags, activity durations, logic changes, and activity float will often provide clues as to the validity of the schedule.

Problems and/or Questions

1. Submit a schedule, along with all necessary reports. Submit your analysis of the project's status.

2. Submit an analysis provided by either a contractor or an owner of a schedule, along with copies of some of the schedule documents.

3. Using the reports in Appendix D, provide a written evaluation of the status of the project.

4. Using the reports in Appendix D, describe what other reports would be helpful in evaluating the schedule and why they would be needed.

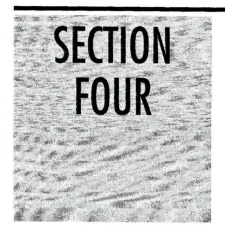

SECTION FOUR

ADVANCED AND ALTERNATE SCHEDULING TECHNIQUES

CHAPTER 14

Linear Scheduling

Goal

Describe the preparation of the linear schedule and describe and demonstrate its uses.

Objectives

- Describe and demonstrate how production relates to activity durations in the Linear Scheduling Method
- Describe and demonstrate the diagram's:
  - Activity placement
  - Durations
  - Relationships among activities
- Describe the use of buffers and the depiction of float.
- Describe how Linear Scheduling Methods are updated.
- Discuss how diagrams are read.

Introduction

The scheduling techniques previously discussed are appropriate for most construction schedules. However, when projects have repetitive activities, such as those for tall buildings, multiple buildings, and highways, linear scheduling may be the most appropriate way to communicate how the work is to be done. Also known as time-space and velocity diagrams, the linear scheduling method (LSM) is an outgrowth of the industrial engineering technique known as the line of balance (LOB),[1] used by Goodyear Tire and Rubber Company to monitor production in 1941.[2] LOB and LSM are effective visual communicators that have been used sparingly in construction. Commercial programs for creating, displaying, updating, and reporting on linear schedule information are limited in number and seem to be less well developed than other commercial programs providing precedence networking tools.

The linear schedule is as visually appealing as the bar chart, but it communicates more information. The linear schedule is a graphical representation of activities on two axes. One axis represents the location of the activity at any point in time. For vertical projects, the location is often a discrete measure, such as the floor of a building, a house, or an apartment. For horizontal projects, the location is usually a measure of distance, such as a station, mile, or mile marker. The other axis depicts time measured in hours, days, months, or years depending on the project's overall duration. Although either axis can represent time or location, this text will designate the abscissa (x-axis) for time and the ordinate (y-axis) for location. Activities are represented as lines, with a slope showing the activity's productivity as measured by its change in location divided by the change in time. Each activity can be composed of one or more line segments, attached or detached, of constant or changing slope. Some activities, such as mobilization, demobilization, the construction of a bridge, or a box culvert, are accomplished at only one location. These activities are depicted as horizontal lines at their location.

Just as with any critical path method (CPM) network, the construction of LSM logic begins with the identification of the appropriate activities. Thus, an activity list might be an appropriate starting point. Although found slightly differently than are the discrete values of most CPMs, LSM durations are still based on the productivity of the activity. However, the productivity in an LSM is related to location (e.g., stations/day) instead of a resource quantity (e.g., cubic yards/hour). Relationships among activities have location and resource utilization linkages in addition to normal CPM-type relationships.

The linear schedule is as easily represented as a precedence network. However, some groups of activities, as in a fragnet, must generally be repeated several times in order to construct the typical network. When the linear schedule represents a highway, the fragnets represent manageable project segments, allowing management control. When they represent a housing development, the fragnets may contain all of the activities for one house. Similarly, a multistory building would be constructed from fragnets representing the work on one floor. The linear schedule reduces the need for multiple iterations of each activity, such as mechanical construction floor 1 and floor 2, by consolidating the multiples into a single activity occurring at multiple floors. If each fragnet that is used to represent a house is only one part of a 100-house tract, 10,000 activities would be needed for the Precedence Diagraming Method. However, to develop the linear schedule, far fewer activities are needed, and the resulting diagram is much easier to interpret. Figure 14.1 shows how the LSM might be used to represent a housing tract.

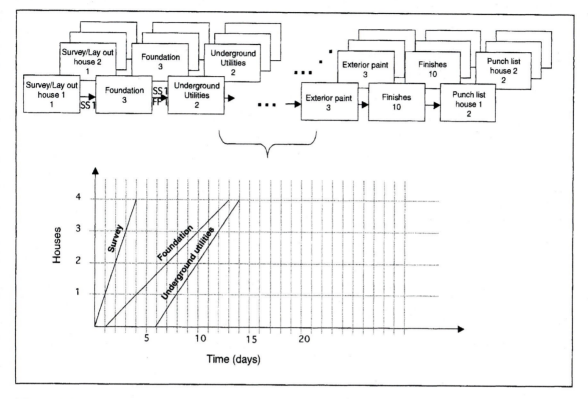

Figure 14.1
Precedence and linear scheduling comparison.

Durations

The productivity of each activity is derived during the estimating process. The slope of the line designating an activity in the linear schedule is a function of its productivity, generally measured in working days. Activities with steeper slopes have a higher production rate (production rate 1) than those with flatter slopes (production rate 3) (Figure 14.2).

Activity slopes need not be constant. Figure 14.3 indicates that, during much of the clearing and grubbing activity duration, the production rate is one station (100 ft.) per day. This may appear to be very slow. However, the length of the project—fifteen stations, or 1,500 feet—is not necessarily indicative of the width of the project site, nor does it describe the density of the above- and below-ground vegetation. Perhaps Figure 14.3 describes the building of a 100-foot-wide road through thick forest and the day 10 to day 18 flat slope represents a section of wet ground.

Each project must have productivities developed for all of its activities. These productivities must be converted to time and distance or location to use the linear scheduling method. Thus, a typical clear and grub activity may normally have its estimated

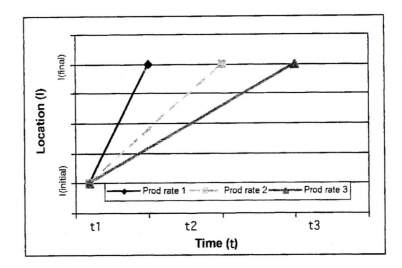

Figure 14.2
Production rate variability.

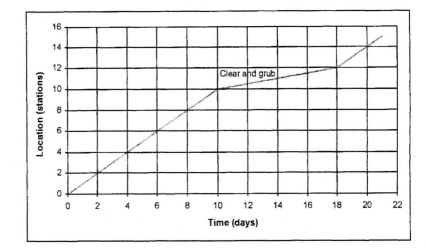

Figure 14.3
Changing slope of an LSM activity.

costs and durations related to the area, such as the acre. The days per acre or acres per day must be converted to linear feet, stations, or another measurement of length per day. When considering this type of conversion for buildings, the scheduler or estimator may need to convert structural steel productivity from tons per day to floors per day. Although this conversion is not a difficult step, it is one more task required for the construction of the linear schedule diagram.

Nonconstant productivity, such as that shown in Figure 14.3, is derived during the estimating process for the work. Changes in productivity can be attributed to planned

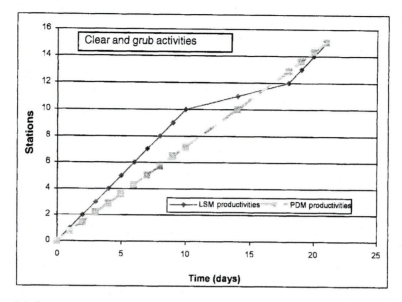

Figure 14.4
Comparison of average productivity versus LSM activity productivity.

changes in crew composition, anticipated weather delays, work of greater scope or complexity, resource constraints, or managerial decisions. The diagram clearly shows these differences, whereas a precedence schedule would not show them unless multiple activities were created to describe the changes in productivities. The outcome in a precedence network with only one clear and grub activity would be to assign an average production rate (Figure 14.4) that would relate to its resources. The result may be to lead the schedule reviewer to believe that the schedule was either ahead or behind, as with earned value, depending on what day the measurement was taken, even though it might be right on schedule and on budget, as can be seen in Figure 14.4. The schedule variance would appear to be good (positive variance) for the first 16 days if an average was used over the duration of the activity.

The Activity Represented on the Diagram

Figure 14.3 shows the basics of the linear schedule activity and diagram. Note that the slope of the line for the activity "clear and grub" (Figure 14.3) has a flatter, less productive slope between stations 10+00 and 12+00 than between any of the other stations. The interpretation of this change in slope and return to the original slope may indicate that the clearing is far more difficult or time-consuming between these two stations and of consistent ease during the remainder of the project.

The Figure 14.3 diagram not only shows the change in slope (productivity) for the clear and grub activity but also shows the location of the activity on any day, its total duration, and its completion date. Date labels are often shown at the beginning and end of the activity line to show the starting and ending date, especially when the scale used for plotting has limited detail. It is obvious in Figure 14.3 that "clear and grub" begins on day 0 and ends on day 21. Note, too, that each activity should be labeled to identify it among the other activities of the network.

Activities need not begin at the lowest station or floor. Activities may begin at more than one location at one time, such as a tunnel that is being driven from two separate headings. When this is the case, it suggests that two or more crews are being used to accomplish the activity.

Activities in the LSM must consider the use and availability of resources. Often, resource use is consolidated into one activity, though it could be two or more activities. A composite activity is often used that requires a specific piece of equipment or a specific labor trade. For example, framers that construct exterior and interior walls as well as erect the roof trusses of houses may have their efforts combined into one LSM activity called framing. If framers are a critical trade, ensuring that this resource is available for all activities needing framers is important. It may be more difficult to identify and control resources in the linear schedule than in a PDM schedule, for example.

Activities Found at One Location

A horizontal line on an LSM diagram normally depicts activities that occur at one location. For example, mobilization may be an activity occurring only when the building is at its first, or ground, floor. In Figure 14.5, the horizontal line is used to show mobilization and a delay, an extension, or a cessation in the work of survey for 2 days. The delay shown is at station (2+10) for the date(s) (days 13 and 14).

Relationships

Just as with the precedence network, the linear schedule relies on relationships among the activities. Usually, most activities occur in parallel, with some delay between the starts and the completions of the activities. Figure 14.1 shows how some of these relationships can be applied to the linear schedule. If the activity line is to remain unbroken, which maintains productivity and the flow of resources, activities with a higher productivity, which are related both start-to-start and finish-to-finish to their followers, have their start-to-start relationships controlling. Figure 14.1 shows "underground utilities," an activity that has a higher productivity and follows the slower "foundation" activity. For this case, the finish-to-finish, lag 1-day relationship controls. Conversely, Figure 14.6 shows the "underground utilities" and "foundation" activities related start-to-start. Here, the start-to-start, lag 1-day relationship is implemented. The activity lines cross, meaning that a logical follower is no longer following but leading and defying the network logic. Thus, a finish-to-finish controlling relationship should have been used between these two activities. Predecessors must always lead and successors must always follow. The lines representing these related activities should not cross.

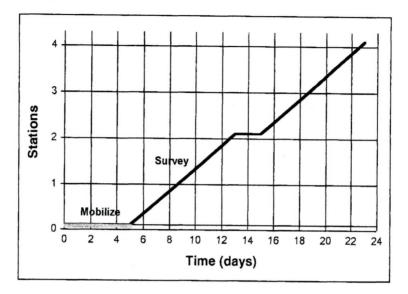

Figure 14.5
Horizontal activities.

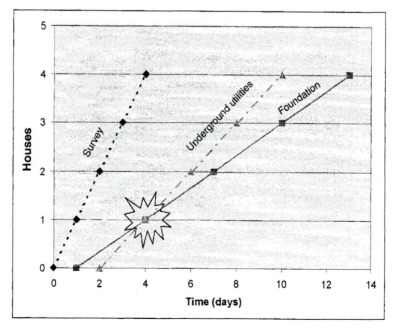

Figure 14.6
Implication of using a start-to-start with a more productive follower.

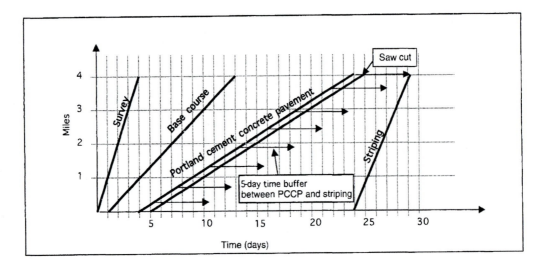

Figure 14.7
Time buffer example.

Buffers

The linear schedule uses two types of buffers: the time buffer and the location, or space, buffer. Instead of being related using only the four conventional relationship types, some activities use buffers to separate the activities. Buffers can be a primary consideration for activities that have important resource requirements and/or constraints.

The time buffer is formed by a horizontal offset from one activity to its follower. Figure 14.7 shows how this time buffer appears as the curing time for Portland cement concrete pavement (PCCP) and its relationship with the striping activity. To keep striping operating at its expected productivity, it should begin on workday 24 and finish on workday 29, never encroaching on the 5-day time buffer with its predecessor, PCCP.

Figure 14.8 shows the location buffer. The base course for the PCCP must stay a ½ mile in front of the paving machine. This provides ample room for the concrete to be delivered to the slipform paver. The vertical arrows in Figure 14.8 represent the ½-mile buffer that must be maintained between base course and PCCP.

Float

Neither the total nor the free float of activities in a linear schedule can be calculated as they can when using other networking techniques. It is clear from Figure 14.8 that there is free float from day 4 to day 13 of the base course activity. It is only the first ½ mile of base course that has no free float resulting from its relationship with its PCCP successor. By the time that the base course reaches mile 4, there appears to be about 7 days of

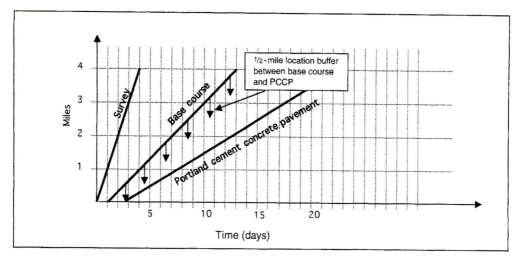

Figure 14.8
Location buffer example.

free float. However, in more traditional networking techniques, free float is on an activity and, in the linear schedule, the activity is represented by the entire line, not just a part of it. Separate fragnets for each mile would show float on base course activities for miles 2 to 4.

Finding the critical path is also more difficult in a linear schedule than with other CPM techniques. However, with effort the longest path through the schedule can still be determined. Usually by beginning at the last activity of the diagram and working toward the beginning, each critically connected activity can be identified. This chain of activities is generally the critical path. However, the most effective method of determining the critical path is to use the underlying network. Even though this network may not have enough detail for good project control, it can be used to determine the available float and critical path. Figures 14.9 and 14.10 show how this can be done.

Figure 14.10 depicts the PDM network that corresponds to the linear schedule in Figure 14.9. All of the activities in the network are critical except "saw cut," which has 4 days of total and free float. The start-to-start and finish-to-finish relationships are needed so that changes in duration or productivity of any of the activities will not result in delays or conflicts among activities.

Updating

Linear schedule activities can be updated by indicating actual progress with lines of different color, texture, or dimension. The updated schedule quickly shows differences between the productivity that was expected and what was achieved. Figure 14.11 is an example of an updated linear schedule.

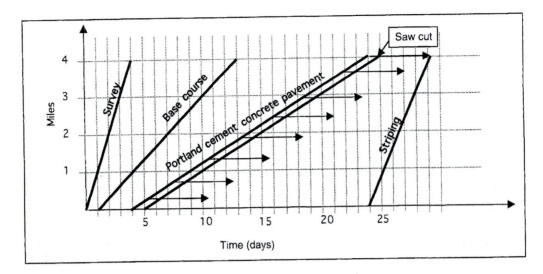

Figure 14.9
Linear schedule.

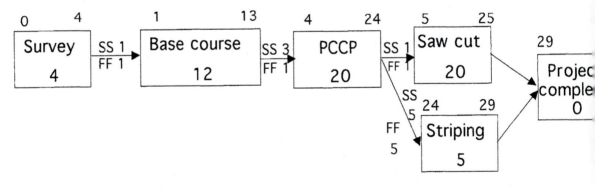

Figure 14.10
PDM network of linear schedule.

In Figure 14.11, the data date is displayed as a dashed vertical line shown at day 75. The diagram also indicates a CPM network that relates to the culvert activity shown at mile 6. The length of the line representing the "culvert" is updated as the CPM is updated. A line that has depth at a location, such as that for earthmoving or base, is indicative of what Johnston calls an *activity interval*. The interval represents work requiring more time at one location, such as rock excavation versus common excavation or excavation to a great depth versus a shallow cut. The dimensioned line depicting earthmoving is of varying width, showing a slowing of progress throughout the length of the activity, possibly due to unanticipated slowed production or delays experienced during the course of the activity. The actual progress on the sub-base has cre-

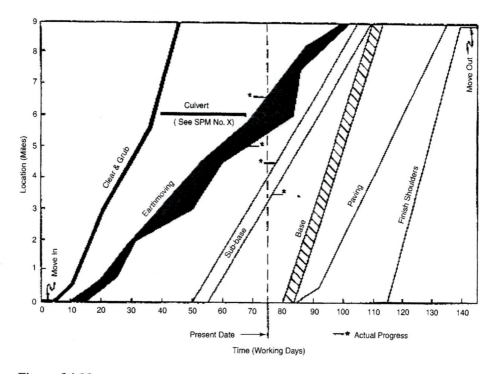

Figure 14.11
An updated linear schedule.
Source: David Johnston, "Linear Scheduling Method for Highway Construction," *Journal of the Construction Division* 107(C02) (1981): 254.

ated a second, parallel line that is delayed by about 5 days and is projected to stay 5 days behind schedule. The hash-marked area shown for base indicates longer durations for this activity at each location.

As progress is monitored, calculations can be made to determine changes in productivity, unit cost, and overall project cost. For example, if the original activity was scheduled to take 10 days to move 10 units of location (1 location unit/day), at a cost of $1,000 per day, after 6 days, the activity has progressed only 4 units. The productivity has diminished to 0.67 units per day, at a cost of $1,000 per day. The original cost was $10,000, or $1,000 per location unit. Now the cost per unit is $1,500, and the total cost will be $15,000 if the productivity remains the same.

Reading the Diagram

The diagrams shown thus far have been rather simplistic, except for Figure 14.11. This section will explore some more complex diagrams and their meanings.

Example 1   Earthwork LSM

The project in Figure 14.12 shows a highway construction project. The proposed earth-work profile plotted adjacent to the location axis shows material being excavated from between approximately stations 35+00 to 75+00. Some of the material is moved to the left to fill the area from station 0+00 to 35+00, and some is moved to the right to fill the area from station 75+00 to 95+00. The bridge, at approximately station 87+00, is shown in two stages, preliminary and finish construction. This activity could appear as a single line, with a supporting CPM network and diagram. Horizontal lines are drawn from the earthwork profile only to clarify the excavation, haul, and em-bankment processes being performed. The line representing top soil excavation crosses the bridge construction area because topsoil is being removed from areas adjacent to the bridge. The first area to be excavated is from station 75+00 to station 35+00. At the same time the excavation is going on, embankment is being placed in the adjacent fill area from 0+00 to 35+00, based on balance lines shown on the earthwork profile. Based on the LSM, the short hauls happen first around station 35+00, but, as the ac-tivities progress, the hauls become longer until the material at station 75+00 is being moved to station 0+00. Similar excavation and embankment activities follow for the material between stations 75+00 and 95+00. The final hauls are for the small volume of material between stations 95+00 and 100+00. This material is moved to the left to about station 90+00.

The activities for sub-base, base course, paving, striping, and repair are typical, easily understood LSM activities. The test traffic activity is vertical, occurring at all stations at the same time and for approximately 1 month.

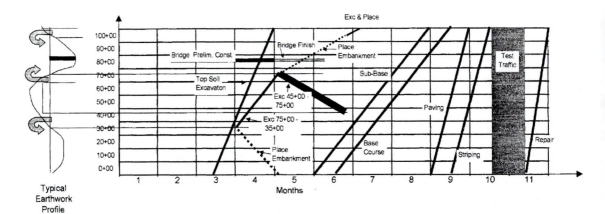

Figure 14.12

Highway construction LSM.

Adapted from Josef Cacha, "Time Space Scheduling Method," *Journal of the Construction Division* 108(C03) (1982): 455.

Example 2   Apartment Building LSM

Figure 14.13 shows a four-floor building with twelve apartment areas and three basement storage areas. One interesting element is the number of parallel activities, all with similar productivities. The description of these activities is noted to the right of the drawing due to the scaling. If possible, scaling should accommodate activity descriptions that are placed alongside the activity line. The activity for pre-cast elements has a steady rate of progress from the basement to the fourth floor and has a noticeably higher productivity for the roof. The stucco application begins at the fourth floor and moves down to the first floor, whereas the two painting activities begin at the bottom floor and move upward.

Advantages and Disadvantages of the Linear Schedule

An advantage of the linear schedule is its ability to communicate with reviewers from all organizational levels, creating a bridge of understanding. It clearly depicts tasks, their durations, and their locations at any point in time. The entire project duration is evident, and the diagram can be used to identify and resolve potential conflicts between tasks.

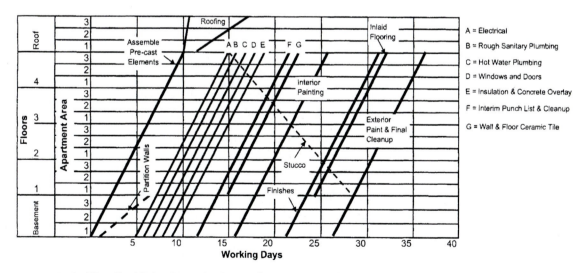

Dashed Lines Used Only to Distinguish One Line from Another

Figure 14.13
LSM for Apartment Building
Adapted from Josef Cacha, "Time Space Scheduling Method," *Journal of the Construction Division* 108(C03) (1982): 451.

However, like a bar chart, the linear schedule fails to show relationships among activities, although, in both cases, the relationships must be determined prior to diagrammatic construction. The LSM fails to communicate resource requirements and potential resource constraints.

Conclusion

The linear schedule is an effective visualization tool that provides some interesting insights for the schedule developer and reviewer. Because this tool is productivity-based, strong links exist between its development for a project and the project's estimate. Divergences from the plan can be identified quickly through a comparison of proposed and actual production, depicted by the slope of the activity line.

Problems and/or Questions

1. Using a published description, create a linear schedule for a tunnel project. Include the description with your linear schedule.

2. Using a published description, create a linear schedule for a housing tract project. Include the description with your linear schedule.

3. Using a published description, create a linear schedule for a high-rise building project. Include the description with your linear schedule.

4. Using a published description, create a linear schedule for a highway project. Include the description with your linear schedule.

5. Using a published description, create a linear schedule for a pipeline project. Include the description with your linear schedule.

6. Using journal articles, discuss the similarities and differences between line of balance and LSM.

7. Using the information in the following LSM diagram and part of this question, redraw the diagram, adding activity E, and answer the questions in parts b–d.

   a. Add activity E to the diagram. It has a constant slope and is related SS 2 and FF 2 with its predecessor, activity D. The duration of activity E is 15 days. Activity F has activity E as its predecessor and is related FS 0. Activity F has a total duration of 10 days. The duration of activity G is 18 days.

   b. What is the productivity rate of activity C in houses per day?

   c. What are the start and finish workday dates for activity E?

   d. What is the project duration (the end date of activity G)?

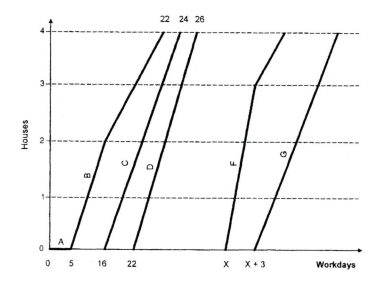

Notes

1. Robert I. Carr and Walter L. Meyer, "Planning Construction of Repetitive Units," *Journal of the Construction Division* 100(CO3) (1974): 403–12.
2. Noel N. Harroff, *Line of Balance, http://www.nnh.com/ev/lob2.html, p.1* (last accessed 9/12/2003).

CHAPTER 15

Activity on Arrow Networks

Goal

Present all facets of arrow diagramming and arrow network calculations.

Objectives

- Discuss the historical context of the arrow diagramming method.
- Demonstrate how activities appear and how they relate to one another:
  - Independent
  - Bursts
  - Merges
- Describe and demonstrate how networks are constructed.
- Discuss and demonstrate network problems:
  - Loops
  - Redundancies
- Discuss and demonstrate network calculations:
  - Forward pass
  - Backward pass
  - Float
    - Total
    - Free
    - Interfering

■ Describe how tables can be used for network calculations.
■ Describe virtual activities.

Introduction

The first networking method to be developed was the arrow diagramming method (ADM). This method is also known as activity on arrow (AOA) or I/J. With this method, activities are linked from the finish of one activity or arrow to the start of the next through a node or an event that connects the two activities. The activity is stated on the arrow, whereas the beginning and terminating nodes or events are diagrammatic. Nodes have no duration and use no resources. Figure 15.1 shows how activities or tasks are represented in an AOA network. Nodes are identified by i and j numbers. The "i" node marks the beginning of the activity, whereas the "j" node marks its completion. The arrow or activity is best diagrammed moving from left to right. The activity identification number in an AOA network is the combination of the "i" and "j" node numbers. The activity description is shown above the arrow, whereas the duration is shown beneath the arrow (Figure 15.2). Thus, activity 10-20 in Figure 15.2 represents mobilization and has a duration of 5 days.

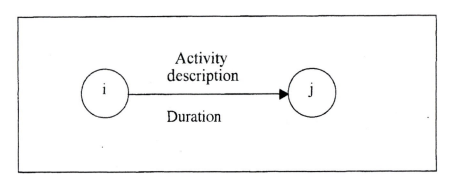

Figure 15.1
An AOA activity.

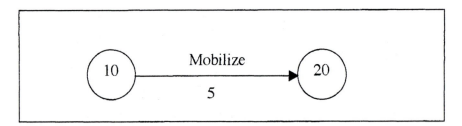

Figure 15.2
An AOA activity.

The activities in Figure 15.3 are related to each other. Activity A, 10-20, begins at node 10 and ends at node 20. Activity B, 20-30, begins at node 20 and ends at node 30. Activity B may not begin until activity A is complete. Activity A precedes activity B, and activity B succeeds activity A. Activity A is the predecessor of activity B; activity B is the successor of activity A.

When two or more activities flow from one node, as shown in Figure 15.4, the result is known as a *burst*. Activities A, B, and C burst from node 10 of Figure 15.4, whereas activities B, C, E, and F burst from node 10 (Figure 15.5).

When two or more activities enter a node, the result is known as a *merge*. Every activity entering a node precedes every activity exiting the same node. Figure 15.6 shows a merge and indicates that activities G, H, and K all precede activity L.

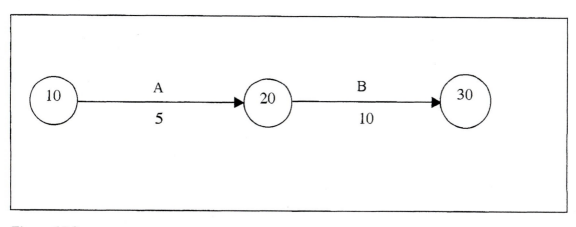

Figure 15.3
Activities A and B are related to each other.

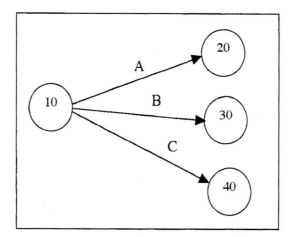

Figure 15.4
A burst at the beginning of the network.

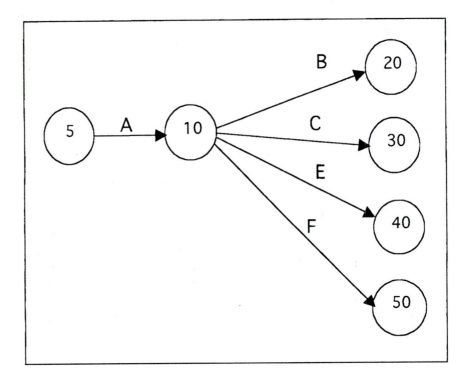

Figure 15.5
A burst node within a network.

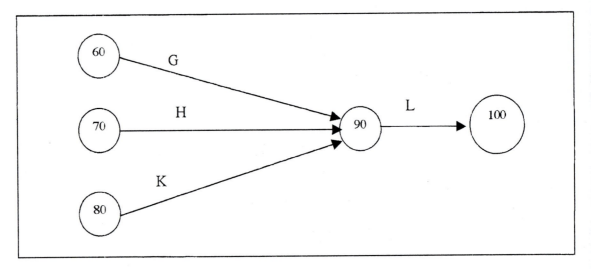

Figure 15.6
Merging activities.

Besides the activities diagrammed as solid arrows, AOA networks use *dummy* activities, depicted by dashed lines. Dummies are used in AOA networks for two reasons. The first reason is to show logic. In Figure 15.7, the dummy between activities E and G shows that activity E precedes activity G. Activity E also precedes activity F. Notice that the dummies are numbered to distinguish one from another, such as D_1 and D_2.

Figure 15.8 shows that activity E precedes activities F and G, but the difference between the logic of Figures 15.7 and 15.8 is that in Figure 15.8, activity C precedes activity F as well as activity G. When activity C precedes activity G only, the dummy is required to show the correct logic.

The second reason to use a dummy is to ensure that each activity has its own unique i-j node pair. If activity C does not precede activity F, but still precedes activity G, and

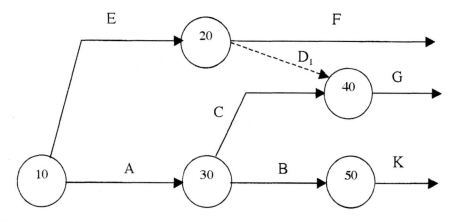

Figure 15.7
Network with a dummy activity, D_1.

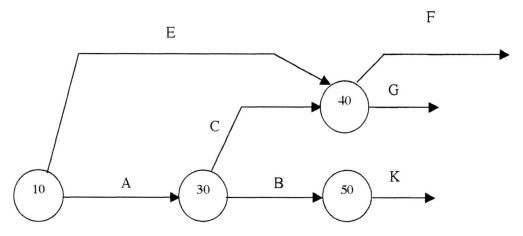

Figure 15.8
Logic change without dummy.

activity B also precedes activity G, then the Figure 15.7 network converts to that shown in Figure 15.9. Without the dummy, D_2, in Figure 15.9, both activity B and activity C would be known as 30-40. With the addition of the dummy, activity B is known as 30-50, activity C as 30-40, and the dummy, D_2, as 50-40. Consequently, each activity maintains its own unique pair of i-j node numbers.

The Network Diagram

Once the dependencies have been established among the activities, a network diagram can be constructed. A list of activities and their relationships is shown in Table 15.1. The resulting network diagram is shown in Figure 15.10.

Table 15.1 shows that neither activity A nor activity B has a predecessor; therefore, each begins the network at a burst. There are four dummies shown in Figure 15.10. Dummies 1 through 3 are used to show the logic of the activities and relationships in Table 15.1. Dummy 4 is used to maintain the uniqueness of activity numbering within the network.

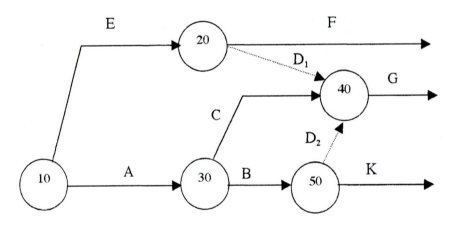

Figure 15.9
D_1 used for logic and D_2 used for unique numbering.

Table 15.1 AOA network dependencies.

Activity	Depends On	Activity	Depends On
A	——	G	C, E
B	——	H	F
C	A, B	K	F, G
E	B	L	H
F	A, C	M	H

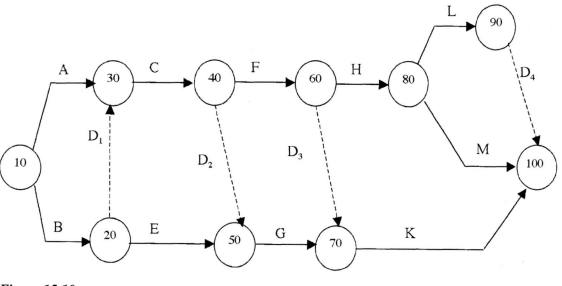

Figure 15.10
Network diagram.

Redundancies

In Table 15.1, the relationships for activity F suggest that both activities A and C are its predecessors. Notice that, in Figure 15.10, there is no event or node that connects activity A to activity F. Any such relationship is redundant because there is already an implicit relationship. Activity A precedes activity C, and activity C precedes activity F; therefore, activity A precedes activity F. Redundancies are most often missed when there is a long chain of activities. AOA networks already carry at least a 15% overage of activities because of the need related to the dummies used for logic and numbering. Adding redundant relationships is another way of increasing the cost (through the additional human resource needed to update and maintain the schedule activities) without increasing the benefit; this is poor scheduling practice.

Loops

Another concern of the network designer is to avoid creating circular logic. Activities that circle, or loop back onto themselves, create fatal flaws, which prevent accurate network calculations. Figure 15.11 shows the simplest loop or logic error, in which P precedes R and R precedes P. Loops may continue through many activities and be difficult to trace without the aid of a computer scheduling program. Most scheduling programs

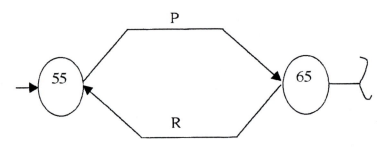

Figure 15.11
Simple network loop.

Loop report -- Scheduling Report Page: 4

Loop #   Activity   Description

-------- ---------- ---

1   AS105   Install Temperature Control Equipment

      AS106   Set & Connect Robots

      AS107   Install System & Misc. Components

      AS310   Site Preparation

      AS315   Install Electrical Power

Figure 15.12
Sample Primavera Project Planner® loop detection report.

routinely check for loops and list the activities included in the unbroken circular chain. Figure 15.12 shows how Primavera Project Planner® reports on loops.

Diagramming Basics

The arrows on the diagram should be drawn from left to right, with arrowheads indicating the direction. Each node should be labeled with an alphanumeric identifier. In most cases, including in this text, these identifiers are only numeric and are generally incremented by 10 for simplicity and to allow for ease in changing the network. Remember that the node numbers identify the activity. When the arrows representing the activity have to cross, one of the arrows should be either broken or looped, as shown in Figure 15.13, to help the reviewer distinguish between the activities.

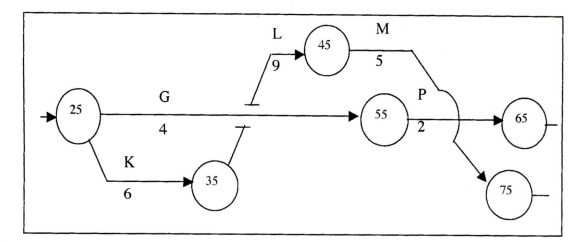

Figure 15.13
Crossing activities.

Network Calculations

When network time calculations are done, both the early dates and the late dates are calculated. These dates enable the reviewer to identify the critical path, the longest path through the network. The calculated dates provide the basis for the calculation of activity float. The calculations are done in two phases, a forward pass and a backward pass.

Forward Pass

To determine the project duration, a forward pass of calculations must be done. The forward pass establishes the early start (ES) and early finish (EF) dates of each activity and/or the early node times for each activity, TE_i and TE; TE_i is the early time at the i node of an activity ij and TE_j is the early time at its j node. The formulae for determining the dates are presented in equations 15-1 through 15-3.

$$Early\ Start_{jk} = \underset{\forall(ij)}{Max}(Early\ Finish_{ij})\ or\ TE_j \qquad (15\text{-}1)$$

$$Early\ Finish_{ij} = Early\ Start_{ij} + Duration_{ij} \qquad (15\text{-}2)$$

$$TE_j = \underset{\forall(ij)}{Max}(Early\ Finish_{ij}) \qquad (15\text{-}3)$$

The max implies that the maximization is to be over all v(ij) links ij terminating at node j.

Figure 15.14 shows where the times are displayed on the nodes and arrows for the forward pass.

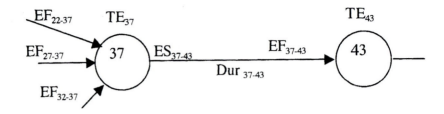

Figure 15.14
Early time notations.

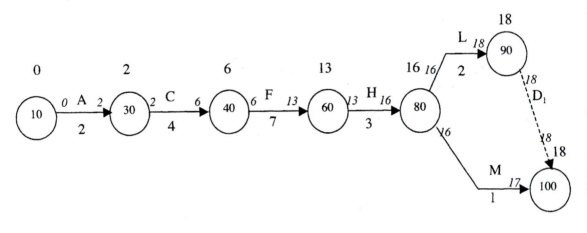

Figure 15.15
Sample I/J, or AOA, network diagram with forward pass calculations.

In Figure 15.14, at a merge, such as node 37, the TE_{37} is the maximum of the early finishes (EFs) of the activities entering the node. The early start of activity 37-43 is equal to the TE_{37}. The early finish of activity 37-43 is equal to the sum of its early start and duration.

The two primary rules to remember when making forward pass calculations are that (1) there should be only one start node and one finish node for a network and (2) the TE of the first node of the network should be zero. Figure 15.15 shows how activity early starts and finishes can be denoted (italics) and how node early times are shown.

Figure 15.15 illustrates two important principles. Dummy activities have no duration, and the largest TE value is used at all merges, although only one merge is shown in this diagram. Thus, when two activities merge at node 100, there are two choices for the TE at that node. TE_{100} equals either 17 (16 + 1) through activity M or 18 (18 + 0) through activity D_1. On the forward pass always use the largest number, in this case18.

Figure 15.16 can be used for practicing the forward pass. Identify the purpose of each dummy and identify the longest path through the network, the critical path. Remember that all of the relationships among activities are finish to start, there is no lag or delay. Figure 15.17 shows the Figure 15.16 calculated network.

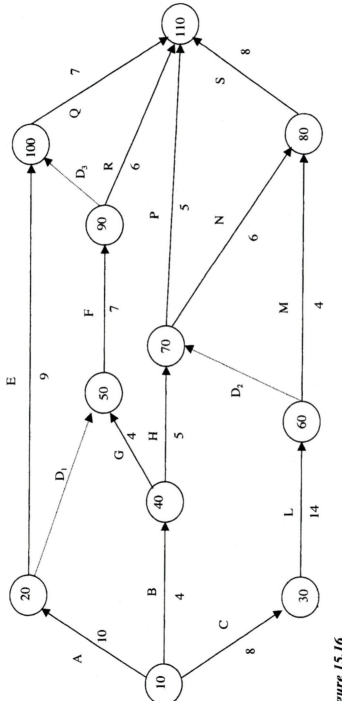

Figure 15.16
AOA network for practice.

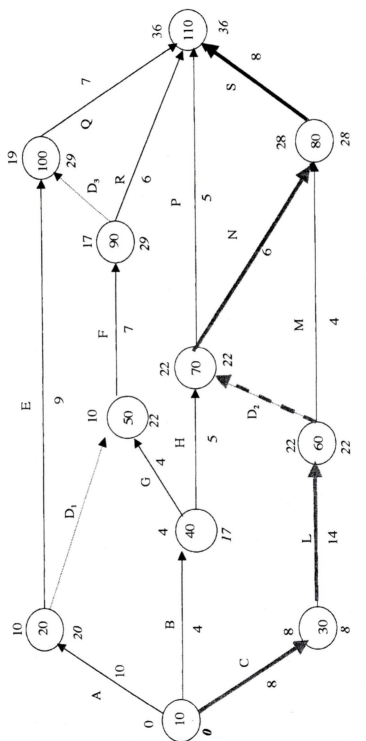

Figure 15.17
Network forward and backward pass calculations with critical path in bold.

214

Backward Pass

The forward pass indicates the earliest dates on which each activity can be accomplished. However, in most construction schedules, only some of the activities are expected to complete on their early dates. These activities are critical to the completion of the project on its expected completion date. The more linear a schedule is—the fewer the subpaths, or branches, it has—the more likely it is that all of the activities will be critical. This means that there will be no time for any unexpected delay without a resulting delay of the completion of the project. Delays to the project completion can result in liquidated damages. Thus, the backward pass provides the late start (LS) and late finish (LF) dates for each activity. These dates are used in conjunction with the early dates to determine the criticality of each activity and its float, if any.

The backward pass begins at the terminal, or last, activity in the network and works backwards toward the beginning of the network. The early date, or TE_j of the last node in the network, is simply copied to the TL_j location. TL_j is the late time at the j node of an activity ij and TL_i is the late time at its i node. When proceeding backward through the network, the forward pass process is conducted in reverse. The late finish (LF) of an activity is equal to the earliest LS of all of its followers, or successors. Equations 15-4 through 15-7 provide backward pass calculation information. *Min* implies that the minimization is to be over all links jk which begin at node j. $\forall jk$

$$Late\ Finish_{ij} = \underset{\forall jk}{Min}(Late\ Start_{jk}) \qquad (15\text{-}4)$$

$$TL_j = \underset{\forall jk}{Min}(Late\ Start_{jk}) \qquad (15\text{-}5)$$

$$Late\ Start_{ij} = Late\ Finish_{ij} - Duration_{ij} \qquad (15\text{-}6)$$

$$TL_i = TL_j - Duration_{ij} \qquad (15\text{-}7)$$

The result of the backward pass is that the LS and TL_i of the first activity should be zero, like its ES (early start) and its TE_i. Figure 15.17 shows the Figure 15.16 network with the backward pass calculations included.

In Figure 15.17, 36 days are required to complete the project, based on the durations of the activities shown. The TL_{10} is equal to zero; this is one indicator that the network was calculated correctly. Another requirement for the properly calculated network is to have all of the early dates or times be smaller than their corresponding late dates or times. This is true as long as there are no imposed time constraints.

Figure 15.18 shows three activities cut from the network. The early finish dates of both G, which is 8 (EF = 4 + 4), and H which is 9 (EF = 4 + 5), are less than the TEs of nodes 50 and 70, because these merge nodes are being "pushed" by the dummy activities shown. At node 50 the incoming dummy must have an EF of 10 and at node 70 the EF of the dummy is 22. The late dates are obtained from the backward pass. The late finish of both G and H is 22 because the TL of nodes 50 and 70 is 22. The late start of G is 22(LF) − 4(duration) or 18, whereas the late start of H is 17 (22 − 5). The *minimum* of these two dates becomes the TL_{40}. The late finish of activity B is 17, the TL_{40}. Although the beginning node of activity B is not shown, its late start is 17 − 4 = 13.

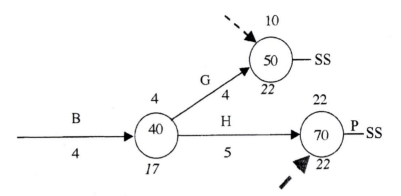

Figure 15.18
Partial network diagram from Figure 15.17.

Float

As discussed in Chapter 4 the most common types of float are total float and free float. It is always good to keep the definitions of each type of float in mind when calculations are done by hand. Simply thinking about the definitions will aid in determining the float values.

The total float on an activity is the amount of time the activity can be delayed and still not delay the project completion date. The word *delay* in the definition means to postpone the start of an activity, to extend an activity's duration, or to do both. Total float can be obtained from one of the following equations:

$$Total\ Float_{activity}\ or\ TF_{ij} = Late\ Finish_{activity} - Early\ Finish_{activity} \qquad (15\text{-}8)$$

$$TF_{ij} = TL_j - Duration_{ij} - TE_i \qquad (15\text{-}9)$$

In Figure 15.19, the TF of activity H equals $TF_H = LF_H - EF_H = 2 - 9 = 13$ or $TL_{70} - Duration_H - TE_{40} = 22 - 5 - 4 = 13$. When the terminating node of an activity, node 70 for activity H, has its TL equal to its TE, then the total and free floats of the activity are equal.

The free float of an activity is the amount of time an activity can be delayed and not delay any following activities or the project completion date. Free float can be obtained from one of the following equations:

$$Free\ Float_{activity}\ or\ FF_{ij} = Early\ Start_{following\ activity} - Early\ Finish_{activity} \qquad (15\text{-}10)$$

$$FF_{ij} = TE_j - Duration_{ij} - TE_i \qquad (15\text{-}11)$$

The reason that *or project completion* is included in the definition of free float is because the last activity in the network has no follower. Therefore, the only way to obtain its FF is to include this phase in the definition. In Figure 15.20, the FF of activity H equals $FF_H = ES_P - EF_H = 22 - 9 = 13$ or $TE_{70} - Duration_H - TE_{40} = 22 - 5 - 4 = 13$. The $FF_G = 10 - 4 - 4 = 2$, while $TF_G = 22 - 4 - 4 = 14$.

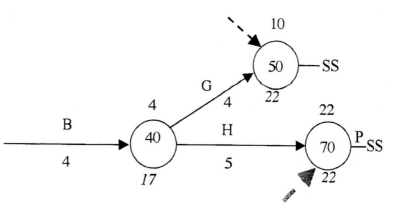

Figure 15.19
Float demonstration.

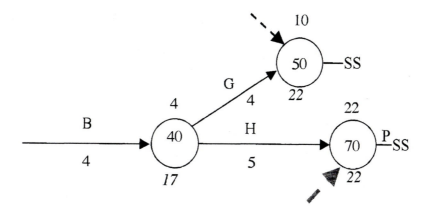

Figure 15.20
Free float demonstration.

Some describe two other types of float, interfering float and independent float. Although these floats describe other relationships among activities, they are seldom used by scheduling programs or professionals. However, interfering float (IF) will be described. The IF is the difference between the TF and the FF. The following equations relate to interfering float:

$$IF_{ij} = TF_{ij} - FF_{ij} \tag{15-12}$$

$$IF_{ij} = (TL_j - Duration_{ij} - TE_j) - (TE_j - Duration_{ij} - TE_i) = TL_j - TE_j \tag{15-13}$$

Equation 15-13 demonstrates that all activities entering a node have the same interfering float.

Tables

Activity early and late dates and their associated floats can be detailed in a table format. Consider the network described in Table 15.2.

Figure 15.21 shows the network resulting from Table 15.2, with the addition of two dummy activities. Both dummies, D_1 and D_2, are needed to preserve the logic described in Table 15.2. In Table 15.3 the calculations of the early and late dates and the total and free floats are shown. Recall that the early start (ES) of an activity is equal to the early time (TE) of its i node, and its early finish (EF) is its early start plus its duration (equations 15-1 and 15-2). Similarly, the late finish (LF) of an activity is equal to the late time (TL) on the j node. The late start (LS) is equal to the late finish minus the activity's duration (equations 15-4 to 15-6). In addition, the total float (TF) is the difference between the late finish and the early finish (equation 15-8), and the free float (FF) is

Table 15.2   Example network.

i j Node	Description	Duration	Depends On
10-20	A	10	—
20-30	B	6	A
30-40	E	17	B
30-35	F	21	B
35-60	H	10	F
40-50	M	8	E, F
50-70	G	11	M
60-70	J	6	M, H
70-80	K	4	G, J

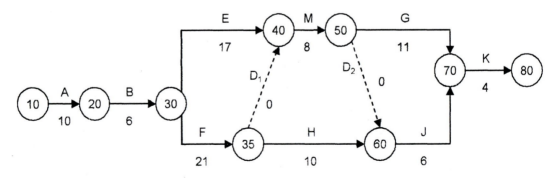

Figure 15.21
Network of Table 15.2 project.

Table 15.3   Tabulated results of Figure 15.21 network.

Activity	Dur	ES	EF	LS	LF	TF	FF	IF
*A	10	0	10	0	10	0	0	0
*B	6	10	16	10	16	0	0	0
E	17	16	33	20	37	4	4	0
*F	21	16	37	16	37	0	0	0
*D$_1$	0	37	37	37	37	0	0	0
H	10	37	47	40	50	3	0	3
*M	8	37	45	37	45	0	0	0
*G	11	45	56	45	56	0	0	0
D$_2$	0	45	45	50	50	5	2	3
J	6	47	53	50	56	3	3	0
*K	4	56	60	56	60	0	0	0

*The critical path

the minimum difference between the early starts of the activity's followers and its early finish (equation 15-10). Last, interfering float (IF) is the difference between the activity's total float and the free float. When completing the table, also consider that the first activity in the network will have an early start date of time zero; dummy activities have dates and floats. The early dates in the table must be completed first, just as the forward pass on a network is calculated first. The late dates are entered next, beginning with the activity with the latest early finish (the last activity in the network). The late finish of this activity is equal to its early finish, and its early start is found by subtracting its duration. Next, the floats are entered into the table using equations 15-8, 15-10, and 15-12. Remember that the first and last activities (A and K) should have early and late dates that are identical; they should be on the critical path. Table 15.3 shows the results of these calculations for the network shown in Figure 15.21. The critical path activities, those activities with zero total and free floats, are identified when the calculations are completed.

The forward pass is typified by the early finish (EF) of activity A becoming the early start (ES) of activity B. Activities E and F both precede activity M. The maximum EF of activity E or F becomes the ES of activity M. When activity K (the last activity in the network) is reached, its EF becomes its LF (late finish), and the backward pass calculations begin. On the backward pass, at bursts such as node 50, where activity G and activity D$_2$ emerge, the LF of activity M (40-50) is the minimum of the late starts of activity G or D$_2$. Because FF (free float) is less than or equal to TF (total float), everywhere TF equals zero, the FF is also zero. The FF on activity E is the difference between the ES of its follower, activity M (37), and its early finish (33), which is 4.

Virtual Activities

A *virtual activity* consists of an unbroken chain of related activities without any bursts or merges until the end of the chain. That means that, in the string of activities that constitute a virtual activity, each activity has an FF equal to zero. However, this may not apply to the last individual activity in the string. Additionally, the total float is the same on all of the activities in the virtual activity. An example of this is shown in Figure 15.22.

In Figure 15.22 there is a virtual activity 10-20, 20-40, and 40-50. The total float along this chain is 10 days for all the individual activities. Nothing changes in the float in this virtual activity until a merge is reached, where another activity becomes the pusher of node 50. Each of the three activities within the virtual activity has a total float equal to 10. The concept behind a virtual activity is that one activity could replace all the activities within the chain. The replacement can occur because there are no bursts or merges; thus, each internal activity (10-20 and 20-40) has a free float equal to zero. Note that there is FF on the last activity (40-50) in the chain; its FF is *not* zero because the ES of 50-70 is forced or pushed by the dummy 30-50.

Conclusion

The AOA method of network diagramming is limited in that all relationships are finish-to-start (FS) without any lag or delay. In reality, activities are related in a variety of ways other than FS 0. Novel ways have been created for solving this problem. One way is to split activities. Prior to the development of activity on node (AON) network diagramming with multiple relationship types, AOA was the only nonstatistical, or deterministic, method used. Today, most owners will accept AON networks, but there are still occasions when an AOA network is required.

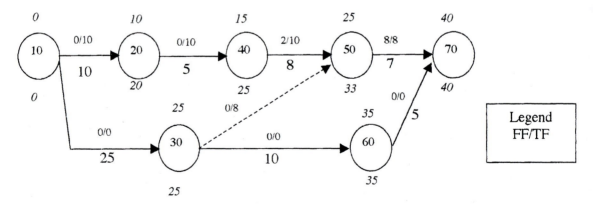

Figure 15.22
Virtual activity float.

Problems and/or Questions

1. Calculate the early and late times for the following network. Show the critical path and calculate the total and free floats. Use the resources given to construct a resource histogram.

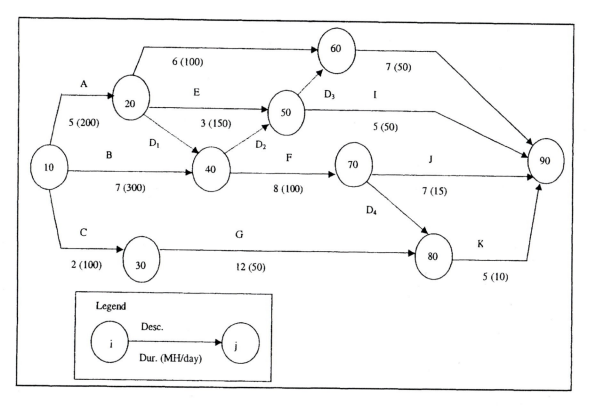

2. Construct an I/J network from the following list of activities and dependencies.

Activity	Depends On	Activity	Depends On
A	——	H	F
B	A	I	F
C	E	J	H and I
E	——	K	D
F	——	D	B, E, F, G
G	A	L	C and K
M	I	N	D and J

3. Construct an I/J network from the following list of activities and dependencies. Do the forward and backward pass calculations (durations are in parentheses). Find the project duration and the total and free floats.

Activity (Dur)	Depends On	Activity	Depends On
A (5)	———	L (6)	F and K
B (8)	———	M (4)	A, G, H
C (16)	———	N (5)	A, G, H
E (9)	B	P (8)	C
F (10)	A	R (9)	F and K
G (3)	B	S (6)	R, L, M
H (5)	E	T (4)	N and P
K (7)	A and G	W (12)	F and K

4. Construct a table from the following list of activities and dependencies. Include the activity, its duration, its early start and finish dates, its late start and finish dates, and its total and free floats.

Activity (Dur)	Depends On	Activity (Dur)	Depends On
A (5)	———	M (6)	A and B
B (7)	———	N (10)	M and P
C (8)	———	P (6)	A, B, L
E (3)	———	Q (8)	P
F (12)	———	R (10)	G
G (4)	E	S (3)	K, Q, W
H (3)	C	T (2)	K, Q, W
K (4)	H and F	W (6)	G
L (7)	C		

5. Construct a table from the following list of activities and dependencies. Include the activity, its duration, its early start and finish dates, its late start and finish dates, and its total and free floats.

Activity (Dur)	Depends On	Activity (Dur)	Depends On
A (5)	——	M (5)	E and F
B (3)	——	N (3)	G
C (2)	——	O (7)	F
E (12)	B	P (7)	H and O
F (8)	B	Q (3)	K and L
G (9)	B	R (6)	C
H (10)	A	S (1)	O and H
K (4)	A	T (2)	N and P
L (4)	A		

6. Describe the purpose of each dummy needed for the diagram constructed in problem 3.

7. You have been given the following schedule information: There are seven activities to be done over the next year. The minimum duration of these activities is 1 month.

Activity	Duration (mo.)	Cost: $ × 1,000	Follower(s)
A	2	50	B and C after 1 mo. of A is complete
B	1	20	None
C	4	120	D after 1 mo. of C
D	3	90	E after 1 mo. of D
E	2	50	F when E is finished
F	4	40	G when F is finished
G	2	40	None

The ABC project, as this is known, must be represented first as an AOA network, then in a bar chart format. Give each activity an activity I.D. The period cost (cost/month) should be tabulated beneath the bar chart, as should the cumulative cost. Then a histogram and an s-curve should be drawn of these costs, using dollars. Answer the following questions:

   a. When is the project 50% complete by resource ($)?

   b. What is the status of the project activities when the project is 50% complete by time?

   c. In what month is the largest expenditure of dollars and what is its value in dollars?

8. Construct an I-J network diagram from the list of activities that follows.

Activity	Depends On
A	———
B	A
C	A
F	C and L
H	B
K	———
L	K
M	R
N	R and S
P	S
R	B and L
S	H and T
T	F

9. For the following network, calculate the early and late dates and total and free floats. Identify the critical path.

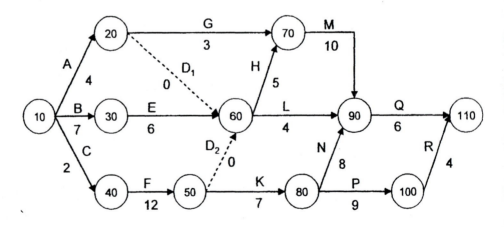

CHAPTER 16

Program Evaluation and Review Technique

Goal

Present many of the facets of PERT diagramming and calculations.

Objectives

- Review the needed statistics.
- Demonstrate how PERT networks are constructed.
- Describe and demonstrate statistical calculations:
  - Activity durations
  - Project duration
  - Standard deviation and variances
- Discuss and demonstrate network calculations, including slack.
- Describe how probabilities are found.

Introduction

The program evaluation and review technique (PERT) is a method of determining the length of a construction project and probability of project or intermediate risky activity completion by a specified date using probabilistic activity durations. Unlike activity on

225

arrow (AOA) and activity on node (AON), which use deterministic durations, the PERT method relies on activity durations that are established either by an analysis of historical data or through estimates of the range of probable activity durations. The scheduler must be aware of the uncertainty actually associated with activity duration estimates. For projects with critical time constraints or those with small windows of opportunity for completion, PERT may be the most appropriate scheduling method.

Statistics Review

Most construction companies engage in work that they have done before. This practice results in multiple occurrences of the same activity and a historical record of durations or productivities. These data can be shown as a frequency histogram such as the one shown in Figure 16.1. No matter the actual distribution, there are three measures of central tendency: *mean, mode,* and *median.* In the normal distribution, these three measures are the same value. Figure 16.1 shows a frequency histogram with the mean, or arithmetic average; the mode; and the median shown. The mean = 287 / 25 = 11.48 days. The mode, or most likely observation, the one occurring most frequently, is 10. Five guardrail activities were completed in 10 days. The median value, or the value with an equal number of observations above and below the value, is approximately 11 days. There are 10 observations below and 11 observations above this value. The durations range is from 8 days to 16 days, or a range of 8 days (16 − 8 = 8).

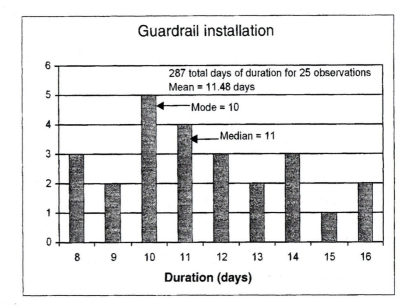

Figure 16.1
Histogram showing measures of central tendency.

Each activity that has been done multiple times has a sample duration distribution that can be obtained and used to determine an estimate of the population duration distribution. Software packages such as BestFit[®][1] can be used to select the statistical distribution most closely related to the sample data. Figure 16.2 shows the most closely related distribution found by BestFit[®] for the data shown in Figure 16.1 using the Kolmogorov-Smirnov goodness-of-fit test. The resulting distribution is known as the Pearson V and has a probability distribution or density function (PDF) with function characteristics that produce the smooth curve in Figure 16.2. The population statistics are presented in Table 16.1. Notice that the mean, mode, and median are similar to those reported for the sample shown in Figure 16.1 but are found by BestFit[®] using the PDF equations for the Pearson V distribution.

If all activities have been performed multiple times in the past enough times to generate a frequency histogram similar to Figure 16.1, a sample can be taken from each distribution that will give a duration for each activity. A network having all activities with historical or estimated distributions can be set up as a PERT network. The sections that follow demonstrate how these statistics are relevant and necessary for PERT network calculations.

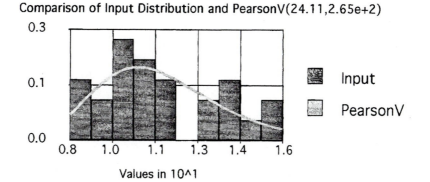

Figure 16.2
Sample data and BestFit[®] population function.

Table 16.1   Pearson V population statistics.

Statistic	Value
Mean	11.489262
Mode	10.586042
Median	11.171523
Standard deviation	2.446558
Variance	5.985648

PERT Diagramming

PERT shares similarities with both the AOA and precedence networking techniques. The diagram most closely resembles the AOA network, in that arrows are used to represent tasks and nodes are used to represent events. It has been said that the PERT network focuses on the events that represent the completion of activities.[2] In the AON network, the node is the entire activity, both start and finish. Some PERT descriptions exclude any activity description from the arrow, noting all activity descriptors to the completions shown in the terminating node. When this is done, sometimes the start of an activity must also be included in the activity-originating node, as with the node in Figure 16.3, "C Complete Begin D."

Another major difference between PERT and either AOA or AON is that PERT uses three estimates for each activity's duration. The three duration estimates are optimistic (t_o), pessimistic (t_p), and most likely (t_m). The optimistic duration estimate assumes that the maximum, or near maximum, productivity is achieved for the activity; so, in the case of the guardrail frequency histogram, Figure 16.1, the optimistic duration is 8 days. The pessimistic duration takes the "worst case" view, in which the pessimistic estimate of activity duration assumes the lowest or nearly lowest productivity. This relates to the 16-day duration for the guardrail activity. The third estimate of activity duration, the most likely, represents a modal duration, meaning that this duration estimate occurs most often when the historical information is available for multiple occurrences of the activity. This is 10 days' duration for the guardrail activity. Figure 16.3 shows a sample PERT network. Activity A has an optimistic duration of 1 day, a most likely duration of 2 days, and a pessimistic duration of 3 days.

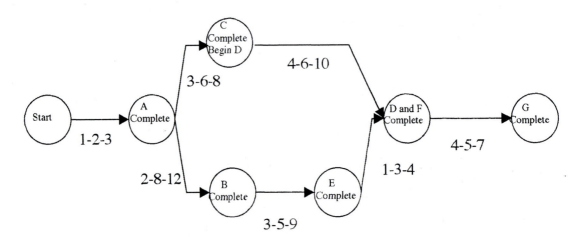

Figure 16.3
Sample PERT network.

Activity Durations

The activity duration is a composite of the three duration estimates and is known as the *activity mean duration* and is denoted as t_e. The t_e for an activity is found by

$$t_e = (t_o + 4t_m + t_p)/6 \qquad (16\text{-}1)$$

The mean duration for activity A is $t_{eA} = (1 + 4*2 + 3)/6 = 2.0$. All activity duration estimates that have t_o and t_p values that are equidistant from the t_m have an activity mean duration, t_e, equal to their most likely duration, t_m. All activity mean durations are a function of 1/6 and frequently have repeating decimals, such as $0.\overline{3}$ and $0.\overline{6}$.

Network Calculations

The *project mean duration* (T_e) is calculated like that used for the network; start at time 0 for the early event time (TE) or early start date on the first activity, activity A. Because all activity mean durations are a function of 1/6, sums should reflect this fact, such that the project mean duration $= 17.83 (17 - 5/6) + 5.16 (5 - 1/6) = 23.0$ $(22 - 6/6)$ or $T_{eProject} = 23.0$.

The forward and backward passes are done using the activity mean durations (t_e) for each activity. Durations are summed, taking the maximum value at all merges, on the forward pass. The backward pass begins with the project duration and works backward, subtracting activity mean durations, and taking the minimum at all bursts. Figure 16.4 shows the activity mean durations calculated based on the t_o, t_m, and t_p values shown in Figure 16.3. The project mean duration of 23.0 days is found along the critical path, or ABEFG.

In the PERT method, there is no *float*. Instead, float is referred to as *slack;* there is *free slack* and *total slack,* both computed the same way as free and total float. There is also *event slack, ES.* Activity total slack (ATS) is found just as total float is found in the arrow diagramming method networks.

$$ATS_{ij} = TL_j - Duration_{ij} - TE_i \qquad (16\text{-}2)$$

For activity D, the $ATS_D = 17.83 - 6.33 - 7.83 = 3.66$ days. The activity free slack (AFS) is the same as ADM free float.

$$AFS_{ij} = TE_j - Duration_{ij} - TE_i \qquad (16\text{-}3)$$

For activity C, the $AFS_C = 7.83 - 5.83 - 2.0 = 0.0$. The *event slack* is similar to the interfering float found in the arrow diagramming method, however, it is related to the event, not the activity.

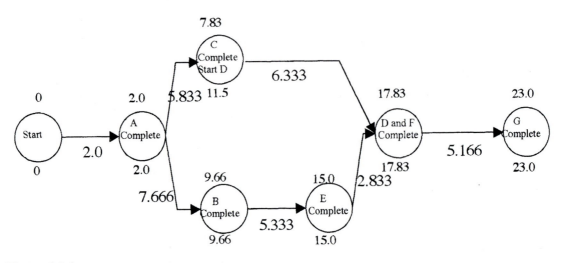

Figure 16.4
PERT network calculation.

$$ES_i = TL_i - TE_i \qquad (16\text{-}4)$$

The $ES_{C\ Complete,\ Start\ D}$ = 11.5 − 7.83 = 3.66. All calculations of mean duration and slack will result in a function of 1/6.

Calculating the Probability of Meeting Deadline Dates

Because the variability of activity durations plays an important role in determining the probability of reaching dates in a specified amount of time, the standard deviation of each activity duration is calculated. The standard deviation is computed as follows:

$$\frac{(t_p - t_o)}{6} \qquad (16\text{-}5)$$

Equation 16-5 says that the standard deviation is equal to the range of activity durations divided by 6. This is generally believed to be the case because ±3 standard deviations from the mean of a normal distribution contains 99.73% of all population values (Figure 16.5 and Table 16.1). Moder, Phillips, and Davis[3] suggest that the standard deviation formula can have a devisor of 3.2 instead of 6. This suggests that t_o, the optimistic duration, would be improved only 5% of the time when the activity was performed repeatedly in similar conditions, and t_p would be exceeded only 5% of the time. This corresponds to the values for ±1.6 in Table 16.2. Therefore, using a devisor of 6 (±3.0) means that t_o would be improved only less than 0.135% of the time and t_p would be exceeded only 0.135% of the time. This text will use equation 16–5 for finding the activity standard deviation. The standard deviation for activity F in Figure 16.3 is (4 − 1) / 6 = 0.50.

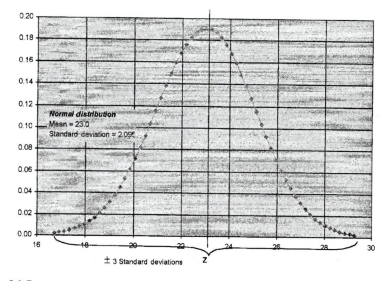

Figure 16.5
Standard normal curve.

The *variance* is equal to the standard deviation squared:

$$V = s^2$$

$$(16\text{-}6)$$

Thus, the variance for activity $F = 0.50^2 = 0.25$.

The *central limit theorem,* one of the results of probability theory, "demonstrates mathematically that the sums of a sufficiently large multiplicity of random variates will tend to produce a normal distribution."[4] If there are n activities in a network that have each been done several times, each has a real duration $t_1, t_2, \ldots t_n$ and an underlying statistical distribution of duration similar to that shown for guardrail installation in Figures 16.1 and 16.2. Because activity durations are continuous random variables, they have population statistics that can be derived from their distributions. Each task or activity duration has a mean $t_{e1}, t_{e2}, \ldots t_{en}$ and variance, $V_1, V_2, \ldots V_n.$[5] The sum of the t_es along the critical path becomes T_e, the project mean duration, which is also a random variable with an underlying distribution. The more samples that are taken from the network (the more activities on the critical path), the stronger the tendency is for the resulting distribution to be normal. In general, four or more activities[6] constitute a large enough number of random variates to approximate the normal distribution. This is significant in that the standard normal distribution function can then be used to determine probabilities. For example, the probability of completing a project by a specified duration, T_S, or less is given by

$$P\{T \le T_s\} = P\left\{Z \le z = \frac{[T_s - T_e]}{s_{cp}}\right\}$$

$$(16\text{-}7)[7]$$

Table 16.2 Standard normal cumulative distribution function.

$$f(z,0,1) = \frac{1}{\sqrt{2\pi}} e^{\frac{-z^2}{2}} \quad \text{for Positive Values} \quad \text{When Z = 1.230, p = 0.8906514 or 89.1\%}$$

Z	0.00	0.01	0.02	0.03	0.04	0.05	0.06	0.07	0.08	0.09
0.00	0.5000000	0.5039894	0.5079784	0.5119665	0.5159535	0.5199389	0.5239223	0.5279032	0.5318814	0.5358565
0.10	0.5398279	0.5437954	0.5477585	0.5517168	0.5556700	0.5596177	0.5635595	0.5674949	0.5714237	0.5753454
0.20	0.5792597	0.5831661	0.5870644	0.5909541	0.5948348	0.5987063	0.6025681	0.6064198	0.6102612	0.6140918
0.30	0.6179114	0.6217195	0.6255158	0.6293000	0.6330717	0.6368306	0.6405764	0.6443087	0.6480272	0.6517317
0.40	0.6554217	0.6590970	0.6627572	0.6664021	0.6700314	0.6736448	0.6772419	0.6808225	0.6843863	0.6879331
0.50	0.6914625	0.6949743	0.6984682	0.7019441	0.7054015	0.7088403	0.7122603	0.7156612	0.7190427	0.7224047
0.60	0.7257469	0.7290692	0.7323712	0.7356528	0.7389138	0.7421540	0.7453732	0.7485712	0.7517478	0.7549030
0.70	0.7580364	0.7611480	0.7642376	0.7673050	0.7703501	0.7733727	0.7763728	0.7793501	0.7823046	0.7852362
0.80	0.7881447	0.7910300	0.7938920	0.7967307	0.7995459	0.8023375	0.8051055	0.8078498	0.8105704	0.8132671
0.90	0.8159399	0.8185888	0.8212136	0.8238145	0.8263912	0.8289439	0.8314724	0.8339768	0.8364569	0.8389129
1.00	0.8413447	0.8437523	0.8461358	0.8484950	0.8508300	0.8531409	0.8554277	0.8576903	0.8599289	0.8621434
1.10	0.8643339	0.8665004	0.8686431	0.8707618	0.8728568	0.8749280	0.8769755	0.8789995	0.8809998	0.8829767
1.20	0.8849303	0.8868605	0.8887675	0.8906514	0.8925122	0.8943502	0.8961653	0.8979576	0.8997274	0.9014746
1.30	0.9031995	0.9049020	0.9065824	0.9082408	0.9098773	0.9114919	0.9130850	0.9146565	0.9162066	0.9177355
1.40	0.9192433	0.9207301	0.9221961	0.9236414	0.9250663	0.9264707	0.9278549	0.9292191	0.9305633	0.9318879
1.50	0.9331928	0.9344783	0.9357445	0.9369916	0.9382198	0.9394292	0.9406200	0.9417924	0.9429466	0.9440826
1.60	0.9452007	0.9463011	0.9473839	0.9484493	0.9494974	0.9505285	0.9515428	0.9525403	0.9535214	0.9544861
1.70	0.9554346	0.9563671	0.9572838	0.9581849	0.9590705	0.9599409	0.9607961	0.9616365	0.9624621	0.9632731
1.80	0.9640697	0.9648522	0.9656206	0.9663751	0.9671159	0.9678433	0.9685573	0.9692582	0.9699460	0.9706211
1.90	0.9712835	0.9719335	0.9725711	0.9731967	0.9738102	0.9744120	0.9750022	0.9755809	0.9761483	0.9767046
2.00	0.9772499	0.9777845	0.9783084	0.9788218	0.9793249	0.9798179	0.9803008	0.9807739	0.9812373	0.9816912
2.10	0.9821356	0.9825709	0.9829970	0.9834143	0.9838227	0.9842224	0.9846137	0.9849966	0.9853713	0.9857379
2.20	0.9860966	0.9864475	0.9867907	0.9871263	0.9874546	0.9877756	0.9880894	0.9883962	0.9886962	0.9889894
2.30	0.9892759	0.9895559	0.9898296	0.9900969	0.9903582	0.9906133	0.9908625	0.9911060	0.9913437	0.9915758
2.40	0.9918025	0.9920237	0.9922397	0.9924506	0.9926564	0.9928572	0.9930531	0.9932443	0.9934309	0.9936128
2.50	0.9937903	0.9939634	0.9941322	0.9942969	0.9944574	0.9946138	0.9947664	0.9949150	0.9950600	0.9952012
2.60	0.9953388	0.9954729	0.9956035	0.9957307	0.9958547	0.9959754	0.9960929	0.9962074	0.9963188	0.9964274
2.70	0.9965330	0.9966358	0.9967359	0.9968332	0.9969280	0.9970202	0.9971099	0.9971971	0.9972820	0.9973645
2.80	0.9974448	0.9975229	0.9975988	0.9976725	0.9977443	0.9978140	0.9978817	0.9979476	0.9980116	0.9980737
2.90	0.9981341	0.9981928	0.9982498	0.9983051	0.9983589	0.9984111	0.9984617	0.9985109	0.9985587	0.9986050
3.00	0.9986500	0.9986937	0.9987361	0.9987772	0.9988170	0.9988557	0.9988932	0.9989296	0.9989649	0.9989991

Table 16.2 *(Continued)*

$$f(z,0,1) = \frac{1}{\sqrt{2\pi}} e^{\frac{-z^2}{2}} \qquad \text{for Negative Values} \qquad \text{When } Z = -1.230, \ p = 0.1093486 \text{ or } 10.9\%$$

z	0.00	0.01	0.02	0.03	0.04	0.05	0.06	0.07	0.08	0.09
0.00	0.5000000	0.4960106	0.4920216	0.4880335	0.4840465	0.4800611	0.4760777	0.4720968	0.4681186	0.4641435
-0.10	0.4601721	0.4562046	0.4522415	0.4482832	0.4443300	0.4403823	0.4364405	0.4325051	0.4285763	0.4246546
-0.20	0.4207403	0.4168339	0.4129356	0.4090459	0.4051652	0.4012937	0.3974319	0.3935802	0.3897388	0.3859082
-0.30	0.3820886	0.3782805	0.3744842	0.3707000	0.3669283	0.3631694	0.3594236	0.3556913	0.3519728	0.3482683
-0.40	0.3445783	0.3409030	0.3372428	0.3335979	0.3299686	0.3263552	0.3227581	0.3191775	0.3156137	0.3120669
-0.50	0.3085375	0.3050257	0.3015318	0.2980559	0.2945985	0.2911597	0.2877397	0.2843388	0.2809573	0.2775953
-0.60	0.2742531	0.2709308	0.2676288	0.2643472	0.2610862	0.2578460	0.2546268	0.2514288	0.2482522	0.2450970
-0.70	0.2419636	0.2388520	0.2357624	0.2326950	0.2296499	0.2266273	0.2236272	0.2206499	0.2176954	0.2147638
-0.80	0.2118553	0.2089700	0.2061080	0.2032693	0.2004541	0.1976625	0.1948945	0.1921502	0.1894296	0.1867329
-0.90	0.1840601	0.1814112	0.1787864	0.1761855	0.1736088	0.1710561	0.1685276	0.1660232	0.1635431	0.1610871
-1.00	0.1586553	0.1562477	0.1538642	0.1515050	0.1491700	0.1468591	0.1445723	0.1423097	0.1400711	0.1378566
-1.10	0.1356661	0.1334996	0.1313569	0.1292382	0.1271432	0.1250720	0.1230245	0.1210005	0.1190002	0.1170233
-1.20	0.1150697	0.1131395	0.1112325	0.1093486	0.1074878	0.1056498	0.1038347	0.1020424	0.1002726	0.0985254
-1.30	0.0968005	0.0950980	0.0934176	0.0917592	0.0901227	0.0885081	0.0869150	0.0853435	0.0837934	0.0822645
-1.40	0.0807567	0.0792699	0.0778039	0.0763586	0.0749337	0.0735293	0.0721451	0.0707809	0.0694367	0.0681121
-1.50	0.0668072	0.0655217	0.0642555	0.0630084	0.0617802	0.0605708	0.0593800	0.0582076	0.0570534	0.0559174
-1.60	0.0547993	0.0536989	0.0526161	0.0515507	0.0505026	0.0494715	0.0484572	0.0474597	0.0464786	0.0455139
-1.70	0.0445654	0.0436329	0.0427162	0.0418151	0.0409295	0.0400591	0.0392039	0.0383635	0.0375379	0.0367269
-1.80	0.0359303	0.0351478	0.0343794	0.0336249	0.0328841	0.0321567	0.0314427	0.0307418	0.0300540	0.0293789
-1.90	0.0287165	0.0280665	0.0274289	0.0268033	0.0261898	0.0255880	0.0249978	0.0244191	0.0238517	0.0232954
-2.00	0.0227501	0.0222155	0.0216916	0.0211782	0.0206751	0.0201821	0.0196992	0.0192261	0.0187627	0.0183088
-2.10	0.0178644	0.0174291	0.0170030	0.0165857	0.0161773	0.0157776	0.0153863	0.0150034	0.0146287	0.0142621
-2.20	0.0139034	0.0135525	0.0132093	0.0128737	0.0125454	0.0122244	0.0119106	0.0116038	0.0113038	0.0110106
-2.30	0.0107241	0.0104441	0.0101704	0.0099031	0.0096418	0.0093867	0.0091375	0.0088940	0.0086563	0.0084242
-2.40	0.0081975	0.0079763	0.0077603	0.0075494	0.0073436	0.0071428	0.0069469	0.0067557	0.0065691	0.0063872
-2.50	0.0062097	0.0060366	0.0058678	0.0057031	0.0055426	0.0053862	0.0052336	0.0050850	0.0049400	0.0047988
-2.60	0.0046612	0.0045271	0.0043965	0.0042693	0.0041453	0.0040246	0.0039071	0.0037926	0.0036812	0.0035726
-2.70	0.0034670	0.0033642	0.0032641	0.0031668	0.0030720	0.0029798	0.0028901	0.0028029	0.0027180	0.0026355
-2.80	0.0025552	0.0024771	0.0024012	0.0023275	0.0022557	0.0021860	0.0021183	0.0020524	0.0019884	0.0019263
-2.90	0.0018659	0.0018072	0.0017502	0.0016949	0.0016411	0.0015889	0.0015383	0.0014891	0.0014413	0.0013950
-3.00	0.0013500	0.0013063	0.0012639	0.0012228	0.0011830	0.0011443	0.0011068	0.0010704	0.0010351	0.0010009

where $S_{cp} = \sqrt{\Sigma V_{cp}}$, the *project standard deviation*   (16-8)

S_{cp} for the project shown in Figures 16.3 and Figure 16.4 =

$$\sqrt{\Sigma V_{cp}} = \sqrt{\Sigma(0.111 + 2.777 + 1.0 + 0.25 + 0.25)} = 2.095$$

Table 16.2 is the standard normal cumulative distribution function table for finding probabilities from the calculation of Z (equation 16-7). Three standard deviations (s = 2.095) on either side of the project mean duration (23.0) takes the values from 16.72 to 29.29 and represents 99.7% of all duration values for the project (Figure 16.5). This can be shown from the Z table (Table 16.2). Z = 3.00 gives a probability of 99.865%, whereas Z = −3.00 = 0.135%. Discarding the probability of completing the project when Z is less than or equal to −3.00, or more than or equal to +3.00 gives a probability of 99.73%.

The probability of completing the project shown in Figure 16.4 in 26 days or less is found by determining the shaded area under the curve in Figure 16.6. From equation 16–7,

$$p\{T_e \le T_s\} = p\left\{ Z \le z = \frac{T_s - T_e}{S_{cp}} \right\} \rightarrow Z = \frac{26.0 - 23.0}{2.095} = 1.432.$$

From Table 16.2, when Z = 1.432, probability falls between 0.9236414 and 0.9250663. Using interpolation to determine the probability, a Z value of 1.43 = 0.9250663 and for 1.44 = 0.9236414 is found. Subtracting the 1.44 value from the 1.43 value = 0.0014249 units between the two values → 0.9236414 + (0.0014249 × 0.2) = 0.92392638, or 92.4%. Thus, the probability of completing the project in 26 days or less is 92.4%.

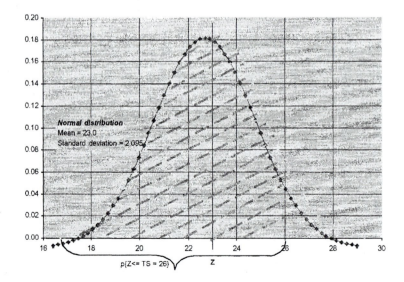

Figure 16.6
Probability and area beneath the normal curve.

To find the project duration that corresponds to an 80% chance of completion, re-arrange the variables in equation 16-7.

$$T_s = ZS_{cp} + T_e \qquad (16\text{-}9)$$

The Z that corresponds to 80% is approximately 0.84 (Table 16.2). Therefore, $T_S = 0.84(2.095) + 23.0 = 24.76$ days would meet the 80% criteria. Therefore, the project has an 80% probability of completing in 24.76 days or less.

The probability that event slack will become zero or less is found by equation 16-10. Event slack is typically zero or positive when there are no constraints in the network. That means it is likely that the calculation will result in a Z value that is a negative number and will produce a probability of 50% or less.

$$Z = \frac{0 - ES}{s_{ES}}, \text{ where } s_{ES} = \sqrt{\Sigma s^2_{TE} + \Sigma s^2_{TL}} \qquad (16\text{-}10)$$

σ_{TE} is the variance on the path that created the TE (time early on the node) and σ_{TL} is the variance on the path that created the TL (time late on the node). Figure 16.7 shows the Figure 16.4 network with the standard deviations and variances calculated. In Figure 16.7, the event slack of node or event C Complete, Start D $= 11.5 - 7.83333 = 3.333$. The TE at this node comes from activity A and then activity C. Therefore, $\Sigma\sigma_{TE} = 0.11111 + 0.69444$. The TL comes from activity D and then activity G → $\Sigma\sigma_{TL} = 1.0 + 0.25$. The Z relating to the probability that the event slack will become zero or less:

$$Z = \frac{0 - ES}{\sqrt{\Sigma\sigma^2_{TE} + \Sigma\sigma^2_{TL}}} = \frac{0 - 3.3333}{\sqrt{0.80555 + 1.250}} = -2.325$$

From Table 16.2, the corresponding probability for this Z value is 1.00%.

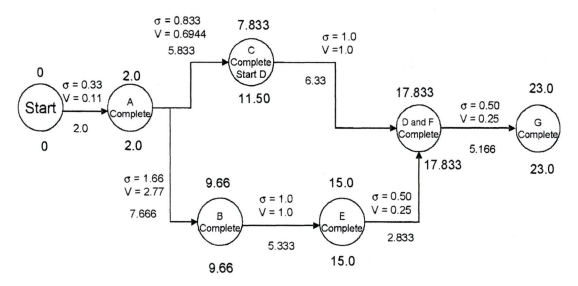

Figure 16.7
Calculated PERT network.

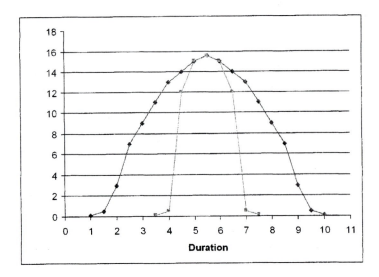

Figure 16.8
Two duration distributions.

PERT ignores *merge event bias,* which can influence the project duration. Assume an activity is on a subcritical path, but is nearly critical, and has an extremely large variance, compared with other activities in the network, including those on the critical path. When durations are sampled from this activity's duration distribution, chances greatly increase that the sampled duration will put this activity on the critical path. Monte Carlo simulation, making thousands of iterations through the calculation of the network where all activities have duration distributions, selecting new durations from each activity's distribution on each run, can provide the percentage of times each activity will become critical. When merge event bias is possible, the scheduler can consider using a tool such as Primavera's Monte Carlo® to determine the possible effects of large variances on subcritical paths.

Figure 16.8 shows one activity with a $t_o = 1$, $t_m = 5.5$, and $t_p = 10$. The activity mean duration for this activity is 5.5. The other activity shown has a $t_o = 3.5$, $t_m = 5.5$, and $t_p = 7.5$. Its mean duration is also 5.5. It is easy to see that the first activity has a greater variability ($\sigma = 1.5$, $V = 2.25$) than does the activity with the narrower range of duration values ($\sigma = 0.66$, $V = 0.44$). The chance that, if durations were selected from these duration distributions multiple times, as with Monte Carlo, the activity with the higher degree of variability, if it is now nearly critical, will appear on the critical path more frequently than the activity with the narrower range of duration values.

Conclusion

As PERT is a technique for determining the length of a project, it has similarities to activity on arrow and activity on node scheduling. Activities durations in PERT are assumed to be variable time estimates with relatively large variances in contrast to the deterministic durations used in AOA and AON scheduling. Because no real activity duration data is available to develop the distributions for individual activity duration time, the technique relies upon assumptions of an optimistic, most likely, and pessimistic activity duration. The advantage of this scheduling technique is that because of its probabilistic framework it permits the computation of the probabilities for meeting a schedule date or a milestone within the schedule.

Problems and/or Questions

1. Using the following diagram,

   a. Calculate the project mean duration, T_e.

   b. Calculate the total and free slack on all activities.

   c. Find the critical path.

   d. Find the probability of completing the project in 38.0 days or less.

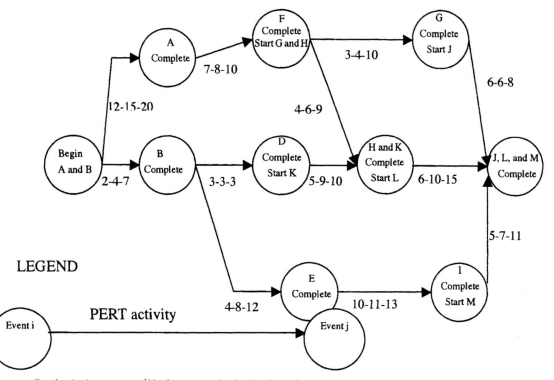

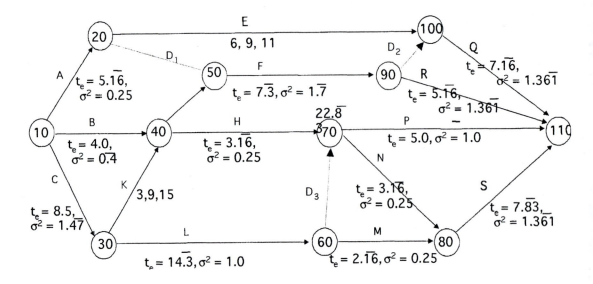

Where σ = s = standard deviation and σ^2 = V = variance

2. Based on the following diagram, find the following:

    a. Project mean duration

    b. AFS_B

    c. ES_{20}

    d. Project standard deviation

    e. ATS_M

    f. Probability of completing the project in 37.5 days or less

    g. Probability of node 80 having zero or less slack

3. Using the table on page 239, create the PERT network diagram, calculate the project mean duration, find the probability of completing the project in 42 days or less, and show all of the slack values.

Activity	Duration			Depends On
	Optimistic	Most Likely	Pessimistic	
A	3	5	8	———
B	5	6	10	A
C	2	4	5	A
E	2	5	6	B, C
F	6	10	12	C
G	4	6	8	B
H	3	6	10	E, F
K	7	9	11	F, G
L	4	5	8	H, K

4. Using the diagram, find the following:
   a. Project mean duration
   b. AFS_F
   c. $ES_{C\ Complete,\ Start\ D}$
   d. Project standard deviation
   e. ATS_E
   f. Probability of completing the project in 37.5 days or less

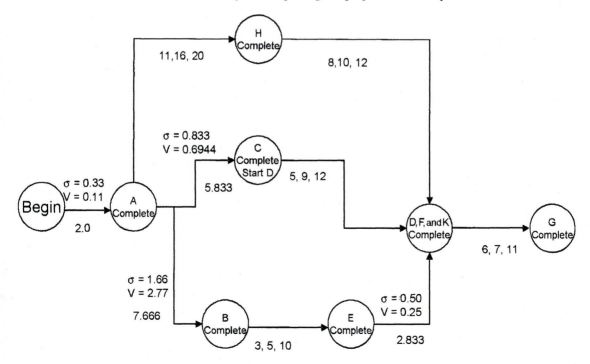

5. Provide the required duration such that the problem 4 network has a 90% probability of completing within.

6. Describe a real project from the construction literature that would have benefited from a PERT schedule and explain why.

Notes

1. BestFit® for Windows, version 2.0d, Palisade Corporation.

2. Robert B. Harris, *Precedence and Arrow Networking Techniques for Construction.* New York: Wiley, 1978.

3. Joseph J. Moder, Cecil R. Phillips, and Edward W. Davis, *Project Management with CPM, PERT, and Precedence Diagramming,* 3rd Ed. New York: Van Nostrand Reinhold Co. 1983.

4. Richard Lowry, *Vassar Stats,* "Central Limit Theorem," *http://faculty.vassar.edu/lowry/central.html,* 7 May 2002, p. 1 (last accessed 9/12/2003).

5. Moder et al., pp. 276, 281.

6. Richard Lowry, *Vassar Stats,* "Central Limit Theorem," *http://faculty.vassar.edu/lowry/central.html,* 7 May 2002, p. 1 (last accessed 9/12/2003).

7. Moder et al., p. 289.

CHAPTER 17

Minimum Moment Leveling Method

Goal

Describe a more advanced method of resource leveling than that presented in Chapter 6.

Objectives

- Describe the leveling process and needed calculations:
  - Resource moment
  - Free float and back float
  - Improvement factor
- Provide an illustrative example using the precedence diagramming method.

Introduction

Although many new methods of leveling using genetic algorithms, neural networks, and linear programming have been developed over the last ten years, this more advanced, yet traditional algorithm may provide a better final resource profile than the traditional or conventional leveling method presented in Chapter 6.

Minimum Moment

The minimum moment method, as described by Harris[1] and the Burgess leveling procedure described by Moder, Phillips, and Davis[2] are similar techniques that require a good deal of bookkeeping to manage each process step in those iterative procedures. The Burgess method is discussed in Chapter 18 on leveling multiple resources.

The minimum moment method (M3) is so termed because the method looks for a minimum histogram moment as is created by the ideal rectangle of resource use. As discussed in Chapter 6, it is extremely unlikely that the uniform distribution of resources is achievable. However, M3 works at improving the leveled histogram as it approaches the minimum moment of the ideal rectangle created by the uniform distribution of the resource. How, then, is the histogram moment calculated to give values for comparison? Consider Figures 17.1, 17.2, and 17.3, the small network, bar chart, and corresponding histogram used in Chapter 6 to illustrate the traditional method of leveling.

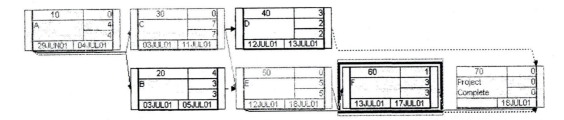

Figure 17.1
Example network for M3.

Activity Information				Workdays														
I.D.	Desc	Dur	Total Resource	1	2	3	4	5	6	7	8	9	10	11	12	13	14
10	A	4	32	8	8	8	8										
20	B	3	6			2	2	2				→					
30	C	7	28			4	4	4	4	4	4	4					
40	D	2	14										7	7			→
50	E	5	25										5	5	5	5	5
60	F	3	9											3	3	3	→
	Sum		114														
Period Sum (Early Start)				8	8	14	14	6	4	4	4	4	12	15	8	8	5
Cumulative Sum				8	16	30	44	50	54	58	62	66	78	93	101	109	114

Figure 17.2
Example bar chart for M3 illustration.

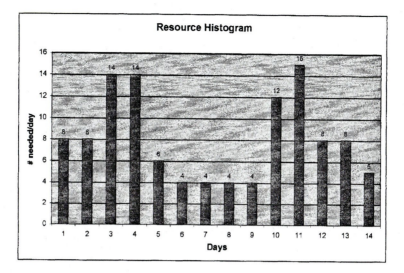

Figure 17.3
M3 example histogram.

Finding the Minimum Moment

Begin by noting the time period i that begins at 1 and proceeds to the project completion time n. For the project in Figures 17.1, 17.2, and 17.3, i ranges from 1 to 14 days. Next, consider the moment created by each histogram bar at about the zero axis for the number of resources. Recall that a structural moment is generally described as a force times the distance over which it acts. Therefore, the moment created by each bar is its resource value or force (r_i) times ½ the resource value that is the average distance of the resource from the zero axis. Equation 17–1 is given for calculating the moment produced by each element when the resource amount is given as r_i, where i is the time period in question.

$$M\,(i)_0 = \frac{1}{2}\,(r_i)^2 \qquad\qquad (17\text{-}1)$$

When equation 17–1 is applied to the histogram in Figure 17.3 for time period 1, the resulting moment is $M(1)_0 = \frac{1}{2}\,(8)^2 = 32$.

The moment for the entire histogram is the sum of the moments for each time interval and is given in equation 17-2, where M_0 is that moment.

$$M_0 = \frac{1}{2}\sum_{i=1}^{n}\,(r_i^2) \qquad\qquad (17\text{-}2)$$

The goal of this resource leveling method is to minimize the entire moment for the histogram. Calculating the moment for the histogram shown in Figure 17.3 yields a total

Table 17.1   Resource histogram moments.

Period	Period Value	$\frac{1}{2}(r)^2 \times \frac{1}{2}$	Period Value	$\frac{1}{2}(r)^2 \times \frac{1}{2}$
1	8	32	8.14	33.15
2	8	32	8.14	33.15
3	14	98	8.14	33.15
4	14	98	8.14	33.15
5	6	18	8.14	33.15
6	4	8	8.14	33.15
7	4	8	8.14	33.15
8	4	8	8.14	33.15
9	4	8	8.14	33.15
10	12	72	8.14	33.15
11	15	112.5	8.14	33.15
12	8	32	8.14	33.15
13	8	32	8.14	33.15
14	5	12.5	8.14	33.15
Total	114	571	114	464.14

value of 571 (see Table 17.1). The sum of the resources is 114 over a 14-day duration (Figure 17.2), so the average resource usage is 114 / 14 = 8.14. Thus, a uniform distribution of resources would create a rectangle of constant value 8.14 for 14 days. Using equation 17-2 and calculating the moment for a project with this uniform resource distribution would give a moment of 464 (see Table 17.1), which is significantly less than 571. Any deviation from the uniform distribution will result in a higher histogram moment value than that derived from the uniform distribution. Thus, the minimum moment would be 464 for the given resource total and duration for the example project.

Finding the Improvement Factor

The purpose of the improvement factor is to determine if moving an activity will create an improved histogram moment. Clearly, the histogram resulting from the beginning traditional leveling moves of activity B for 2 days could be used to calculate the new histogram moment. However, this calculation is not of an improvement factor and is not a totally different leveling process. This suggests that the improvement factor will be applied in another, unique way.

Recall that, in the traditional method, a running period tabulation was carried out at the bottom of the bar chart and the histogram, reducing 1 day's period value as an activity was shifted and raising another day's value an equal amount. Using the bar

I.D.	Desc	Dur	Total Resource	1	2	3	4	5	6	7	8	9	10	11	12	13	14
10	A	4	32	8	8	8	8										
20	B	3	6			X	X	2	2	2	→						
30	C	7	28			4	4	4	4	4	4	4	4				
40	D	2	14										7	7	→		
50	E	5	25										5	5	5	5	5
60	F	3	9											3	3	3	→
	Sum		114														
	Original Period Sum			8	8	14	14	6	4	4	4	4	12	15	8	8	5
						t1	t2		s1	s2							
	Revised Period Sum			8	8	12	12	6	6	6	4	4	12	15	8	8	5
	Resource Rate (r)					2	2		2	2							

Figure 17.4
Histogram with activity B moved 2 days.

chart and the histogram in Figures 17.2 and 17.3, and knowing that activity B does have free float greater than zero, if B delayed in starting until day 5, the days 3 and 4 totals would be reduced by B's resource contribution of 2, while two additional resources would be added to days 6 and 7, as shown in Figure 17.4. The result is a lower peak on days 3 and 4 (= 12 each) and a higher peak on days 6 and 7 (= 6 each). Thus, there must be a way to capture the result of movements such as these mathematically, as they apply to the histogram moment.

To begin the improvement factor computation, sum the resource daily rates for the periods where resources will be deducted. For the movement of activity B 2 days, the value would be 14 for each of days 3 and 4 (Figure 17.4—"Original Period Sum"). Next, sum the resource daily rates for the periods where resources will be added, days 6 and 7 at four each day. Then, to find the current histogram moment for the proposed changed days, M_1, begin by eliminating the constant from equation 17-2. This simplification does not affect the results of the calculations described. Consider Figure 17.5. Let t represent the daily resource rates where resources will be deducted and let s represent the daily resource rates where resources will be added. Let r represent the resource amount to be deducted and added.

Then,

$$M_1 = \sum_1^j t_j^2 + \sum_1^j s_j^2 \qquad (17\text{-}3)$$

where j is the *minimum* of the number of days the activity is moved or its duration.

Applying equation 17-3,

$$M_1 = (14^2 + 14^2) + (4^2 + 4^2) = 424$$

I.D.	Desc	Dur	Total Resource	1	2	3	4	5	6	7	8	9	10	11	12	13	14
10	A	4	32	8	8	8	8										
20	B	3	6			X	X	2	2	2 →							
30	C	7	28			4	4	4	4	4	4	4					
40	D	2	14										7	7 →			
50	E	5	25										5	5	5	5	5
60	F	3	9											3	3	3 →	
Sum			114														
Original Period Sum				8	8	14	14	6	4	4	4	4	12	15	8	8	5
						t1	t2		s1	s2							
Revised Period Sum				8	8	12	12	6	6	6	4	4	12	15	8	8	5
Resource Rate (r)						2	2		2	2							

Figure 17.5
Movement of activity B.

Then, take the histogram moment of the revised totals for the changed days, M_2.

$$M_2 = \sum_1^j (t_j - r)^2 + \sum_1^j (s_j + r)^2 \qquad (17\text{-}4)$$

where the resource rate, r, is 2. The resulting histogram moment for the example is

$$M_2 = (12^2 + 12^2) + (6^2 + 6^2) = 360$$

As long as M_2 is less than M_1, there is improvement in the histogram. However, we still need to find the improvement factor so that alternative strategies can be compared. The corresponding equation showing M_2 less than M_1 becomes $M_2 < M_1$; substituting equations 17-3 and 17-4 gives

$$\sum_1^j (t_j - r)^2 + \sum_1^j (s_j + r)^2 < \sum_1^j t_j^2 + \sum_1^j s_j^2$$

Expanding →

$$\sum_1^j t_j^2 - 2r \sum_1^j t_j + jr^2 + \sum_1^j s_j^2 + 2r \sum_1^j s_j + jr^2 < \sum_1^j t_j^2 + \sum_1^j s_j^2$$

Combining terms →

$$-2r \sum_1^j t_j + 2jr^2 + 2r \sum_1^j s_j < 0$$

Divide by $-2 \rightarrow$

$$r\left(\sum_1^j t_j - \sum_1^j s_j - jr \right) > 0$$

The improvement factor (IF)

$$IF(Activity, shift) = r\left(\sum_1^j t_j - \sum_1^j s_j - jr \right) \qquad (17\text{-}5)$$

and it must be greater than zero to be an improvement. Applying equation 17-5 to the example gives

$$IF(Act\_B, 2) = 2((14 + 14) - (4 + 4) - (2 \times 2))$$
$$IF = 2(28 - 8 - 4) = 32$$

The positive improvement factor indicates that the shift of activity B 2 days will improve the resource profile. The value of the factor also enables the reviewer to compare the movement of activity B with other potential activity movements to determine which one gives the largest improvement factor.

Back Float

Because the minimum moment process moves from the last activity in the network in reverse order to the beginning of the network and then from the beginning of the network back to the end, back float and free float must be calculated so that moves can be made backward. Back float is a means of moving activities in the second cycle from the front to the back. Harris defines back float as "the time span in which an activity can be started and not cause a preceding activity to be finished earlier than its early finish date." Thus, for a finish-to-start, zero lag relationship, the back float, BF, is

$$BF_{activity} = ES_{activity} - \underset{\forall predeccessors}{Max} (EF_{predecessor}) \qquad (17\text{-}6)$$

Similar equations can be written for all precedence relationship types and lag values.

As free float tends to collect at the end of a chain of activities when it ties into a chain of more critical activities, there is seldom an occasion for free float. This is because all activities that are not constrained have pushers. However, when an activity is scheduled at its late time, it can be moved backward toward its early times; the amount of this movement is the back float. Figures 17.6 through 17.8 show the before and after of the back float calculation.

The early and late dates are the same for activities A, C, E, and Project Complete because they are on the critical path. Figure 17.7 shows a portion of this network, whereas Figure 17.8 shows the bar chart version of this network portion, along with the back float on activity F.

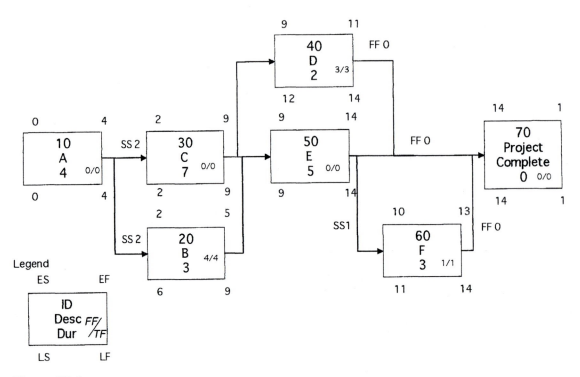

Legend

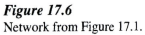

Figure 17.6
Network from Figure 17.1.

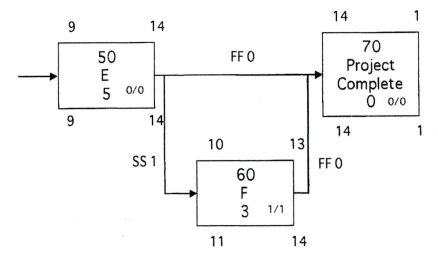

Figure 17.7
Portion of the network in Figure 17.6.

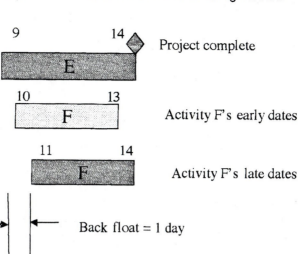

Figure 17.8
Bar chart representation of Figure 17.7.

It is clear from Figure 17.8 that if activity F is moved to its late time, there is 1 day of back float. This example is uncomplicated and fails to include multiple predecessors (F's only predecessor is activity E). However, using the early and late date comparison will enable the calculation of back float.

Minimum Moment Procedure

As with most leveling methods, the initial phase includes ordering activities on a bar chart by their early start dates, identifying the resource rates per day for each activity, and totaling the period resource amounts for each day of the project duration for the resource to be leveled. Both the early and late dates for each activity must be determined, too.

Figure 17.9 shows the example bar chart with early and late resource tabulations at the bottom. The locations of the late date bars for the three activities with float are shown as hash-marked bars.

Organize your network so that there are what Harris terms "sequence steps." Skip any step, beginning with the last one that has only critical activities or activities with no free float. Figure 17.10 shows the network with sequence steps included. In the last step, step 5, only the critical activity Project Complete is present, and it has zero free float, so this step is skipped. Step 4 has activity F only, which has a free float of 1 day.

Calculate the improvement factor for activity F. This means moving from the late start histogram to one with activity F shifted backward. The resources will be deducted from workday 14, which has a late period amount of 15. The three resources will be added to workday 11, which currently has a late period total of five resources. The shift is 1 day and the resource rate is three per day for activity F. If more than one activity

Activity Information				Workdays														
I.D.	Desc	Dur	Total Resource	1	2	3	4	5	6	7	8	9	10	11	12	13	14
10	A	4	32	8	8	8	8										
20	B	3	6			2	2	2									
30	C	7	28			4	4	4	4	4	4	4					
40	D	2	14										7	7			
50	E	5	25										5	5	5	5	5
60	F	3	9											3	3	3	
	Sum		114														
Period Sum (Early Start)				8	8	14	14	6	4	4	4	4	12	15	8	8	5
Period Sum (Late Start)				8	8	12	12	4	4	6	6	6	5	5	8	15	15

Figure 17.9
Bar chart with early and late resource tabulation.

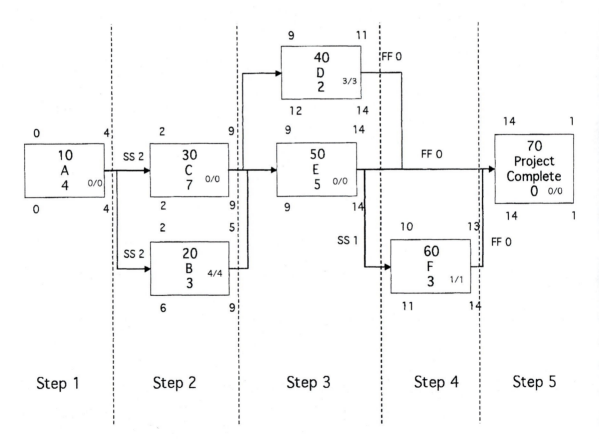

Figure 17.10
Network diagram showing sequence steps.

Activity Information   Workdays

I.D.	Desc	Dur	Total Resource	1	2	3	4	5	6	7	8	9	10	11	12	13	14
10	A	4	32	8	8	8	8										
20	B	3	6			2	2	2									
30	C	7	28			4	4	4	4	4	4	4					
40	D	2	14										7	7			
50	E	5	25										5	5	5	5	5
60	F	3	9											3	3	3	
Sum			114														
Period Sum (Early Start)				8	8	14	14	6	4	4	4	4	12	15	8	8	5
Period Sum (Late Start)				8	8	12	12	4	4	6	6	6	5	5	8	15	15
Revised Period Amount				8	8	14	14	6	4	4	4	4	12	12	8	8	8

F moved 1 day

Figure 17.11
Revised histogram.

were available to move backwards, all improvement factors would be created and the activity with the largest positive IF would be moved. Recalculate the IF for any remaining activities in the current sequence step. If the value of the IF is zero or negative, do not move the activity.

$$IF(Act\_F, 1) = 3((15) - (5) - (3 \times 1))$$
$$IF(Act\_F, 1) = 3(15 - 5 - 3) = 21$$

Since the IF for activity F is positive, the activity is moved forward to the 1-day limit of its free float. The revised tabulation should be calculated so further changes can be done based on this update. Figure 17.11 shows the updated values.

In the network diagram in Figure 17.10, activity D is in sequence step 3 and is the next one for review. Calculating the improvement factor for the minimum move, 1 day, to the maximum move of 3 days (amount of free float) gives the following results:

$$IF(Act\_D, 1) = 7((12) - (8) - (7 \times 1))$$
$$IF(Act\_D, 1) = 7(12 - 8 - 7) = -21$$
$$IF(Act\_D, 2) = 7((12 + 12) - (8 + 8) - (7 \times 2))$$
$$IF(Act\_D, 2) = 7(24 - 16 - 14) = -42$$
$$IF(Act\_D, 3) = 7((12 + 12) - (8 + 8) - (7 \times 2))$$
$$IF(Act\_D, 3) = 7(24 - 16 - 14) = -42$$

Because all of the results of the IF calculations are negative, activity D is not moved.

At sequence step 2, activities B and C occur. As activity C is critical, it is ignored. Activity B can be moved up to 4 days. The IF calculations follow:

$$IF(Act\_B, 1) = 2((14) - (4) - (2 \times 1))$$
$$IF(Act\_B, 1) = 2(14 - 4 - 2) = 16$$

Activity Information   **Workdays**

I.D.	Desc	Dur	Total Resources	1	2	3	4	5	6	7	8	9	10	11	12	13	14
10	A	4	32	8	8	8	8										
20	B	3	6		2	2	2										
30	C	7	28			4	4	4	4	4	4	4					
40	D	2	14										7	7			
50	E	5	25										5	5	5	5	5
60	F	3	9											3	3	3	
Sum			114														
Period Sum (Early Start)				8	8	14	14	6	4	4	4	4	12	15	8	8	5
Period Sum (Late Start)				8	8	12	12	4	4	6	6	6	5	5	8	15	15
Revised Period Amount				8	8	12	12	4	4	6	6	6	12	12	8	8	8

F moved 1 day and B moved 4 days

Figure 17.12
Revised tabulation with activities F and B moved.

$$IF(Act\_B, 2) = 2((14 + 14) - (4 + 4) - (2 \times 2))$$
$$IF(Act\_B, 2) = 2(28 - 8 - 4) = 32$$
$$IF(Act\_B, 3) = 2((14 + 14 + 6) - (4 + 4 + 4) - (2 \times 3))$$
$$IF(Act\_B, 3) = 2(34 - 12 - 6) = 32$$
$$IF(Act\_B, 4) = 2((14 + 14 + 6) - (4 + 4 + 4) - (2 \times 3))$$
$$IF(Act\_B, 4) = 2(34 - 12 - 6) = 32$$

The results of all possible moves of activity B are positive improvement factors, and because moves 2, 3, and 4 all give an IF of 32, move activity B 4 days.

Activity A cannot be moved; thus, the process now begins at sequence step 1 and continues to the last sequence step using the back float. Note that back float is created in activity B (4 days) and activity F (1 day).

Sequence step 1 has only activity A with no free or back float, so skip to sequence step 2. The improvement factor is again calculated for activity B. The only difference is that if the largest IF is zero, the activity will be moved. Again, activity C is eliminated from the IF calculations because it is a critical activity.

$$IF(Act\_B, 1) = 2((6) - (4) - (2 \times 1))$$
$$IF(Act\_B, 1) = 2(6 - 4 - 2) = 0$$
$$IF(Act\_B, 2) = 2((6 + 6) - (4 + 4) - (2 \times 2))$$
$$IF(Act\_B, 2) = 2(12 - 8 - 4) = 0$$
$$IF(Act\_B, 3) = 2((6 + 6 + 6) - (4 + 4 + 12) - (2 \times 3))$$
$$IF(Act\_B, 3) = 2(18 - 20 - 6) = -16$$
$$IF(Act\_B, 4) = 2((6 + 6 + 6) - (4 + 12 + 12) - (2 \times 3))$$
$$IF(Act\_B, 4) = 2(18 - 28 - 6) = -32$$

Activity Information   **Workdays**

I.D.	Desc	Dur	Total Resources	1	2	3	4	5	6	7	8	9	10	11	12	13	14
10	A	4	32	8	8	8	8										
20	B	3	6			2	2	2									
30	C	7	28			4	4	4	4	4	4	4					
40	D	2	14										7	7			
50	E	5	25										5	5	5	5	5
60	F	3	9											3	3	3	
Sum			114														
Period Sum (Early Start)				8	8	14	14	6	4	4	4	4	12	15	8	8	5
Period Sum (Late Start)				8	8	12	12	4	4	6	6	6	5	5	8	15	15
Revised Period Amount				8	8	12	12	6	6	6	4	4	12	12	8	8	8

B moved back 2 days

Figure 17.13
Updated histogram period amount.

Since the first two moves of B produce an IF of zero, B will be moved the 2 days. The revised bar chart tabulation is shown in Figure 17.13.

Activities in step 3 have no back float, so skip to step 4. Activity F has 1 day of back float.

$$IF(Act\_F, 1) = 3((8) - (12) - (3 \times 1))$$
$$IF(Act\_F, 1) = 3(8 - 12 - 3) = -21$$

Since F's improvement factor is negative, it is not moved. Early in this chapter, the resource moment was calculated at 571 and the minimum moment at 464. Table 17.2 shows the current resource moment tabulation. Shown in Table 17.2, the resulting histogram has a moment of 518, improved from the original 571.

Resource Improvement Coefficient

The resource improvement coefficient (RIC) helps the construction manager determine the magnitude of the improvement of one move over another, which is not easily seen in the improvement factor (IF). The RIC shows how close the current histogram is to the ideal, rectangular shape. Equation 17–7 shows that the current histogram moment is divided by the minimum moment (that derived from the rectangular-shaped histogram of average resource use). The closer the RIC value is to 1, the closer the shape is to the ideal.

$$RIC = \frac{\sum_{1}^{n} y_i^2}{\frac{1}{2} \frac{\left(\sum_{1}^{n} y_i\right)^2}{n}} \cong \frac{n \sum y_i^2}{\left(\sum y_i\right)^2} \cong \frac{CurrHistogramMoment}{MinMoment} \qquad (17\text{-}7)$$

Table 17.2   Revised improvement factor.

Period	Period Value	$\frac{1}{2}(r)^2 \times \frac{1}{2}$
1	8	32
2	8	32
3	12	72
4	12	72
5	6	18
6	6	18
7	6	18
8	4	8
9	4	8
10	12	72
11	12	72
12	8	32
13	8	32
14	8	32
Total	114	518

When the current values are entered into the RIC equation, the result is

$$RIC = \frac{n \sum y_i^2}{\left(\sum y_i\right)^2} = \frac{14,504}{12,996} = 1.116,$$ which is the same result as would have been

obtained from the values from Table 17.2 and the minimum moment of 464 →

$$RIC = \frac{518}{464} = 1.116.$$ If the initial network were calculated, the result would be

$$RIC = \frac{571}{464} = 1.231.$$ Therefore, the current histogram has moved significantly closer

to the ideal profile.

A modified minimum moment method program for leveling is given by Dr. Photius Ioannou at the University of Michigan and is called CPMLevel. It can be downloaded at *http://www.engin.umich.edu/cem/Ioannou/CPMLevel/cpmlevel.htm.*

Table 17.3   Resource histogram moments.

Period (n)	Period Value (y)	y^2	$\acute{y}$	
1	8	64	8.14	
2	8	64	8.14	
3	12	144	8.14	
4	12	144	8.14	
5	6	36	8.14	
6	6	36	8.14	
7	6	36	8.14	
8	4	16	8.14	
9	4	16	8.14	
10	12	144	8.14	
11	12	144	8.14	
12	8	64	8.14	
13	8	64	8.14	
14	8	64	8.14	
	Sum	1,036	114.00	
	n (sum y^2)	14,504	12,996	= (sum $\acute{y}$)^2

Conclusion

The minimum moment method of leveling activity resources is structured on the assumption that there is a histogram moment of the used resources that is a minimum. The criterion for judging an activity shift, from its original position to a better position, is the change in the statistical moment of the resource histogram before and after such movement. The activity, found for each possible day of shifting, with the maximum improvement factor is selected first. The process is then repeated for all remaining activities using the updated histogram resulting from the previously shifted activity. This method of resource leveling does not extend the project duration, as do traditional approaches.

Problems and/or Questions

1. Using the network and budgeted total quantity resources that follow, level the network resource using the minimum moment algorithm.

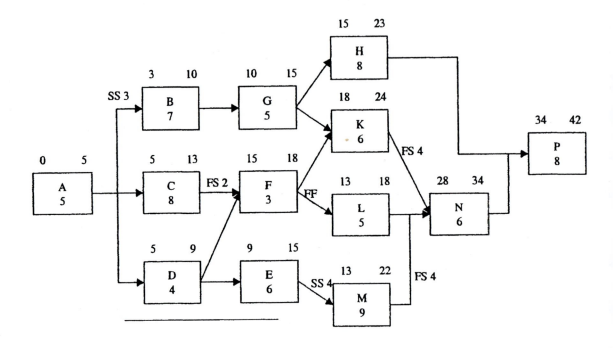

Activity	Resource	Activity	Resource
A	15,000	H	6,000
B	14,700	K	3,000
C	12,000	L	2,500
D	4,000	M	13,500
E	12,000	N	4,200
F	6,000	P	4,000
G	7,500		

2. Using the following network and the resources from problem 1, use the minimum moment algorithm to level the network resource.

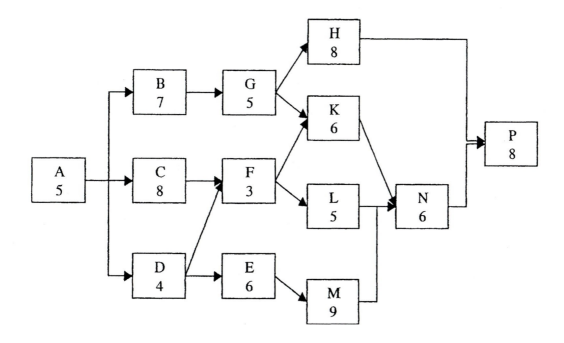

3. Using the network and resources that follow, level the network using the minimum moment algorithm.

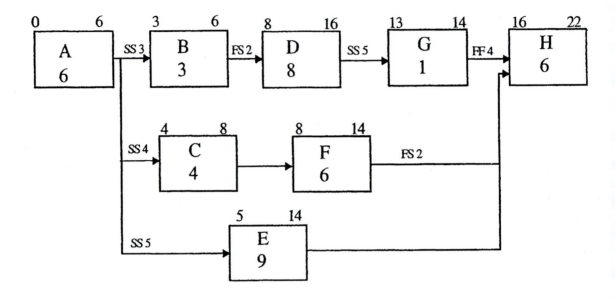

Activity	Resource Rate/Day
A	8
B	16
C	10
D	12
E	12
F	9
G	7
H	4

4. Level the following network, using the minimum moment algorithm.

Activity	Duration	Depends On	Resource Rate
A	4	——	100
B	6	A	50
C	5	A (FS 2)	200
D	3	A (FF 2)	150
F	2	B	100
G	4	C	75
H	3	C (FS 0), D (FS 2)	125
J	3	F, G	200
K	7	H, G	100
L	4	J, K	100

5. From the network and resources provided, level the network resource using the minimum moment algorithm. Supply a bar chart and an early start histogram with your solution.

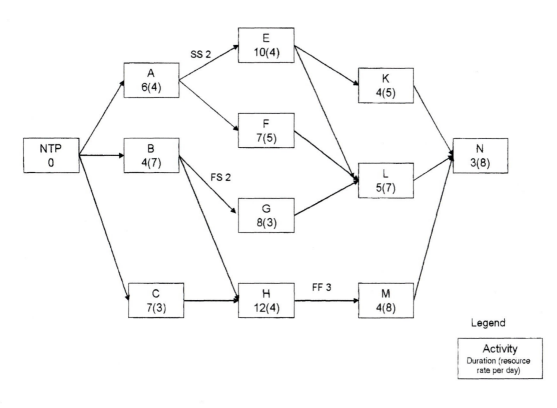

Notes

1. Robert B. Harris, *Precedence and Arrow Networking Techniques for Construction.* New York: Wiley, 1978, p. 29.
2. Joseph J. Moder, Cecil R. Phillips, and Edward W. Davis, *Project Management with CPM, PERT, and Precedence Diagramming,* 3rd ed. New York: Van Nostrand Reinhold Co., 1983, p. 129.

CHAPTER 18

Burgess Method for Leveling Multiple Resources

Goal

Describe the Burgess method for leveling multiple resources.

Objectives

- Describe the Burgess method of sum of the least squares.
- Provide an example to demonstrate the Burgess method that can be used in part as a comparison with the minimum moment method.

Introduction

When schedules are produced that are resource-loaded, they frequently track more than one resource. A monetary resource, such as cost or bid price, is frequently combined with limited material, labor, or equipment resources. Because labor is the most variable of project costs, it is often tracked in resource-loaded schedules. The Burgess method, as described by Moder et al.,[1] is presented in this chapter to show a manual method of multiple-resource leveling. Programs such as P3® have their own algorithms for handling this tricky task. It may seem obvious that leveling one resource could as easily harm the distribution profile of another project resource as it would help it. The more resources that are leveled simultaneously, the more difficult the process. Thus, the example used in this chapter will consider only two resources.

Burgess Method

As with all leveling methods, the Burgess method begins by arranging the activities, their durations, their floats, and their resource requirements. This can be done effectively with a bar chart. The Burgess method will be demonstrated in this section using the same example as used to demonstrate the minimum moment method in Chapter 17 (Figure 18.1) with the addition of one more resource.

Like the M3, the Burgess method begins with the last activity. Instead of calculating a moment and an improvement factor, the Burgess method uses the least sum of squares. Begin by calculating the sum of the squares for each resource and each period day. Figure 18.2 shows that the original sum of squares for resource 1 was 1,142 and the sum for resource 2 was 1,099, or a sum of 2,241. Beginning with the last activity with float (activity F), test the sum of squares for each possible day of movement. For activity F, that is only 1 day. Delaying activity F 1 day gives a sum of squares equal to 2,119. Since this total is less than the original, move activity F 1 day. If more than one move of an activity yields the same least square sum, move the activity as late as possible to potentially provide activities earlier in the network with more float.

Leaving activity F in its new position, move to the next to last activity with float, activity D. Activity D can move up to 3 days. Testing all of the sums of the squares shows that none of the values is less than 2,119. Therefore, do not move activity D.

Activity Information					Workdays													
I.D.	Desc	Dur	Total Resource 1	Total Resource 2	1	2	3	4	5	6	7	8	9	10	11	12	13	14
10	A	4	32		8	8	8	8										
20	B	3	6				2	2	2								
30	C	7	28				4	4	4	4	4	4	4				
40	D	2	14											7	7		
50	E	5	25											5	5	5	5	5
60	F	3	9												3	3	3
	Sum		114															
Period Sum Resource 1					8	8	14	14	6	4	4	4	4	12	15	8	8	5
10	A	4		20	5	5	5	5										
20	B	3		15			5	5	5								
30	C	7		21			3	3	3	3	3	3	3				
40	D	2		16										8	8		
50	E	5		20										4	4	4	4	4
60	F	3		15											5	5	5
	Sum			107														
Period Sum Resource 2					5	5	13	13	8	3	3	3	3	12	17	9	9	4
Period Sum Resc 1 and Resc 2					13	13	27	27	14	7	7	7	7	24	32	17	17	9

Figure 18.1
The beginning bar chart example.

Activity Information

I.D.	Desc	Dur	Total Resource 1	Total Resource 2
10	A	4	32	
10	A	4		20
20	B	3	6	
20	B	3		15
30	C	7	28	
30	C	7		21
40	D	2	14	
40	D	2		16
50	E	5	25	
50	E	5		20
60	F	3	9	
60	F	3		15
Sum			114	92

Workdays

I.D.	1	2	3	4	5	6	7	8	9	10	11	12	13	14
10 A	8	8	8	8										
10 A	5	5	5	5										
20 B			2	2	2									
20 B			5	5	5									
30 C				4	4	4	4	4	4	4				
30 C				3	3	3	3	3	3	3				
40 D										7	7			
40 D										8	8			
50 E										5	5	5	5	5
50 E										4	4	4	4	4
60 F											3	3	3	3
60 F											6	5	5	5
Period Sum Resc 1	8	8	14	14	6	4	4	4	4	12	15	8	8	5
Period Sum Resc 2	5	5	13	13	8	3	3	3	3	12	17	9	9	4
Revised Resc 1	8	8	12	12	4	4	4	4	3	12	12	8	8	8
Revised Resc 2	5	5	8	8	3	6	6	6	8	12	12	8	8	9

	Original	Move F 1 day	Move D 3 days	Move D 2 days	Move D 1 day	Move B 4 days	Move B 3 days	Move B 2 days
Period Sum Resc 1	1142	1100	1194	1194	1142	1036	1036	1036
Period Sum Resc 2	1099	1018	1179	1179	1099	919	919	919
	2241	2119	2363	2363	2241	1955	1955	1955

Figure 18.2
Sum of squares for resources 1 and 2.

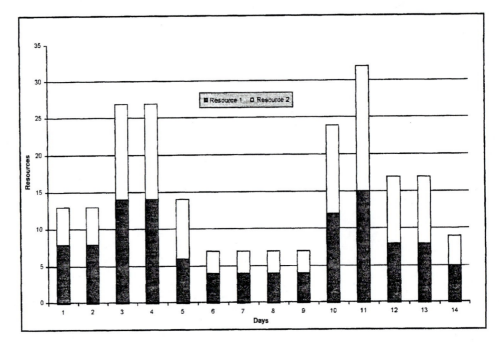

Figure 18.3
Original histogram for resources 1 and 2.

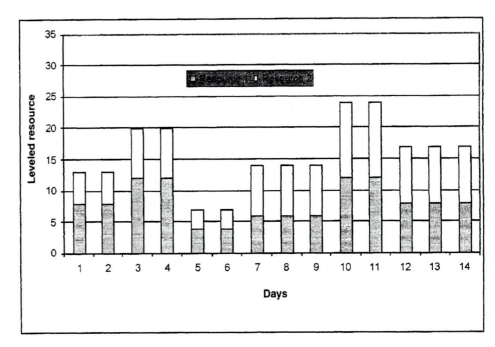

Figure 18.4
Burgess leveled histogram for resources 1 and 2.

Final Bar Chart Showing Activities, Final Position

I.D.	Desc	Dur	Total Resource 1	Total Resource 2	1	2	3	4	5	6	7	8	9	10	11	12	13	14
10	A	4	32		8	8	8	8										
10	A	4		20	5	5	5	5										
20	B	3	6								2	2	2					
20	B	3		15														
30	C	7	28				4	4	4	4	4	4	4					
30	C	7		21			3	3	3	3	3	3	3					
40	D	2	14											7	7			
40	D	2		18														
50	E	5	25											5	5	5	5	5
50	E	5		20										4	4	4	4	4
60	F	3	9													3	3	3
60	F	3		15														
Sum			114	92														
Period Sum Resc 1					8	8	12	12	4	4	6	6	6	12	12	8	8	8
Period Sum Resc 2					5	5	8	8	3	3	8	8	8	12	12	9	9	9

Figure 18.5
Final resource leveled bar chart.

Move backward again, to activity B. When testing all of the possible moves of B, moving it from any of 2 to 4 days produces the same smaller square sum of 1,955. Therefore, move activity B 4 days. The Burgess method can be used for any number of resources but requires careful tabulation and a strong desire to have a composite best resource profile. The original and final histograms are shown in Figures 18.3 and 18.4. The resources are shown stacked to give the true picture of leveling both resources 1 and 2. Both histograms are shown on the same scale for better comparison of the before and after leveling profile.

Figure 18.5 shows the bar chart with activities B and F moved to their new leveled positions. The period values are tabulated at the bottom of the bar chart for both resources, and they correspond to the values shown in the histogram in Figure 18.4.

Conclusion

The scheme of resource leveling is to minimize resource fluctuations by rescheduling activities within their float. The Burgess method for leveling multiple resources, like the minimum moment method, seeks a solution to the limited resource challenge while not extending the project duration. Burgess, by calculating the sum of the squares for the daily resource demands, measures the quality of the leveling. This measure is based on the fact the least possible sum occurs in the case of constant resource usage.

Problems and/or Questions

1. Using the network and budgeted total quantity resources that follow, level the network resources using the Burgess method.

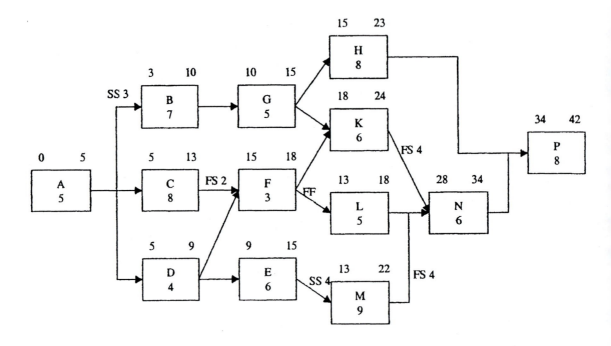

Activity	Resources	Activity	Resources
A	15,000–2,200	H	6,000–6,000
B	14,700–1,950	K	3,000–4,500
C	12,000–1,800	L	2,500–2,000
D	4,000–3,800	M	13,500–12,000
E	12,000–13,000	N	4,200–3,800
F	6,000–6,000	P	4,000–3,000
G	7,500–6,200		

2. Using the following network and the resources from problem 1, use the Burgess method to level the network resource.

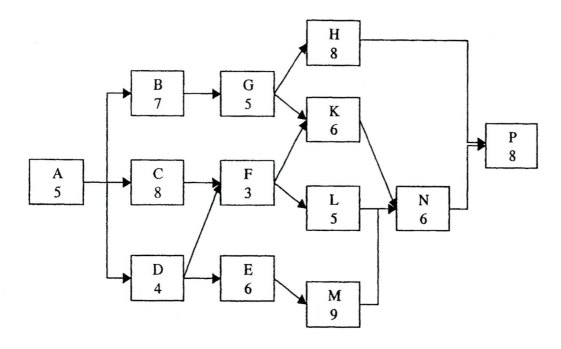

3. Using the network and resources that follow, level the network using the Burgess method.

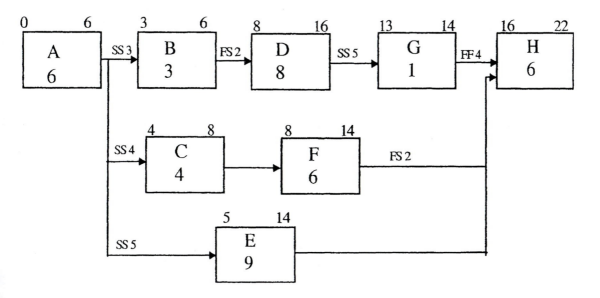

Activity	Resource 1 Rate/Day	Resource 2 Rate/Day
A	8	25
B	16	17
C	10	22
D	12	18
E	12	12
F	9	10
G	7	20
H	4	6

4. Level the following network using the Burgess method.

Activity	Duration	Depends On	Resource 1 Rate	Resource 2 Rate
A	4	——	100	1,250
B	6	A	50	600
C	5	A (FS 2)	200	2,500
D	3	A (FF 2)	150	2,500
F	2	B	100	2,500
G	4	C	75	500
H	3	C (FS 0), D (FS 2)	125	1,000
J	3	F, G	200	1,500
K	7	H, G	100	1,500
L	4	J, K	100	700

5. From the network and resources provided, level the network resource using the Burgess method. Supply a bar chart and an early start histogram with your solution.

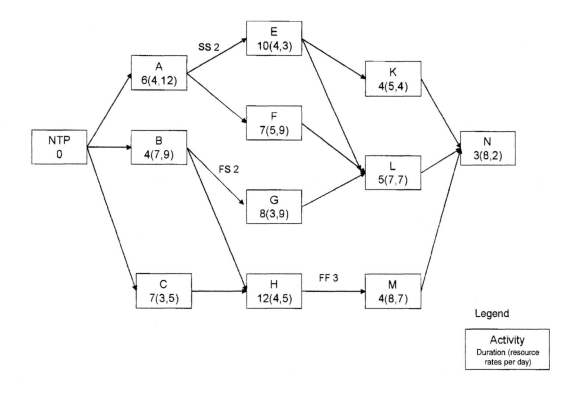

Notes

1. Joseph J. Moder, Cecil R. Phillips, and Edward W. Davis, *Project Management with CPM, PERT, and Precedence Diagramming,* 3rd ed. New York: Van Nostrand Reinhold Co., 1983, p. 129.

CHAPTER 19

Multiple Project Scheduling

Goal

Describe the use of master schedules to manage resources for multiple projects.

Objectives

- Discuss companywide resources and their use.
- Demonstrate the use of the schedule to manage resources in the larger context.
- Create summary activities.
- Demonstrate how projects can be merged into a master schedule using P3®, SureTrak®, and MS Project®.
- Discuss reports that will help managers make resource decisions.

Introduction

Many companies work on more than one project at a time and actually attempt to achieve a measurable backlog of work. The amount of backlog is considered a measure of a company's sustainability. When managing its companywide resources, the company often considers it important to construct and maintain a *master schedule* that captures the details from all current projects. If the master schedule is resource loaded, adjustments can be made in an attempt to optimize resource use. The resources companies may want to track usually include financial resources as well as management staff assignments, designer or engineer hours, critical trade work hours, and/or specialized equipment use.

Companywide Resources

For the purpose of illustration, this chapter will consider a constructor that has a limited number of crews and needs to plan their use based on the projects the company is currently constructing and the ones it hopes to be awarded from projects being bid. The company owner keeps all of his or her specialized crews from project to project. Right now, the owner has three trained crews for this specialty work. For simplicity, each project has five activities, including at least one that uses the specialty crew.

When considering the resource allocation and distribution for an entire company, the person responsible for overall schedule control must be in close communication and collaboration with the responsible project team members who will collect and analyze the project data. The *master schedule* is constructed from the accurate portrayal of each project. As the individual supporting projects are updated, the master schedule must reflect all resulting changes.

The baseline schedules for the four projects currently in progress and the two potential projects due to bid soon by the example contractor are presented in Figures 19.1 and 19.2. The crew type is specified on each bar chart activity. When the crew type is denoted as "SPC," the crew requires one of the specialty crews. All other crews are considered normal crews and are denoted "NML." A portion of the master schedule of the merged projects is presented in Figure 19.3, whereas Figure 19.4 shows the resulting histogram of specialty crew assignments on a daily basis for a 30-day period. If today is workday 10, the overallocation of the specialty crews (more than three crews required) begins in 2 days, on workday 12. It can be seen from the bar charts that projects 1, 2, 3, and 4 all need a specialty crew on that day. Specialty crews in projects 3 and 4 are needed for activities that are not critical; they have total float and may be delayed through resource leveling or management changes to the relationships among the activities or their organization.

Resource Management in a Larger Context

Thus far, the figures in this chapter have shown that aggregating a company's projects into one master schedule can help the decision maker clearly identify when the need for limited resources exceeds the available supply. In order to merge projects effectively, the scheduler must consider how to identify activities so they merge successfully

Project 4 -- In Progress — Workdays

I.D.	Desc	Dur	Crew
310	A	5	NML
320	C	4	SPC
330	F	6	SPC
340	G	4	NML
350	H	3	SPC

Workday	8	9	10	11	12	13	14	15	16	17	18	19	20	21	22	23
Period Sum NML Crew	1	1	1	1	1	0	0	0	0	1	1	1	1	0	0	0
Period Sum SPC Crew			1	1	1	2	1	1	1	1	1	1	1	1	1	1
Total Crews	1	1	2	2	2	2	1	1	1	2	2	2	2	1	1	1

Project 5 -- Planned — Workdays

I.D.	Desc	Dur	Crew
410	B	3	NML
420	D	4	NML
430	G	7	NML
440	H	6	SPC
450	K	5	NML

Workday	17	18	19	20	21	22	23	24	25	26	27	28	29	30
Period Sum NML Crew	1	1	1	2	2	2	2	1	1	2	1	1	1	1
Period Sum SPC Crew								1	1	1	1	1	1	
Total Crews	1	1	1	2	2	2	2	2	2	3	2	2	2	1

Project 6 -- Planned — Workdays

I.D.	Desc	Dur	Crew
510	A	7	NML
520	B	2	NML
530	F	7	SPC
540	G	4	NML
550	H	3	SPC

Workday	15	16	17	18	19	20	21	22	23	24	25	26	27	28
Period Sum NML Crew	1	1	1	1	1	2	2	1	1	1	1	0	0	0
Period Sum SPC Crew						1	1	1	1	1	1	2	1	1
Total Crews	1	1	1	1	1	3	3	2	2	2	2	2	1	1

Total Normal Crew	1	1	2	2	1	1	1	3	3	5	6	4	2	2	2	2	6	5	6	6	3	3	3	2	2	2	1	1	1	1
Total Specialty Crew	0	0	1	1	1	1	1	1	1	2	3	4	5	4	3	3	2	2	3	3	3	3	3	2	2	2	2	2	1	0
Total All Crews	1	1	3	3	2	2	2	4	4	7	9	8	7	6	5	5	8	7	9	9	6	6	6	4	4	4	3	3	2	1

Figure 19.1
Bar charts for projects 1 through 3.

and are easily identified as corresponding to each project. This means using activity identification number schemes that are recognizable. The example use the letter "A," followed by a new number for each new project, so that all activities in the first project have an I.D. beginning with "A0." Once there is a logical means of identifying individual projects, resource pools can be created and shared.

When the overallocation of available resources is identified, the company decision maker can level or constrain the master schedule to see how the results change the resource requirements. Noting again that the specialty crews of the example contractor are overcommitted on workdays 12, 13, and 14, it is clear that the contractor cannot train a new crew in the next 2 days (the data date is day 10). If this condition were noted early enough and if there were a trend toward needing one or two more specialty crews, the company could consider its options: training new crews, hiring a specialty subcontractor, or eliminating some of the planned projects.

Project 4 -- In Progress — Workdays

I.D.	Desc	Dur	Crew	8	9	10	11	12	13	14	15	16	17	18	19	20	21	22	23
310	A	5	NML																
320	C	4	SPC			1	1	1	1										
330	F	6	SPC																
340	G	4	NML																
350	H	3	SPC																

				8	9	10	11	12	13	14	15	16	17	18	19	20	21	22	23
Period Sum NML Crew				1	1	1	1	1	0	0	0	0	1	1	1	1	0	0	0
Period Sum SPC Crew						1	1	1	2	1	1	1	1	1	1	1	1	1	1
Total Crews				1	1	2	2	2	2	1	1	1	2	2	2	2	1	1	1

Project 5 -- Planned — Workdays

I.D.	Desc	Dur	Crew	17	18	19	20	21	22	23	24	25	26	27	28	29	30
410	B	3	NML														
420	D	4	NML			1	1	1	1								
430	G	7	NML														
440	H	6	SPC									1	1	1	1	1	1
450	K	5	NML														

				17	18	19	20	21	22	23	24	25	26	27	28	29	30
Period Sum NML Crew				1	1	1	2	2	2	2	1	1	2	1	1	1	1
Period Sum SPC Crew											1	1	1	1	1	1	
Total Crews				1	1	1	2	2	2	2	2	2	3	2	2	2	1

Project 6 -- Planned — Workdays

I.D.	Desc	Dur	Crew	15	16	17	18	19	20	21	22	23	24	25	26	27	28
510	A	7	NML														
520	B	2	NML						1	1							
530	F	7	SPC						1	1	1	1	1	1	1		
540	G	4	NML														
550	H	3	SPC														

				15	16	17	18	19	20	21	22	23	24	25	26	27	28
Period Sum NML Crew				1	1	1	1	2	2	1	1	1	1	1	0	0	0
Period Sum SPC Crew								1	1	1	1	1	1	1	1	1	1
Total Crews				1	1	1	1	3	3	2	2	2	2	2	1	1	1

Total Normal Crew	1	1	2	2	1	1	1	3	3	5	6	4	2	2	2	2	6	5	6	6	3	3	3	2	2	2	1	1	1	1
Total Specialty Crew	0	0	1	1	1	1	1	1	1	2	3	4	5	4	3	3	2	2	3	3	3	3	3	2	2	2	2	2	1	0
Total All Crews	1	1	3	3	2	2	2	4	4	7	9	8	7	6	5	5	8	7	9	9	6	6	6	4	4	4	3	3	2	1

Figure 19.2
Bar charts for projects 4 through 6 with total resource tabulations.

When the example project is leveled, there is no change in the placement of activities that have specialty crews. Figures 19.5 and 19.6 show the leveling report and the resulting leveled specialty crew histogram. Although one activity moved (A4340), there are no changes to the profile.

The darker peaks on the histogram clearly show the overallocation of the specialty crew resource. Note, too, that the resources are still present for the entire 29 days, as they were prior to leveling (Figure 19.4).

If the master schedule is constrained to only three specialty crews, project 4 gets delayed, with most of its five activities being delayed 4 days. The leveling report shows the negative total float clearly (Figure 19.7), whereas the combined early start and late start histogram depicts the resulting anomalies another way (Figure 19.8).

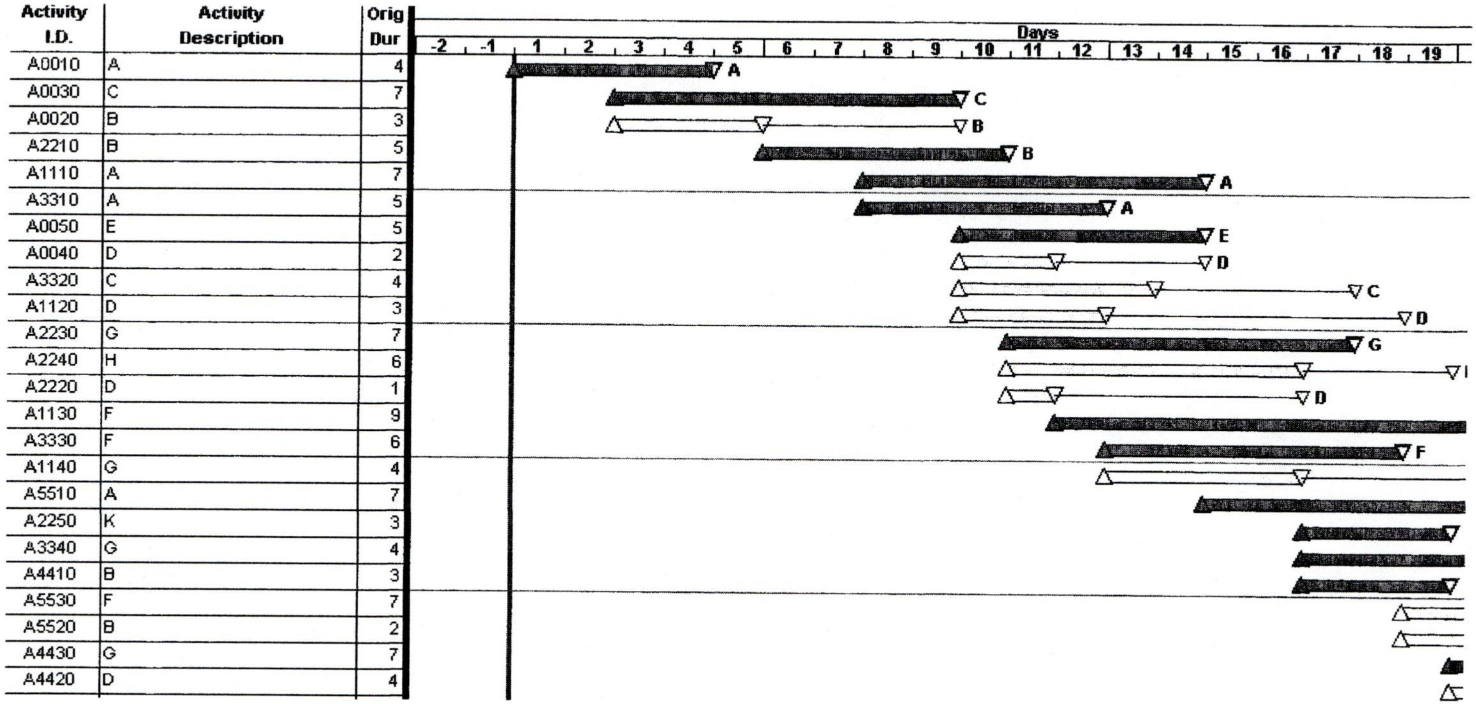

Figure 19.3
Portion of the master schedule bar chart shown in P3®.

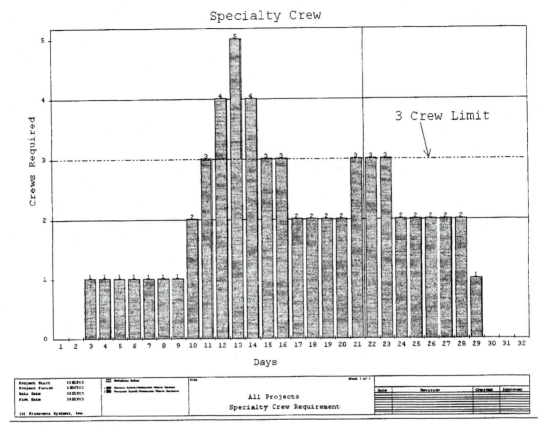

Figure 19.4
Specialty crew master schedule resource needs.

The late start peaks of the histogram (Figure 19.8) are higher than the limit of 3 and continue out to workday 30, whereas the early start peaks are limited to 3 and finish on workday 28, 1 day earlier than the baseline schedule.

These changes are not the result of the constraining as much as they are a result of having six projects merged into a master schedule without any interconnecting links. Each time a master schedule is created, tests should be made to ensure that the desired results of leveling or constraining match the expected result. In the example, a common milestone start and finish or other interconnections between common activities may have prevented the negative float because the one start, one finish premise of the Critical path method would not have been violated. Each company must work out the most effective solution to its own set of projects contained in the master schedule.

Primavera Project Planner — Project 1 -- In Progress

Report Date 13SEP03 9:28 — Forward Resource Leveling Analysis Report — Start Date 12SEP03 Fin Date 11OCT03

Data Date 12SE P03 — Page no. 2

Activity Id	Resource	Daily Usage	Res Lag	Rem Dur	Early Start Date	Early Start Tf	Early Start Norm	Early Start Max	Delayed by Pred Date	Delayed by Pred Tf	Delayed by Pred Norm	Delayed by Pred Max	Delayed by Res. Date	Delayed by Res. Tf	Delayed by Res. Norm	Delayed by Res. Max	Early Leveled Start	Early Leveled Finish
A0030	C			7	14SEP03	0											14SEP03	20SEP03
	SPC	1.00		7	14SEP03		3.00	6.00									14SEP03	20SEP03
A0050	E			5	21SEP03	0											21SEP03	25SEP03
	SPC	1.00		5	21SEP03		3.00	6.00									21SEP03	25SEP03
A1130	F			9	23SEP03	0											23SEP03	01OCT03
	SPC	1.00		9	23SEP03		2.00	5.00									23SEP03	01OCT03
A2240	H			6	22SEP03	3											22SEP03	27SEP03
	SPC	1.00		6	2 2SEP03		2.00	5.00									22SEP03	27SEP03
A3220	C			4	21SEP03	4											21SEP03	24SEP03
	SPC	1 .00		4	21SEP03		2.00	5.00									21SEP03	24SEP03
A3230	F			6	24SEP03	0											24SEP03	29SEP03
	SPC	1.00		6	24SEP03		0.00	2.00									24SEP03	29SEP03
A1150	H			3	02OCT03	0											02OCT03	04OCT03
	SPC	1.00		3	02OCT03		3.00	6.00									02OCT03	04OCT03
A3250	H			3	02OCT03	0											02 OCT03	04OCT03
	SPC	1.00		3	02OCT03		2.00	5.00									02OCT03	04OCT03
A5430	F			7	30SEP03	3											30SEP03	06OCT03
	SPC	1.00		7	30SEP03		2.00	5.00									30SEP03	06OCT03
A4340	H			6	01OCT03	5							05O CT03	1			05OCT03	10OCT03
	SPC	1.00		6	01OCT03		1.00	4.00					05OCT03		2.00	5.00	05OCT03	10OCT03
A5450	H			3	07OCT03	0											07OCT03	09OCT03
	SPC	1.00		3	07OCT03		2.00	5.00									07OCT03	09OCT03

Figure 19.5
Leveling report.

Creation of Summary Activities

There are times when company personnel are interested in the macroscopic view, or overview, of the company's work. At times like these, providing information in aggregate forms is worthwhile. Using the idea of the work breakdown structure can describe the many summary levels available for display. At the most summary level, one activity can be used to represent all of the projects contained in the master schedule. The composite resource use can be shown in histogram or cumulative curve form. Figure 19.9 shows the result for the company with the four ongoing projects depicted in Figures 19.1 through 19.4. This single summary bar might be useful if the company were a division of a multifaceted organization with many projects for its many companies. If that were the case, there would be multiple bars, not just one. There would also be another layer to the work breakdown structure.

Figures 19.10 and 19.11 show the next level, where each summary activity represents an entire project. At this level, the stacking of needed resources can be seen in a resource

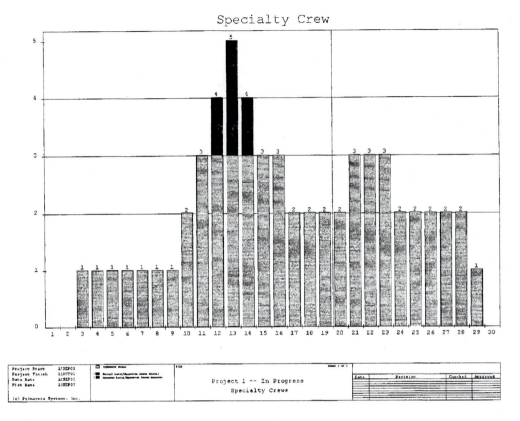

Figure 19.6
Leveled specialty crew histogram.

histogram in Figure 19.9. The projects illustrated on the histogram are limited to those that the company has already been awarded. The summary bars in Figure 19.11 show all of the projects summarized as one bar each. Each project is shown as critical because each summary bar is connected to the start and end of the critical path in its network.

Merging of Projects

For P3®, the master schedule can be set up when starting a new project by adding the new project to a new or an existing project group. The new project addition screen is shown in Figure 19.12. Each new project can be worked on as an independent project. The project group can be worked on and the resulting changes will be shown in the individual projects. This includes the ability to establish relationships across project boundaries. Projects can be merged similarly in MS Project® and in SureTrak®.

```
-------------------------------------------------------------------------------------------------------
                                 Primavera Project Planner              Master Schedule
 Report Date 13SEP03 10:11       Forward Resource Leveling Analysis Report    Start Date 12SEP03  Fin Date 11OCT03
                                                                              Data Date 12SEP03   Page no. 2
 ----------  --------  ----- --- --- ------------------------  ---------------------------  --------------------------  ----------------
                      Daily Res Rem --------Early Start------  -----Delayed by Pred------  -----Delayed by Res.-----  Early Leveled
 Activity Id Resource Usage Lag Dur Date   Tf  Norm   Max      Date   Tf  Norm   Max       Date   Tf  Norm   Max     Start   Finish
 ----------  --------  ----- --- --- ------------------------  ---------------------------  --------------------------  ----------------
 A0030       C              7 14SEP03  0                                                                              14SEP03 20SEP03
             SPC      1.00  7 14SEP03     3.00   3.00                                                                 14SEP03 20SEP03

 A0050       E              5 21SEP03  0                                                                              21SEP03 25SEP03
             SPC      1.00  5 21SEP03     3.00   3.00                                                                 21SEP03 25SEP03

 A1130       F              9 23SEP03  0                                                                              23SEP03 01OCT03
             SPC      1.00  9 23SEP03     2.00   2.00                                                                 23SEP03 01OCT03

 A2240       H              6 22SEP03  3                                                                              22SEP03 27SEP03
             SPC      1.00  6 22SEP03     2.00   2.00                                                                 22SEP03 27SEP03

 A3220       C              4 21SEP03  4                                      26SEP03  -1                             26SEP03 29SEP03
             SPC      1.00  4 21SEP03     2.00   2.00                         26SEP03       1.00   1.00               26SEP03 29SEP03

 A3230       F              6 24SEP03  0               25SEP03  -1            28SEP03  -4                             28SEP03 03OCT03
             SPC      1.00  6 24SEP03     0.00   0.00   25SEP03      0.00  0.00  28SEP03      1.00   1.00              28SEP03 03OCT03

 A1150       H              3 02OCT03  0                                                                              02OCT03 04OCT03
             SPC      1.00  3 02OCT03     2.00   2.00                                                                 02OCT03 04OCT03

 A3250       H              3 02OCT03  0               06OCT03  -4                                                    06OCT03 08OCT03
             SPC      1.00  3 02OCT03     1.00   1.00   06OCT03      3.00  3.00                                        06OCT03 08OCT03

 A5430       F              7 30SEP03  3                                                                              30SEP03 06OCT03
             SPC      1.00  7 30SEP03     1.00   1.00                                                                 30SEP03 06OCT03

 A4340       H              6 01OCT03  5                                      04OCT03   2                             04OCT03 09OCT03
             SPC      1.00  6 01OCT03     0.00   0.00                         04OCT03       1.00   1.00               04OCT03 09OCT03

 A5450       H              3 07OCT03  0                                                                              07OCT03 09OCT03
             SPC      1.00  3 07OCT03     1.00   1.00                                                                 07OCT03 09OCT03
```

Figure 19.7
Constrained master schedule report.

Reports to Aid Company Decision Makers

In addition to the resource graphics that can be produced from the master schedule, generally all other reports are also available. This means that earned value reporting for all projects can be used to help manage at this higher, macro level. Management by exception allows the company leadership to quickly identify projects that are showing negative schedule and/or cost variances and to delve into these projects in more detail.

Reports that compare and contrast activities that are common among all projects can provide estimators with insight into changes in productivity that are occurring or changes that are location- or management-specific. Insights such as these are often the key to better future estimates and improved company profitability.

Other reports that compare and contrast the baseline schedules with the current up-dated schedules contained in the master schedule can give a clear indication of the changes in expected dates. Although these changes in dates may not affect the project completions of the networks they are a part of, they can erode total float assets and threaten profitability. Finding such conditions early can help decision makers test potential schedule changes and provide them with tools for evaluating the changes' effects early enough to make a difference to individual project outcomes and to the company's overall success.

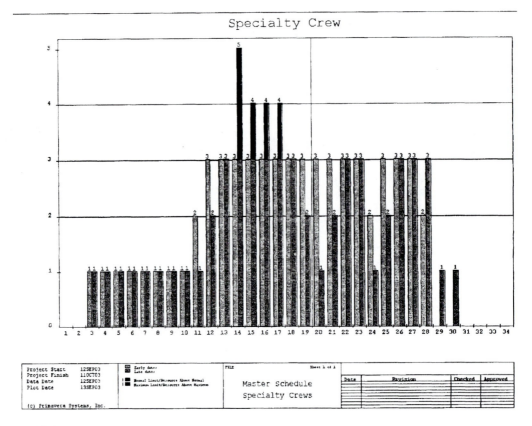

Project Start	12SEP03		Early date	FILE		Sheet 1 of 1				
Project Finish	11OCT03		Late date							
Data Date	12SEP03		Normal Limit/Resource Above Normal	Master Schedule		Date	Revision	Checked	Approved
Plot Date	13SEP03		Maximum Limit/Resource Above Maximum	Specialty Crews					
(c) Primavera Systems, Inc.										

Figure 19.8
Combined early and late start constrained histogram.

Figure 19.9
Single activity representation that combines all of the projects.

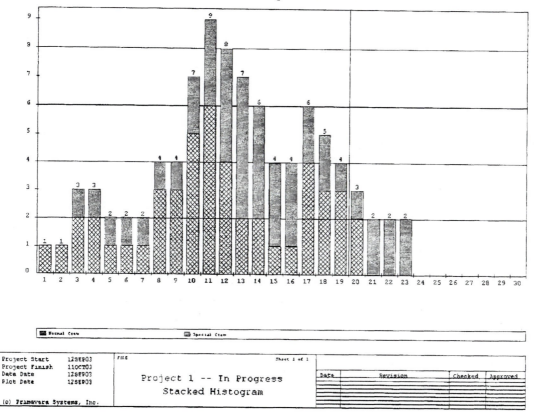

Crew Requirements

Project Start   12SEP03
Project Finish   11OCT03
Data Date   12SEP03
Plot Date   12SEP03

(c) Primavera Systems, Inc.

Project 1 -- In Progress
Stacked Histogram

Figure 19.10
Stacked histogram of normal and specialized crew needs.

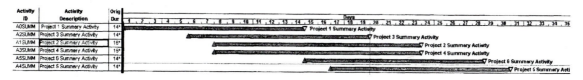

Figure 19.11
Summary bars for each of the six projects.

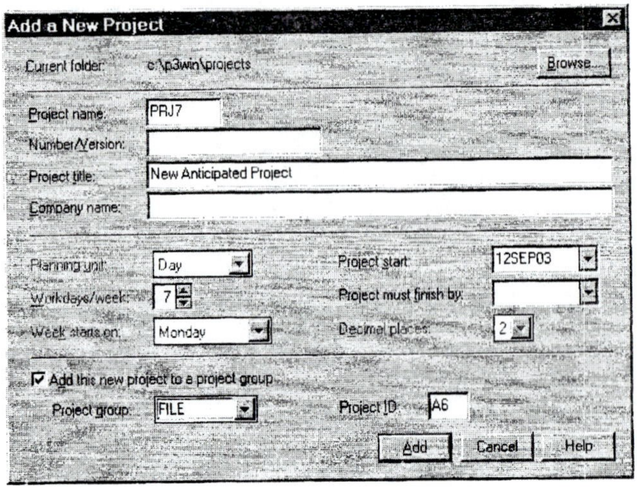

Figure 19.12
P3® master schedule setup.

Conclusion

Most companies that use project-scheduling tools are actually involved in a number of interrelated projects. A common and important characteristic of such situations is that resources needed by the multiple projects are drawn from a common pool—a pool of limited resources. Therefore, at the upper levels of management the concern is planning and monitoring of tasks and resources across a portfolio of projects. To do this, individual projects are scheduled first and then a master schedule of multiple projects is built to facilitate management control at a macro level. This master schedule can expose interproject conflicts and aid in the identification of problems, especially multiproject resource demands.

Problems and/or Questions

1. Document the use of multiple project schedules by a local construction company or owner. Provide evidence to support your discussion of how these schedules are used.

2. Use P3®, SureTrak®, or MS Project® to create five resource-loaded projects, each with five activities. Merge the projects and discuss the results. Then, select a resource level, level the master schedule, and discuss the outcome. Support your statements with reports from the merged project.

3. Given this chapter's example projects, link the individual projects so that the thirty activities are occurring as shown in Figures 19.1 and 19.2. Constrain the specialty crews to three by hand and discuss the results. Compare the results with the computer-generated results provided in the chapter.

4. Given this chapter's example projects, link the individual projects so that the thirty activities are occurring as shown in Figures 19.1 and 19.2. Level both of the crews using the Burgess method and discuss the results. Compare the results with the computer-generated results provided in the chapter.

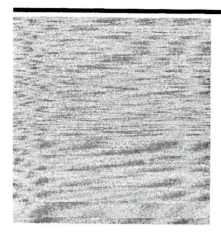

Glossary

activity—The procurement, production, and management tasks needed to comply with construction contract requirements and to describe the work needed to construct the project. The scope or content of the activity may be made up of several tasks, such as fabricate, order, and deliver a piece of equipment that must be installed by the contractor.

activity codes—A way of attaching activity attributes, such as responsibility, location, phase, type of work, or work breakdown structure component.

activity interval—A term relating to an LSM diagram—the width of the activity line is larger, representing more work time at one location.

activity mean duration (t_e)—The activity duration found in PERT by using equation 16-1 to manipulate the optimistic, most likely, and pessimistic durations provided for each activity.

activity on arrow (AOA)—A schedule diagramming method—the method of choice in early, computerized scheduling programs that places the activity on the arrow that connects two nodes or events. This method of scheduling is also known by the names arrow diagramming method (ADM) and I/J, which relates to the subscripts given to the generic nodes preceding and following the activity arrow.

activity standard deviation—A measure of the range of duration values for the activity, obtained using equation 16-5.

actual cost of work performed (ACWP)—The reported actual cost of an activity or the summation of actual costs for a project.

actual finish—The date that is recorded for the completion of an activity.

actual start—The date that is recorded for the beginning of an activity.

algorithm—A series of steps that are often repeated.

backward pass calculation—A calculation that begins with the last activity and works backward through the network to the beginning activity.

bar chart—A common graphical method of depicting a construction schedule.

baseline schedule—The original schedule, before any progress has been reported.

benchmark—A measure of performance with which to compare personal or project performance—for example, the industry average (benchmark) for profit is 3.5% for similar projects.

bi-modal distribution—A distribution with two modes and characterized by two peaks.

budgeted cost of work performed (BCWP)—The earned value; it represents the cost of the work completed to-date either on an activity or for the project.

budgeted cost of work scheduled (BCWS)—The value of the work that was planned to be put in place to-date, calculated using the baseline schedule.

central limit theorem—A mathematical theorem that suggests that, given a number of events with varying duration distributions, when aggregated, the result tends to be a normal distribution. This theorem is key to PERT's ability to use the standard cumulative normal distribution to determine probabilities.

change order—A legal document that can be initiated by an owner or a contractor.

claim—The result of an unresolved change order request for an extension in time, money, or both.

clearing (site)—Removing the plant material and debris above the ground.

compensable delay—A delay that is not the constructor's fault and for which the owner will pay for in terms of time and money, often caused by the owner or owner's agent.

constraining—A network with a specified resource limit. There is a cap on the availability of that resource. A constrained network may have its duration extended to stay within the specified resource limit.

constraint—Something that limits. With regard to an activity, a constraint is an imposed date affecting either the activity's start or its finish.

constructability—The ease with which a designed structure can be built. The constructability of a design is in question when there are frequent design changes, omissions or errors, conflicts, or interferences or when the contractor must frequently request information to clarify design ambiguities.

construction plan—The plan for meeting the contractual construction requirements; it includes several subplans.

contract documents—The graphic plans and written specifications that describe work to be done for a bid or negotiated price.

contract duration—The amount of time allotted to the construction of a project and specified in the contract documents. If the contract duration is exceeded, some owners impose disincentives, such as liquidated damages, on the contractor.

crash—To shorten. A crash duration is the shortest duration for an activity or a project.

crew—The labor and equipment needed or used to complete tasks.

critical path—The longest path through the network; if it is delayed, it will delay the project completion. The critical path is the path with the least total float and the one that usually has the total and free floats of the activities in the path equal to zero.

critical path method (CPM)—The calculation process that requires one start and one finish, so that the longest, or critical, path can be found. CPM was developed by John Fondahl, Stanford University, in the 1960s.

cumulative—The summation of the period amounts such that period amounts 10, 10, 20 become cumulative amounts 10, 20, 40.

data date—The day on which project date information is collected and reported. All date information prior to the data date is known, whereas date information after the data date is calculated by the program or constrained by the user.

dummy activity—An activity used in the arrow diagramming method to show logical connections between or among activities or to preserve the uniqueness of each activity's i-j node pair.

early start—The earliest date on which an activity can begin. Early start order is used to depict activities in a bar chart, with the earliest activity listed first, the next earliest second, and so on until the latest early start activity appears last. This produces a cascade of activities from left to right across the bar chart.

earned value—The budget cost of work performed; the value of the work put in place. Earned value reporting can be used to measure cost and schedule performance.

event slack (ES)—A measure of impact of the slippage of a PERT event's occurrence. It is the difference between the *time late* and the *time early* of an event $(ES_i = TL_i - TE_i)$.

excusable delay—A delay that is not the fault of the owner or the contractor and results in a contract time extension but no additional money compensation.

expendable material—Generally, material that does not become a permanent part of the structure, such as concrete forms.

extranet—A private network that uses the Internet protocol and the public telecommunications system to securely share business information. Provides a means for specific users to enter an intranet network from outside. For example, a prime contractor may want subcontractors to have information about the projects they are working on together. The information is already available on the company's intranet. By creating a portal for the subcontractors to enter and a means of limiting the information they may see, an extranet space is provided.

finish milestone—A marker of the finish of a prominent project feature, such as building enclosed.

finish-to-start relationship—The relationship used when one activity's finish is required before the following activity may begin.

forward pass calculation—A calculation done from the first, or initial, activity to each follower until the last activity in the network is reached. The forward pass is used to find the project duration.

fragnet—A segment of a network that is often repeated, either in the current schedule, such as the activities that represent house 1, house 2, and house 3, or in multiple networks, such as the activities that represent the installation and testing of HVAC equipment. Fragnets are usually stored in computer programs for easy recall and use.

free float—An indication of an activity's most closely related successor. It is the amount of time an activity can be delayed or extended without creating an impact on downstream successors.

grub (site)——To remove the roots and plant material below ground that would adversely affect construction.

histogram—The period-by-period graphic representation of the one or more resources needed for a project.

horizontal sight lines—Sight lines frequently used in bar charts to help the reader relate information on the left of the chart with the corresponding activities on the right. If a specific activity is three activities down from a sight line, the reviewer can follow the sight line left and then count three down and read the corresponding information.

Internet—The global network of computers linked together through a common set of communication tools that allow the military, universities, businesses, and individuals to communicate via e-mail, file transfer, and the World Wide Web.

intranet—A communications network based on Internet protocols belonging to an organization—provides a means of communications within a company or an organization where file transfer, data exchange, and collaboration can occur. There is generally a "firewall" that protects intranet information from being viewed or borrowed by people not within the company.

lag value—The number of days an activity is delayed for a specific relationship type—for example, an FS 3 has a relationship type of finish-to-start and a lag value of 3, meaning that 3 days after the predecessor finishes, the successor may start.

leveling—Moving activities within the limits of their total float to achieve a more uniform resource profile.

logic diagrams—Graphic representations of the linkages among activities in a network.

mainframe—A type of large computer that filled an entire room, used by many companies into the 1970s and 1980s to process business and engineering functions, including scheduling.

management activity—An activity, required to complete a project, that is neither production nor procurement and may be at the discretion of the manager, such as when permits are obtained or when inspections are done.

management by exception—A means of limiting the information presented to a manager, so that only problems and successes are easily apparent. Tools that enable management by exception include the cost and schedule variance on the earned value report.

master schedule—Often the schedule that contains the networks from multiple projects. It can be used by the company to balance resource use.

mean—The arithmetic average of the observed values that are characterized by a frequency distribution.

median—The point in a distribution where half the values are above and the other half are below. In a true normal distribution, the mean, median, and mode are all the same value.

merge event bias—The potential for the subcritical path to become critical. Merge event bias is introduced into the schedule when subcritical activities with high duration variability join the critical path.

milestone—An event in time, not an activity. It has no duration, nor does it consume resources.

mode—A statistical property of a frequency distribution. The mode, along with the mean and the median, helps describe an underlying variable. The mode is also known as the mostly likely value to occur in the distribution.

Monte Carlo simulation—In scheduling, the iterative calculation of the network using statistically distributed activity durations to determine the probability of each activity's criticality and a calculated distribution of the project duration.

MS Project®—A scheduling program developed and sold by Microsoft Corporation, Redmond, WA, and its distributors.

narrative report—A text report that describes the status of a project, highlighting important activities since the last narrative report or schedule update.

necking—The reduction in width of horizontal bars on a bar chart to indicate periods when no work occurs, such as weekends and holidays.

negative float—The amount of time that the early date of an activity exceeds its late date. Negative total or free float indicates a problem with the schedule. Negative total float means that the project or a portion of it is taking longer than allowed. Negative free float indicates that the relationship between two activities is not controlling; instead, a constraint has made their relationship impractical. Negative float can happen only when constraints are introduced into the network.

network—The graphical representation of one or more linked chains of activities or tasks. In the critical path method, these chains are linked in such a way as to have one start and one finish activity.

noncompensable delay—Delay that is not compensated with a time extension or money; it is generally contractor-caused and can lead to liquidated damages.

normal durations—Activity or project durations that are generally the longest. Normal durations for activities are the least expensive. The project normal duration may not be the least expensive, due to the addition of overhead costs to direct costs.

overhead—Indirect costs that cannot be assigned to an individual activity. Company overhead, also known as general and administrative costs, are estimated each year, and a portion is applied to each project. Many overhead costs escalate with time, depending on the economy (inflation and cost of living) and increases in costs for business operation.

parallel activity placement—The simultaneous occurrence of activities. Parallel activities are usually related start-to-start or finish-to-finish, so that they overlap or occur during similar time periods.

period resource contribution—The number of resources an activity uses in 1 day (or another selected period). The total period resource on a day, which is the summation of all activity resources being consumed that day, is the value that appears on the vertical bar of the histogram for that period.

permanent material—Material that will become a part of a final structure, such as wood for framing or concrete for slabs.

plot—The printed output of a network diagram. Many printers act as plotters and can print the output of these diagrams.

precedence diagramming method (PDM)—The method that uses up to four different relationships to link activities, which are placed on nodes and linked by arrows.

Primavera Project Planner® (P3®)—A scheduling software package provided by Primavera Systems, Inc., Bala Cynwyd, PA.

procurement activities—Activities that represent the fabrication, ordering, and delivery of specialty, owner-furnished, or long-lead-time materials or equipment—for example, turbines and generators, Carrara marble, and ebony hardwood.

production activities—Activities that are used to describe the work of building (action verbs)—for example, erecting formwork, setting trusses, installing electrical systems, and paving lane miles of freeway.

productivity—In the classic sense, a ratio of the number of inputs used to generate a number of outputs. In construction, it may be measured in cubic yards per hour or square feet per day. Thus, productivity is normally measured as a quantity per unit of time.

program evaluation and review technique (PERT)—A statistical method of scheduling developed to help manage work with high degrees of costly risk.

project duration—The time it is expected to take to complete a project based on early finish of the last activity in the network. The calculated project duration should be compared with the specified project duration.

project mean duration—The sum of the activity mean durations along the critical path.

project standard deviation—A measure of the variability and range of project mean duration. In PERT, it is obtained using equation 16-8.

redundant relationships—Relationships in which a direct connection between two activities can be eliminated because one or more implied relationships create dependencies that are the same as the direct connection.

relationships—Linkages between activities; activities are preceded and followed by other activities.

remaining duration—The amount of time an activity is expected to take beyond the current data date. A remaining duration should be specified if an activity has begun but is not yet complete when updating a network schedule.

resources—Sometimes described as the four *m*'s and a *t*, *m*en (labor), *m*oney, *m*aterials, *m*achines (equipment), and *t*ime.

scheduled early start (SES)—A constraint used to limit when an activity may begin. This constraint means "start no earlier than," which means the activity cannot start earlier than the constraint date, but it can start later.

scheduled late finish (SLF)—A constraint used to limit when an activity can finish; it means "finish no later than." An activity can finish earlier but no later than this date.

serial activity placement—A string of serial activities related end to end with finish-to-start relationships and no overlapping activities.

simulate—To model the real world in a computer program and evaluate the results of taking certain actions. Simulation is an inexpensive way of testing problem-solving approaches to find the one that gives the best expected result before implementing the changes in the real world.

slack—The PERT equivalent of float. Both activity free slack and activity total slack can be calculated, as can event slack.

special conditions—Conditions that modify or add to standard conditions and are specific to a project. They often give the expected project duration and scheduling requirements, among other project-specific elements.

spoil—The excess earth or soil material that cannot be replaced in the location from which it was excavated.

start milestone—The beginning of an important event in a schedule, such as "Notice to Proceed" or "Open Detour."

status—To update a project with actual start and finish dates, remaining durations, and actual resource use.

summary activity—The aggregation of two or more linked activities. When shown in a bar chart, the duration of the activity, and hence the length of the bar, can change as the durations of the aggregated activities change—for example, one summary activity may represent all of the activities needed to control the site work and underground work for a building.

target schedule—A schedule used for comparison with the current schedule. Frequently, the baseline, or original, schedule is used as a target. Sometimes, a resource-leveled schedule is used as a target.

task—The lowest level of work controlled in a project schedule; an activity.

total float—The amount of time an activity can be delayed without delaying the project completion. A chain of activities with the same total float shares the total float amount. Thus, if one activity is delayed 2 days, every activity in the chain has its total float reduced by 2 days.

update—To make regular, periodic incorporation of progress in the schedule and to apply the changes needed to meet project requirements.

variance—A non-negative number that gives an idea of how widely spread the values of the variable can be. The variance in a PERT network is found for each activity by squaring the activity standard deviation.

vertical sight lines—Vertical lines used on a bar chart to help the reader correlate activity placement with time.

virtual activity—A replacement for several activities done in an uninterrupted, serial fashion. The total float on all activities in the chain is the same, whereas the free float is zero on all of the activities except, perhaps, the last one in the chain.

work breakdown structure (WBS)—A way of subdividing a project into finer and finer detail until the task level is reached; it is a hierarchical means of project organization. If the hierarchy is top to bottom, the organizational breakdown structure (OBS) can be aligned on the adjacent axis and a comparison between task and responsible party can be made.

work profile—The characterization of a company's project requirements, such as the type of work, the project location, the dollar value of the contract, and the owner for whom the work is to be done.

workday duration—Construction projects often have two calendars: one on which workdays are counted and the other for calendar days. Unless a project is working every day of the week, the workday duration, 5 days per week, of a project is different from the calendar day duration, 7 days per week, typically.

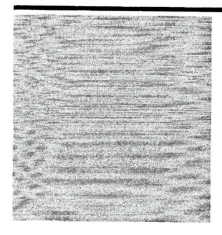

List of Acronyms and Abbreviations

ACWP—actual cost of work performed

ADM—arrow diagramming method

AF—actual finish

AFS—activity free slack

AOA—activity on arrow

AS—actual start

ATF—activity total slack

BCWP—budgeted cost of work performed

BCWS—budgeted cost of work scheduled

CLT—central limit theorem

Dur—duration

EF—early finish

ES—early start; event slack

FF—free float; finish-to-finish

IF—interfering float

I/J—activity on arrow network method; I/J refers to the activity that links the nodes known as i and j

LF—late finish

LOB—line of balance

LS—late start

LSM—linear scheduling method

MAX—maximum

MIN—minimum

OD—original duration

P3®—Primavera Project Planner®

PDM—precedence diagramming method

PERT—program evaluation and review technique

RD—remaining duration

SES—scheduled early start

SF—start-to-finish

SLF—scheduled late finish

SMS—scheduled must start

SS—start-to-start

T_e—project mean duration

t_e—activity mean duration

TF—total float

WBS—work breakdown structure

Z—The cumulative normal distribution function

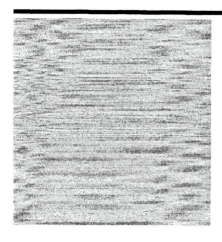

List of Mathematical Symbols

∀—for all or for every

Σ—summation

Updated Network Information

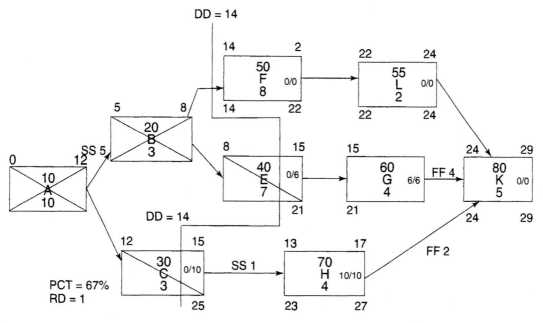

Figure A.1
Updated network diagram from Chapter 9.

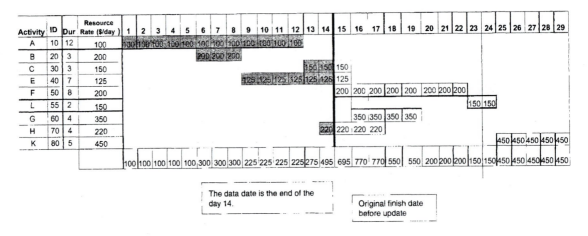

Figure A.2
Updated bar chart.

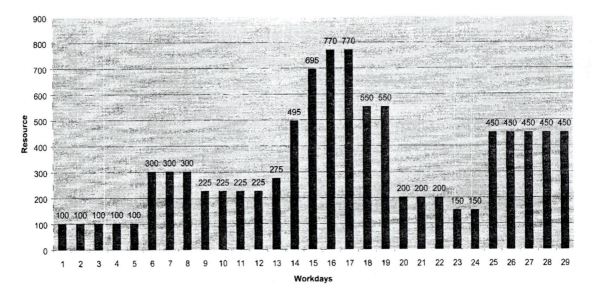

Figure A.3
Updated histogram.

APPENDIX
B

Sample Request for Payment Form

	DPW PROJECT NO.	
State of Idaho DIVISION OF PUBLIC WORKS **CONTRACTOR REQUEST FOR PAYMENT** SUBMIT ONE ORIGINAL	Code #	AMOUNT
	CC	
	Date	

Name and Location of Project

Name and Address of Contractor

Request No.	For Period
	_____ TO _____

ANALYSIS OF CONTRACT AMOUNT TO DATE

Original Contract Amount $_____ (1)

Net Amount of Change Orders through CO#_____ $_____ (2)

Adjusted Contract Amount *(Line 1 + Line 2)* $_____ (3)

ANALYSIS OF WORK PERFORMED (Attach Pay Estimate Breakdown)

Value of Work Performed from Column 4 of Estimate Breakdown $_____ (4)

Less Amount Retained Per Contract Terms

    (5% of Line 4 above, show % if different)   _____% $_____ (5)

Net Amount Earned to Date $_____ (6)

LessPrevious Payments $_____ (7)

BALANCE DUE THIS PAYMENT *(Line 6 - Line 7)* $_____(8)

CERTIFICATION OF CONTRACTOR:

I certify that the foregoing is just and correct and the amount claimed is legally due after showing all just credits.

Certified by Contractor	Date

I certify that I have inspected the above work, that to the best of my knowledge it is in accord with contract requirements and that the estimated quantities are correct.

Certified by (Architect/Engineer)	Date
Inspected by DPW FR	Date

Recommended by SFR	Recommended by PM	Final Documents Received (DPW Coordinator)
Approved by Administrator of Public Works		Date

APPENDIX C

Reports for Analysis

Project Description

There are a total of 13 activities in the project, which are a part of the two major subdivisions, site work and foundation. There is a milestone activity called "Lines Complete," which denotes the completion of electric, water, and sewer line activities. The project start date is **September 9, 2002,** and the **data date is September 30, 2002.** Some activities are completed, some are in progress, and some have not yet started. There are two resources MH (man-hours) and $ (cost in dollars). Some activities had different resource usage than was budgeted in the target. The appendix consists of the following reports.

Updated Project Reports	Baseline Project Reports
Early Start Report	Early Start Report
Early Start with Target Comparison	Relationship Report
Relationship Report	TFES
TFES	Histogram
Histogram	Network Diagram
Network Diagram	
Earned Value Report	

Use these reports to write a narrative on the status of the project.

```
CON 495                          PRIMAVERA PROJECT PLANNER              Updating Sample Project

REPORT DATE  3OCT02  RUN NO.   5                                        START DATE  7SEP02  FIN DATE  9OCT02
             15:38
ES Report Original                                                      DATA DATE  7SEP02  PAGE NO.    1
```

ACTIVITY ID	ORIG DUR	REM DUR	%	ACTIVITY DESCRIPTION	EARLY START	EARLY FINISH	LATE START	LATE FINISH	TOTAL FLOAT
10	2	2	0	Clear and Grub	9SEP02	10SEP02	9SEP02	10SEP02	0
20	3	3	0	Survey	11SEP02	13SEP02	11SEP02	13SEP02	0
30	4	4	0	Bulk Excavation	16SEP02	19SEP02	16SEP02	19SEP02	0
50	1	1	0	Trenching	20SEP02	20SEP02	20SEP02	20SEP02	0
53	1	1	0	Underground Electric lines	23SEP02	23SEP02	26SEP02	26SEP02	3
56	1	1	0	Water lines	25SEP02	25SEP02	26SEP02	26SEP02	1
58	0	0	0	Lines Complete		26SEP02		26SEP02	0
59	1	1	0	Sewer lines	26SEP02	26SEP02	26SEP02	26SEP02	0
40	3	3	0	Backfill	27SEP02	10OCT02	27SEP02	10OCT02	0
60	1	1	0	Compaction	2OCT02	2OCT02	2OCT02	2OCT02	0
70	2	2	0	Form Isolated Footing	3OCT02	4OCT02	3OCT02	4OCT02	0
80	1	1	0	Reinforce Footing	7OCT02	7OCT02	7OCT02	7OCT02	0
90	2	2	0	Pour Footing	8OCT02	9OCT02	8OCT02	9OCT02	0

BASELINE: Early Start Report.

```
CON 495                          PRIMAVERA PROJECT PLANNER              Updating Sample Project
REPORT DATE  7SEP02  RUN NO.   2                                        START DATE  7SEP02  FIN DATE  9OCT02
             11:07
Relationship Report                                                     DATA DATE  7SEP02  PAGE NO.    1
```

	ACTIVITY ID	ORIG DUR	REM DUR	%			ACTIVITY DESCRIPTION	EARLY START	EARLY FINISH	LATE START	LATE FINISH	TOTAL FLOAT
	10	2	2	0			Clear and Grub	9SEP02	10SEP02	9SEP02	10SEP02	0
..	20*	3	3	0	SU		Survey	11SEP02	13SEP02	11SEP02	13SEP02	0
	20	3	3	0			Survey	11SEP02	13SEP02	11SEP02	13SEP02	0
..	10*	2	2	0	PR		Clear and Grub	9SEP02	10SEP02	9SEP02	10SEP02	0
..	30*	4	4	0	SU		Bulk Excavation	16SEP02	19SEP02	16SEP02	19SEP02	0
	30	4	4	0			Bulk Excavation	16SEP02	19SEP02	16SEP02	19SEP02	0
..	20*	3	3	0	PR		Survey	11SEP02	13SEP02	11SEP02	13SEP02	0
..	50*	1	1	0	SU		Trenching	20SEP02	20SEP02	20SEP02	20SEP02	0
	40	3	3	0			Backfill	27SEP02	10OCT02	27SEP02	10OCT02	0
..	58*	0	0	0	PR		Lines Complete		26SEP02		26SEP02	0
..	60*	1	1	0	SU		Compaction	2OCT02	2OCT02	2OCT02	2OCT02	0
	50	1	1	0			Trenching	20SEP02	20SEP02	20SEP02	20SEP02	0
..	30*	4	4	0	PR		Bulk Excavation	16SEP02	19SEP02	16SEP02	19SEP02	0
..	53*	1	1	0	SU		Underground Electric lines	23SEP02	23SEP02	26SEP02	26SEP02	3
..	56*	1	1	0	SU FS	2	Water lines	25SEP02	25SEP02	26SEP02	26SEP02	1
..	59*	1	1	0	SU SS	4	Sewer lines	26SEP02	26SEP02	26SEP02	26SEP02	0
	53	1	1	0			Underground Electric lines	23SEP02	23SEP02	26SEP02	26SEP02	3
..	50*	1	1	0	PR		Trenching	20SEP02	20SEP02	20SEP02	20SEP02	0
..	58	0	0	0	SU		Lines Complete		26SEP02		26SEP02	0
	56	1	1	0			Water lines	25SEP02	25SEP02	26SEP02	26SEP02	1
..	50*	1	1	0	PR FS	2	Trenching	20SEP02	20SEP02	20SEP02	20SEP02	0
..	58	0	0	0	SU		Lines Complete		26SEP02		26SEP02	0
	58	0	0	0			Lines Complete		26SEP02		26SEP02	0
..	53	1	1	0	PR		Underground Electric lines	23SEP02	23SEP02	26SEP02	26SEP02	3
..	56	1	1	0	PR		Water lines	25SEP02	25SEP02	26SEP02	26SEP02	1
..	59*	1	1	0	PR		Sewer lines	26SEP02	26SEP02	26SEP02	26SEP02	0
..	40*	3	3	0	SU		Backfill	27SEP02	10OCT02	27SEP02	10OCT02	0
	59	1	1	0			Sewer lines	26SEP02	26SEP02	26SEP02	26SEP02	0
..	50*	1	1	0	PR SS	4	Trenching	20SEP02	20SEP02	20SEP02	20SEP02	0
..	58*	0	0	0	SU		Lines Complete		26SEP02		26SEP02	0

ID	DUR	DUR	%			START	FINISH	START	FINISH	FLOAT
60	1	1	0		Compaction	2OCT02	2OCT02	2OCT02	2OCT02	0
.. 40*	3	3	0 PR		Backfill	27SEP02	1OCT02	27SEP02	1OCT02	0
.. 70*	2	2	0 SU		Form Isolated Footing	3OCT02	4OCT02	3OCT02	4OCT02	0
70	2	2	0		Form Isolated Footing	3OCT02	4OCT02	3OCT02	4OCT02	0
.. 60*	1	1	0 PR		Compaction	2OCT02	2OCT02	2OCT02	2OCT02	0
.. 80*	1	1	0 SU		Reinforce Footing	7OCT02	7OCT02	7OCT02	7OCT02	0
80	1	1	0		Reinforce Footing	7OCT02	7OCT02	7OCT02	7OCT02	0
.. 70*	2	2	0 PR		Form Isolated Footing	3OCT02	4OCT02	3OCT02	4OCT02	0
.. 90*	2	2	0 SU		Pour Footing	8OCT02	9OCT02	8OCT02	9OCT02	0
90	2	2	0		Pour Footing	8OCT02	9OCT02	8OCT02	9OCT02	0
.. 80*	1	1	0 PR		Reinforce Footing	7OCT02	7OCT02	7OCT02	7OCT02	0

BASELINE: Relationship Report.

```
------------------------------------------------------------------------------------------------
CON 495                              PRIMAVERA PROJECT PLANNER              Updating Sample Project
REPORT DATE  3OCT02  RUN NO.   3                                  START DATE  7SEP02  FIN DATE  9OCT02
             15:35
Original Project - Sort by TF, ES                                DATA DATE  7SEP02  PAGE NO.   1
------------------------------------------------------------------------------------------------
```

ACTIVITY ID	ORIG DUR	REM DUR	%	CODE	ACTIVITY DESCRIPTION	EARLY START	EARLY FINISH	LATE START	LATE FINISH	TOTAL FLOAT
10	2	2	0		Clear and Grub	9SEP02	10SEP02	9SEP02	10SEP02	0
20	3	3	0		Survey	11SEP02	13SEP02	11SEP02	13SEP02	0
30	4	4	0		Bulk Excavation	16SEP02	19SEP02	16SEP02	19SEP02	0
50	1	1	0		Trenching	20SEP02	20SEP02	20SEP02	20SEP02	0
58	0	0	0		Lines Complete		26SEP02		26SEP02	0
59	1	1	0		Sewer lines	26SEP02	26SEP02	26SEP02	26SEP02	0
40	3	3	0		Backfill	27SEP02	1OCT02	27SEP02	1OCT02	0
60	1	1	0		Compaction	2OCT02	2OCT02	2OCT02	2OCT02	0
70	2	2	0		Form Isolated Footing	3OCT02	4OCT02	3OCT02	4OCT02	0
80	1	1	0		Reinforce Footing	7OCT02	7OCT02	7OCT02	7OCT02	0
90	2	2	0		Pour Footing	8OCT02	9OCT02	8OCT02	9OCT02	0
56	1	1	0		Water lines	25SEP02	25SEP02	26SEP02	26SEP02	1
53	1	1	0		Underground Electric lines	23SEP02	23SEP02	26SEP02	26SEP02	3

BASELINE: Schedule Report sorted by Total Float first, then Early Start.

303

File   Edit   View   Tools   Window   Help

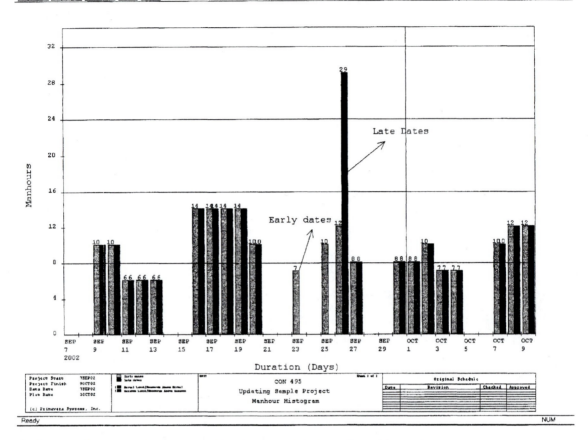

BASELINE: Resource Histogram for Man-Hours with both early and late values.

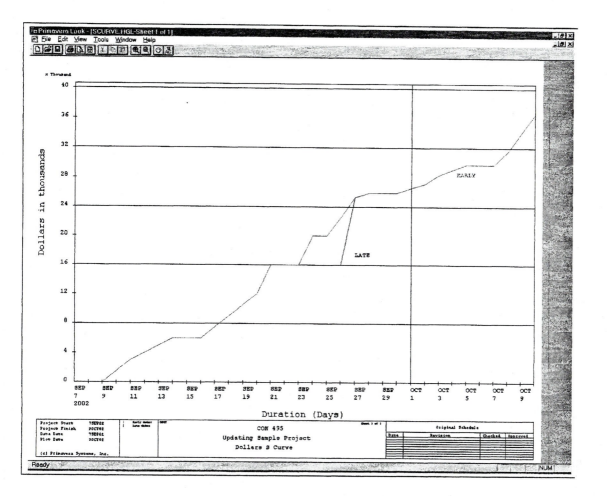

BASELINE: Network Diagram.

```
----------------------------------------------------------------------------------------------------------------------
CON 495                                           PRIMAVERA PROJECT PLANNER              Updating Sample Project
REPORT DATE 7SEP02 RUN NO.  3                                                 START DATE 7SEP02  FIN DATE  9OCT02
            10:22
Current ES Report                                                            DATA DATE  30SEP02  PAGE NO.   1
----- ---- ---- - ---  ---------- --------------------------------------- -------- -------- -------- -------- -----
  ACTIVITY   ORIG REM                                                        EARLY    EARLY    LATE     LATE   TOTAL
    ID       DUR  DUR    %                ACTIVITY DESCRIPTION               START   FINISH   START   FINISH  FLOAT
----- ---- ---- - ---  ---------- --------------------------------------- -------- -------- -------- -------- -----
        10    2    0   100          Clear and Grub                         9SEP02A 10SEP02A
        20    3    0   100          Survey                                11SEP02A 16SEP02A
        30    2    0   100          Bulk Excavation                       17SEP02A 18SEP02A
        50    2    0   100          Trenching                             23SEP02A 24SEP02A
        53    1    0   100          Underground Electric lines            24SEP02A 25SEP02A
        59    1    0   100          Sewer lines                           26SEP02A 26SEP02A
        40    3    2    33          Backfill                              27SEP02A  1OCT02                     1OCT02        0
        56    1    0   100          Water lines                           27SEP02A 27SEP02A
        58    0    0   100          Lines Complete                                 27SEP02A
        60    1    1     0          Compaction                             2OCT02   2OCT02   2OCT02   2OCT02       0
        70    2    2     0          Form Isolated Footing                  3OCT02   4OCT02   3OCT02   4OCT02       0
        80    1    1     0          Reinforce Footing                      7OCT02   7OCT02   7OCT02   7OCT02       0
        90    2    2     0          Pour Footing                           8OCT02   9OCT02   8OCT02   9OCT02       0
```

UPDATED: Early Start Report.

```
----------------------------------------------------------------------------------------------------------------------
CON 495                                           PRIMAVERA PROJECT PLANNER              Updating Sample Project
REPORT DATE 7SEP02 RUN NO.  4                                                 START DATE 7SEP02  FIN DATE  9OCT02
            10:23
ES Report with Comparision to Target                                         DATA DATE  30SEP02  PAGE NO.   1
----- ---- ---- - ---  ---------- --------------------------------------- -------- -------- -------- -------- -----
  ACTIVITY   TAR  CUR                                                       CURRENT  EARLY   TARGET   EARLY
    ID       DUR  DUR    %                ACTIVITY DESCRIPTION               START   FINISH   START   FINISH  VAR.
----- ---- ---- - ---  ---------- --------------------------------------- -------- -------- -------- -------- -----
        10    2    2   100          Clear and Grub                         9SEP02A 10SEP02A  9SEP02  10SEP02     0
        20    3    4   100          Survey                                11SEP02A 16SEP02A 11SEP02  13SEP02    -1
        30    4    2   100          Bulk Excavation                       17SEP02A 18SEP02A 16SEP02  19SEP02     1
        50    1    2   100          Trenching                             23SEP02A 24SEP02A 20SEP02  20SEP02    -2
        53    1    2   100          Underground Electric lines            24SEP02A 25SEP02A 23SEP02  23SEP02    -2
        59    1    1   100          Sewer lines                           26SEP02A 26SEP02A 26SEP02  26SEP02     0
        40    3    2    33          Backfill                              27SEP02A  1OCT02  27SEP02   1OCT02     0
        56    1    1   100          Water lines                           27SEP02A 27SEP02A 25SEP02  25SEP02    -2
        58    0    0   100          Lines Complete                                 27SEP02A          26SEP02    -1
        60    1    1     0          Compaction                             2OCT02   2OCT02   2OCT02   2OCT02     0
        70    2    2     0          Form Isolated Footing                  3OCT02   4OCT02   3OCT02   4OCT02     0
        80    1    1     0          Reinforce Footing                      7OCT02   7OCT02   7OCT02   7OCT02     0
        90    2    2     0          Pour Footing                           8OCT02   9OCT02   8OCT02   9OCT02     0
```

UPDATED: An Early Start Report that compares the Current Updated schedule with the Target or Baseline schedule.

```
----------------------------------------------------------------------------------------------------------------------
                                                  PRIMAVERA PROJECT PLANNER              Updating Sample Project
REPORT DATE 28SEP02 RUN NO.  7                                                START DATE 7SEP02  FIN DATE  9OCT02
             15:06
Schedule Report - Sort by TF, ES                                             DATA DATE  30SEP02  PAGE NO.   1
----- ---- ---- - ---  ---------- --------------------------------------- -------- -------- -------- -------- -----
  ACTIVITY   ORIG REM                                                        EARLY    EARLY    LATE     LATE   TOTAL
    ID       DUR  DUR    %   CODE          ACTIVITY DESCRIPTION               START   FINISH   START   FINISH  FLOAT
----- ---- ---- - ---  ---------- --------------------------------------- -------- -------- -------- -------- -----
        10    2    0   100          Clear and Grub                         9SEP02A 10SEP02A
        20    3    0   100          Survey                                11SEP02A 16SEP02A
        30    2    0   100          Bulk Excavation                       17SEP02A 18SEP02A
        50    2    0   100          Trenching                             23SEP02A 24SEP02A
        53    1    0   100          Underground Electric lines            24SEP02A 25SEP02A
        59    1    0   100          Sewer lines                           26SEP02A 26SEP02A
        56    1    0   100          Water lines                           27SEP02A 27SEP02A
        58    0    0   100          Lines Complete                                 27SEP02A
        40    3    2    33          Backfill                              27SEP02A  1OCT02                     1OCT02        0
        60    1    1     0          Compaction                             2OCT02   2OCT02   2OCT02   2OCT02     0
        70    2    2     0          Form Isolated Footing                  3OCT02   4OCT02   3OCT02   4OCT02     0
        80    1    1     0          Reinforce Footing                      7OCT02   7OCT02   7OCT02   7OCT02     0
        90    2    2     0          Pour Footing                           8OCT02   9OCT02   8OCT02   9OCT02     0
```

UPDATED: Report Sorted by Total Float, then Early Start.

CON 495   PRIMAVERA PROJECT PLANNER   Updating Sample Project
REPORT DATE 3OCT02 RUN NO. 8   START DATE 7SEP02 FIN DATE 9OCT02
16:10
DATA DATE 30SEP02 PAGE NO. 1
Relationship Report

ACTIVITY ID	ORIG DUR	REM DUR	%	CODE	ACTIVITY DESCRIPTION	EARLY START	EARLY FINISH	LATE START	LATE FINISH	TOTAL FLOAT
10	2	0	100	01	Clear and Grub	9SEP02A	10SEP02A			
.. 20	3	0	100 SU		Survey	11SEP02A	16SEP02A			
20	3	0	100	03	Survey	11SEP02A	16SEP02A			
.. 10	2	0	100 PR		Clear and Grub	9SEP02A	10SEP02A			
.. 30	2	0	100 SU		Bulk Excavation	17SEP02A	18SEP02A			
30	2	0	100	02	Bulk Excavation	17SEP02A	18SEP02A			
.. 20	3	0	100 PR		Survey	11SEP02A	16SEP02A			
.. 50	2	0	100 SU		Trenching	23SEP02A	24SEP02A			
40	3	2	33		Backfill	27SEP02A	1OCT02		1OCT02	0
.. 58*	0	0	100 PR		Lines Complete		27SEP02A			
.. 60*	1	1	0 SU		Compaction	2OCT02	2OCT02	2OCT02	2OCT02	0
50	2	0	100	04	Trenching	23SEP02A	24SEP02A			
.. 30	2	0	100 PR		Bulk Excavation	17SEP02A	18SEP02A			
.. 53	1	0	100 SU		Underground Electric lines	24SEP02A	25SEP02A			
.. 56	1	0	100 SU FS	2	Water lines	27SEP02A	27SEP02A			
.. 59*	1	0	100 SU SS	4	Sewer lines	26SEP02A	26SEP02A			
53	1	0	100	02	Underground Electric lines	24SEP02A	25SEP02A			
.. 50	2	0	100 PR		Trenching	23SEP02A	24SEP02A			

CON 495   PRIMAVERA PROJECT PLANNER   Updating Sample Project
REPORT DATE 3OCT02 RUN NO. 8   START DATE 7SEP02 FIN DATE 9OCT02
16:10
DATA DATE 30SEP02 PAGE NO. 2
Relationship Report

ACTIVITY ID	ORIG DUR	REM DUR	%	CODE	ACTIVITY DESCRIPTION	EARLY START	EARLY FINISH	LATE START	LATE FINISH	TOTAL FLOAT
.. 58	0	0	100 SU		Lines Complete		27SEP02A			
56	1	0	100	03	Water lines	27SEP02A	27SEP02A			
.. 50	2	0	100 PR FS	2	Trenching	23SEP02A	24SEP02A			
.. 58	0	0	100 SU		Lines Complete		27SEP02A			
58	0	0	100	02	Lines Complete		27SEP02A			
.. 53	1	0	100 PR		Underground Electric lines	24SEP02A	25SEP02A			
.. 56	1	0	100 PR		Water lines	27SEP02A	27SEP02A			
.. 59	1	0	100 PR		Sewer lines	26SEP02A	26SEP02A			
.. 40*	3	2	33 SU		Backfill	27SEP02A	1OCT02		1OCT02	0
59	1	0	100	04	Sewer lines	26SEP02A	26SEP02A			
.. 50*	2	0	100 PR SS	4	Trenching	23SEP02A	24SEP02A			
.. 58	0	0	100 SU		Lines Complete		27SEP02A			
60	1	1	0	03	Compaction	2OCT02	2OCT02	2OCT02	2OCT02	0
.. 40*	3	2	33 PR		Backfill	27SEP02A	1OCT02		1OCT02	0
.. 70*	2	2	0 SU		Form Isolated Footing	3OCT02	4OCT02	3OCT02	4OCT02	0
70	2	2	0	02	Form Isolated Footing	3OCT02	4OCT02	3OCT02	4OCT02	0
.. 60*	1	1	0 PR		Compaction	2OCT02	2OCT02	2OCT02	2OCT02	0
.. 80*	1	1	0 SU		Reinforce Footing	7OCT02	7OCT02	7OCT02	7OCT02	0

CON 495   PRIMAVERA PROJECT PLANNER   Updating Sample Project
REPORT DATE 3OCT02 RUN NO. 8   START DATE 7SEP02 FIN DATE 9OCT02
16:10
DATA DATE 30SEP02 PAGE NO. 3
Relationship Report

ACTIVITY ID	ORIG DUR	REM DUR	%	CODE	ACTIVITY DESCRIPTION	EARLY START	EARLY FINISH	LATE START	LATE FINISH	TOTAL FLOAT
80	1	1	0	04	Reinforce Footing	7OCT02	7OCT02	7OCT02	7OCT02	0
.. 70*	2	2	0 PR		Form Isolated Footing	3OCT02	4OCT02	3OCT02	4OCT02	0
.. 90*	2	2	0 SU		Pour Footing	8OCT02	9OCT02	8OCT02	9OCT02	0
90	2	2	0		Pour Footing	8OCT02	9OCT02	8OCT02	9OCT02	0
.. 80*	1	1	0 PR		Reinforce Footing	7OCT02	7OCT02	7OCT02	7OCT02	0

UPDATED: Relationship Report.

```
CON 495
REPORT DATE   7SEP02  RUN NO.    6                    PRIMAVERA PROJECT PLANNER              Updating Sample Project
              10:48                                   EARNED VALUE REPORT - QUANTITY         START DATE 7SEP02  FIN DATE  9OCT02
Earned Value Report - Units                                                                 DATA DATE 30SEP02    PAGE NO.    1
```

COST ACCOUNT	RESOURCE	ACTIVITY ID	PCT CMP	ACTUAL	EARNED	PLANNED	COST	SCHEDULE	BUDGET	ESTIMATE
				..........CUMULATIVE TO DATE..........			.......VARIANCE.........		......AT COMPLETION......	
$	–									
$		10	100.0	3200.00	3000.00	3000.00	-200.00	.00	3000.00	3200.00
$		20	100.0	3100.00	3000.00	3000.00	-100.00	.00	3000.00	3100.00
$		30	100.0	2000.00	2000.00	2000.00	.00	.00	2000.00	2000.00
$		40	33.3	632.70	632.70	633.33	.00	-.63	1900.00	1900.00
$		50	100.0	4000.00	4000.00	4000.00	.00	.00	4000.00	4000.00
$		53	100.0	4000.00	4000.00	4000.00	.00	.00	4000.00	4000.00
$		56	100.0	2500.00	2500.00	2500.00	.00	.00	2500.00	2500.00
$		59	100.0	2800.00	2800.00	2800.00	.00	.00	2800.00	2800.00
$		60	.0	.00	.00	.00	.00	.00	1200.00	1200.00
$		70	.0	.00	.00	.00	.00	.00	1400.00	1400.00
$		80	.0	.00	.00	.00	.00	.00	1800.00	1800.00
$		90	.0	.00	.00	.00	.00	.00	5000.00	5000.00
$	TOTAL		67.3	22232.70	21932.70	21933.33	-300.00	-.63	32600.00	32900.00

```
CON 495
REPORT DATE   7SEP02  RUN NO.    6                    PRIMAVERA PROJECT PLANNER              Updating Sample Project
              10:48                                   EARNED VALUE REPORT - QUANTITY         START DATE 7SEP02  FIN DATE  9OCT02
Earned Value Report - Units                                                                 DATA DATE 30SEP02    PAGE NO.    1
```

COST ACCOUNT	RESOURCE	ACTIVITY ID	PCT CMP	ACTUAL	EARNED	PLANNED	COST	SCHEDULE	BUDGET	ESTIMATE
				..........CUMULATIVE TO DATE..........			.......VARIANCE.........		......AT COMPLETION......	
MH	–									
	MH	10	100.0	20.00	20.00	20.00	.00	.00	20.00	20.00
	MH	20	100.0	16.00	18.00	18.00	2.00	.00	18.00	16.00
	MH	30	100.0	20.00	20.00	20.00	.00	.00	20.00	20.00
	MH	40	33.3	7.99	7.99	8.00	.00	-.01	24.00	24.00
	MH	50	100.0	10.00	10.00	10.00	.00	.00	10.00	10.00
	MH	53	100.0	7.00	7.00	7.00	.00	.00	7.00	7.00
	MH	56	100.0	10.00	10.00	10.00	.00	.00	10.00	10.00
	MH	59	100.0	12.00	12.00	12.00	.00	.00	12.00	12.00
	MH	60	.0	.00	.00	.00	.00	.00	10.00	10.00
	MH	70	.0	.00	.00	.00	.00	.00	14.00	14.00
	MH	80	.0	.00	.00	.00	.00	.00	10.00	10.00
	MH	90	.0	.00	.00	.00	.00	.00	24.00	24.00
	MH	TOTAL	58.7	102.99	104.99	105.00	2.00	-.01	179.00	177.00
	REPORT	TOTALS	67.2	22335.69	22037.69	22038.33	-298.00	-.64	32779.00	33077.00

UPDATED: Earned Value Report for both Dollars and Man-Hours.

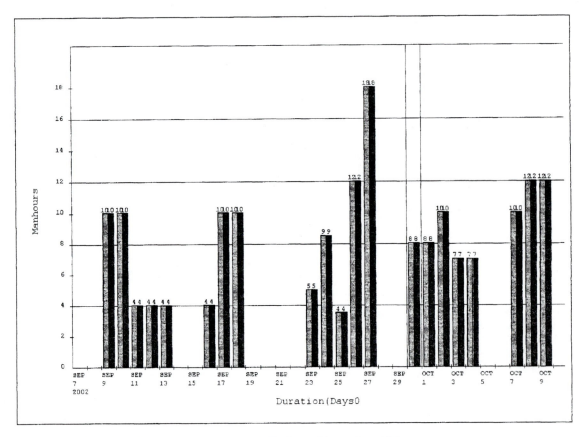

UPDATED: Man-Hour Histogram showing both Early and Late Start Values.

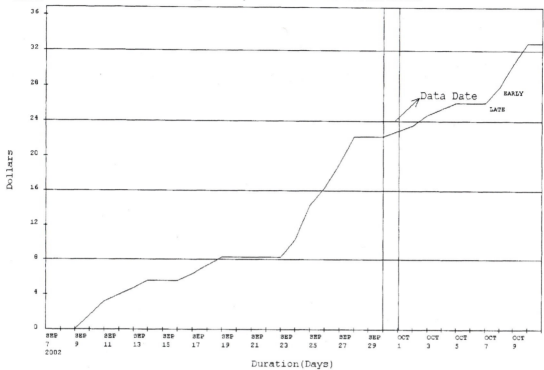

UPDATED: Dollar S-curve showing both Early and Late Start Values and a data date line.

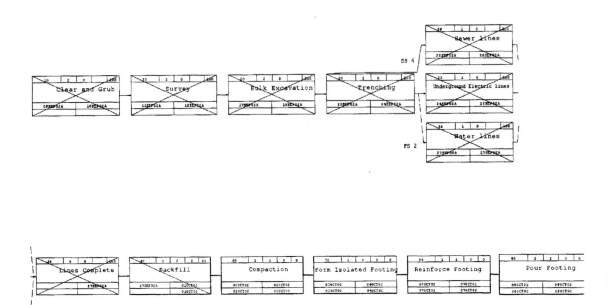

UPDATED: Network Diagram.

APPENDIX D

Representative Scheduling Specifications

Sample Specification 1

Progress Schedule (Critical Path)

Progress schedules will be required for this contract. Progress schedules shall utilize the critical path method (CPM).

Definitions—The following definitions apply to this section "Progress Schedule (Critical Path):"

1. **Activity:** Any task, or portion of a project that takes time to complete.
2. **Baseline Schedule:** The initial CPM schedule representing the contractor's original work plan, as accepted by the engineer.
3. **Critical Path Method:** A mathematical calculation to determine the longest path of work and relative float represented by a graphic representation of the sequence of activities that shows the interrelationships and interdependencies of the elements composing a project.
4. **Current Contract Completion Date:** The extended date for completion of the contract shown on the weekly statement of working days furnished by the engineer in accordance with Section 8–1.06, "Time of Completion," of the standard specifications.
5. **Early Completion Time:** The difference in time between the current contract completion date and the contractor's scheduled early completion as shown on the accepted baseline schedule, or schedule updates and revisions.
6. **Float:** The amount of time between the early start date and the late start date, or the early finish date and the late finish date, of any activities in the network.

7. **Fragnet:** A section or fragment of the network diagram comprised of a group of activities.

8. **Hammock Activity:** An activity added to the network to span an existing group of activities for summarizing purposes.

9. **Milestone:** A marker in a network that is typically used to mark a point in time or denote the beginning or end of a sequence of activities. A milestone has zero duration, but will otherwise function in the network as if it were an activity.

10. **Revision:** A change in the future portion of the schedule that modifies logic, adds or deletes activities, or alters activities, sequences, or durations.

11. **Tabular Listing:** A report showing schedule activities, their relationships, durations, scheduled and actual dates, and float.

12. **Total Float:** The amount of time that an activity may be delayed without affecting the total project duration of the critical path.

13. **Update:** The modification of the CPM progress schedule through a regular review to incorporate actual progress to date by activity, approved time adjustments, and projected completion dates.

Preconstruction Scheduling Conference—The engineer will schedule and conduct a Preconstruction Scheduling Conference with the contractor's project manager and construction scheduler within 7 days after the bidder has received the contract for execution. At this meeting, the requirements for this section of the special provisions will be reviewed with the contractor. The contractor shall be prepared to discuss its schedule methodology, proposed sequence of operations, and any deviations it proposes to make from the Stage Construction Plans. At this meeting, the contractor shall submit its proposed work breakdown structure, the associated alphanumeric coding structure to implement the work breakdown structure, and the activity identification system for labeling all work activities. The engineer shall review and comment on the work breakdown structure, the coding structure, and the activity identification system within 7 days after submission by the contractor. The contractor shall make all modifications to the proposed work breakdown structure, the coding structure, and activity identification system that are requested by the engineer, and shall employ that coding, structure, and system in its baseline schedule submission.

Interim Baseline Schedule—Within 10 days after approval of the contract, the contractor shall submit to the engineer an interim baseline project schedule, which will serve as the progress schedule for the first 120 days of the project, or until the baseline schedule is accepted, whichever is sooner. The interim baseline schedule shall utilize the critical path method. The interim baseline schedule shall depict how the contractor plans to perform the work for the first 120 days of the contract. Additionally, the interim baseline schedule shall show all submittals required early in the project, and shall provide for all permits, and other nonwork activities necessary to begin the work. The interim baseline schedule submittal shall include a diskette that contains the data files used to generate the schedule.

The engineer shall be allowed 15 calendar days to review and accept or reject the interim baseline schedule submitted. Rejected schedules shall be resubmitted to the engineer within 5 calendar days of receipt by the contractor of the engineer's comments, at which time a new 15-calendar day review period by the engineer will begin.

Baseline Schedule—Within 30 days after approval of the contract, the contractor shall submit to the engineer a baseline project schedule. The baseline schedule shall include the activities shown on the interim baseline schedule in the same order and logical relationship as shown in the interim baseline schedule. The baseline project schedule shall have a data date of the day prior to the first working day of the contract and shall not include any completed work to-date. The baseline progress schedule shall meet interim target dates, milestones, stage construction requirements, and internal time constraints; shall show logical sequence of activities; and must not extend beyond the number of days originally provided for in the contract.

The baseline CPM schedule submitted by the contractor shall have a sufficient number of activities to assure adequate planning of the project and to permit the monitoring and evaluation of progress and the analysis of time impacts. The baseline schedule shall depict how the contractor plans to complete the whole work involved and shall show all activities that define the critical path.

The baseline progress schedule shall be supplemented with resource allocations for every activity, to a level of detail that facilitates report generation based on labor craft and equipment class for the contractor and subcontractors. The contractor shall use average composite crews to display the labor loading of on-site construction activities. The contractor shall optimize and level labor to reflect a reasonable plan for accomplishing the work of the contract and to assure that resources are not duplicated in concurrent activities. The contractor shall require each subcontractor to submit in writing a statement certifying that the subcontractor has concurred with the contractor's CPM, including major updates, and that the subcontractor's related schedule has been incorporated accurately, including the duration of activities and labor and equipment loading. Along with the baseline progress schedule, the contractor shall also submit to the engineer time-scaled resource histograms of the labor crafts and equipment classes to be utilized on the contract.

The engineer shall be allowed 15 calendar days to review and accept or reject the baseline project schedule submitted. Rejected schedules shall be resubmitted to the engineer within 5 calendar days, at which time a new 15-calendar-day review period by the engineer will begin.

Project Schedule Reports—Schedules submitted to the engineer including baseline and interim baseline schedules shall include time-scaled network diagrams. Network diagrams shall be based on early start and early finish dates of activities shown. The network diagrams submitted to the engineer shall also be accompanied by the computer-generated mathematical analysis tabular reports for each activity included in the project schedule. Three different report sorts shall be provided: early start, total float, and activity number, which shall show all predecessors and successors for each activity. The mathematical analysis tabular reports (8½″ × 11″ size) shall be submitted to the engineer and shall include, at a minimum, the following:

1. Data date;
2. Predecessor and successor activity numbers and descriptions;
3. Activity number and description;
4. Activity codes;
5. Schedule and actual and remaining duration for each activity;
6. Earliest start date (by calendar date);
7. Earliest finish date (by calendar date);
8. Actual start date (by calendar date);
9. Actual finish date (by calendar date);
10. Latest start date (by calendar date);
11. Latest finish date (by calendar date);
12. Actual nonworking days;
13. Activity calendar type;
14. Float, in workdays:
15. Percentage of activity complete and remaining duration for incomplete activities; and
16. Imposed constraints.

Networks shall be drafted time-scaled to show a continuous flow of information from left to right. The primary paths of criticality shall be clearly and graphically identified on the networks. The network diagram shall be prepared on E-size sheets (36″ × 48″) and shall have a title block on the lower right-hand corner and a time line on each page. Exceptions to the size of network sheets and the use of computer graphics to generate the networks shall be subject to the approval of the engineer.

Schedule network diagrams and computer tabulations shall be submitted to the engineer for acceptance in the following quantities:

A. Two sets of the network diagrams;
B. Two copies of the computer tabulation reports (8½″ × 11″ size); and
C. Three computer diskettes.

Should the baseline schedule or schedule update, submitted for acceptance, show variances from the requirements of the contract, the contractor shall make specific mention of the variations in the letter of transmittal, in order that, if accepted, proper adjustments to the project schedule can be made. The contractor will not be relieved of the responsibility for executing the work in strict accordance with the requirement of the contract documents. In the event of a conflict between the requirements of the contract documents and the information provided or shown on an accepted schedule, the requirements of the contract document shall take precedence.

Each schedule submitted to the engineer shall comply with all limits imposed by the contract, with all specified intermediate milestone and completion dates, and with all constraints, restraints, or sequences included in the contract. The degree of detail should include factors including, but not limited to:

1. Physical breakdown of the project;

2. Contract milestones and completion dates, substantial completion dates, constraints, restraints, sequences of work shown in the contract, the planned substantial completion date, and the final completion date;

3. Type of work to be performed and the sequences and the major subcontractors involved;

4. All purchase, submittals, submittal reviews, manufacture, tests, deliver and installation activities for all major materials and equipment;

5. Preparation, submittal, and approval of shop and working drawing samples, showing time, as specified elsewhere, for the engineer's review (the same time frame shall be allowed for at least one resubmittal on all major submittals so identified in the contract documents);

6. Identification of interfaces and interdependencies with preceding. Concurrent and follow on contractors, railroads and utilities as shown on the plans or specified in the specifications;

7. Identification of every utility relocation and interface as a separate activity, including activity description and responsibility coding that identifies the type of utility and the name of the utility company involved;

8. Actual tests, submission of test reports, and approval of test results;

9. All start-up testing, training, and assistance required on the contract;

10. Punchlist and final cleanup;

11. Identification of any manpower, material, or equipment restrictions, as well as any activity requiring unusual shift work, such as double shifts, 6-day weeks, specified overtime, or work at times other than regular days or hours; and

12. Identification of every ramp closing and opening event as a separate one-day activity, including designation by activity coding and description that it is a north-bound, south-bound, east-bound, west-bound, and entry or exit ramp activity.

Each construction activity shall have duration of not more than 20 working days, and not less than 1 working day unless permitted otherwise by the engineer. All activities in the schedule, with the exception of the first and last activities, shall have a minimum of one predecessor and one successor. The baseline schedule shall not attribute negative float to any activity. Float shall not be considered as time for the exclusive use of or benefit of either the state or the contractor but shall be considered as a jointly owned, expiring resource available to the project and shall not be used to the financial detriment of either party. Any accepted schedule, revision, or update having an early completion date shall show the time between early completion date and the current contract completion date as "project float."

The contractor shall be responsible for assuring that all work sequences are logical and that the network shows a coordinated plan for complete performance of the work. Failure of the contractor to include any element of work required for the performance of the contract in the network shall not relieve the contractor from completing all work within the time limit specified for completion of the contract. If the contractor fails to define any element of work activity or logic, and the omission or error is discovered by either the contractor or the engineer, it shall be corrected by the contractor at the next monthly update or revision of the schedule.

Monthly Update Schedules—The contractor shall submit a monthly update schedule to the engineer once in each month. The proposed update schedule prepared by the contractor shall include all information available as of the 20th calendar day of the month, or another date as established by the engineer. A detailed list of all proposed schedule changes, such as logic, duration, lead/lag, additions, and deletions, shall be submitted with the update.

The monthly update schedule submitted to the engineer shall be accompanied by a schedule narrative report. The schedule narrative report shall describe the physical progress during the report period, plans for continuing the work during the forthcoming report period, actions planned to correct any negative float predictions, and an explanation of potential delays or problems and their estimated impact on performance, milestone completion dates, and the overall project completion date. In addition, alternatives for possible schedule recovery to mitigate any potential delay or cost increases shall be included for consideration by the engineer. The report shall follow the outline set forth as follows:

Contractor's Schedule Narrative Report Outline

1. Contractor's transmittal letter
2. Work completed during the period
3. Description of the current critical path
4. Description of problem areas
5. Current and anticipated delays
   A. Cause of the delay
   B. Corrective action and schedule adjustments to correct the delay
   C. Impact of the delay on other activities, milestones, and completion dates
6. Changes in construction sequences
7. Pending items and status thereof
   A. Permits
   B. Change orders
   C. Time extensions
   D. Noncompliance notices

8. Contract completion date(s) status

    A. Ahead of schedule and number of days

    B. Behind schedule and number of days

9. Updated network diagram and reports

The contractor shall provide to the engineer a 3½″ electronic disk of the schedule, together with printed copies of the network diagrams and tabular reports described in the section "Project Schedule Reports," and the schedule narrative report.

The monthly update of the schedule shall be for the period from the last update to the current cut-off date and for the remainder of the project. The current period's activities shall be reported as they actually take place and designated as actually complete, if actually completed, in the schedule updates.

Portions of the network diagram on which all activities are complete need not be reprinted and submitted in subsequent updates. However, the electronic disk file of the submitted schedule and the related reports shall constitute a clear record of progress of the work from award of contract to final completion.

The contractor will be permitted to show early or late completion on schedule updates and revisions. The engineer may use the updates and the revisions, and other information available, in evaluating the effect of changes, delays, or time savings on the critical path and the accepted schedule current at the time to determine if there is an applicable adjustment of time, if any, to any target date or completion date due to the changes, delays, or time savings.

On a date determined by the engineer, the contractor shall meet with the engineer to review the monthly schedule update. At the monthly progress meeting, the contractor and the engineer will review the updated schedule and will discuss the content of narrative report. The engineer shall be allowed 15 days after the meeting to review and accept or reject the update schedule submitted. Rejected schedules shall be resubmitted to the engineer within 15 calendar days, at which time a new 15-calendar-day review period by the engineer will begin.

Schedule Revisions—If the contractor desires to make a change to the accepted schedule, the contractor shall request permission from the engineer in writing, stating the reasons for the change and proposed revisions to activities, logic, and duration. The contractor shall submit for acceptance the affected portions of the project schedule and an analysis to show the effect on the entire project. The engineer will provide a response within 10 days. No revision to the accepted baseline schedule or the schedule updates shall be made without the prior written approval of the engineer.

The engineer will request the contractor to submit a proposed revised schedule within 15 days when:

    A. There is a significant change in the contractor's operations that will affect the critical path;

    B. The current updated schedule indicates that the contract progress is 30 calendar days or more behind the planned schedule, as determined by the engineer; or

C. The engineer determines that an approved or anticipated change will impact the critical path, milestone or completion dates, contract progress, or work by other contractors.

The engineer shall be allowed 15 days to review and accept or reject a schedule revision. Rejected schedule revisions shall be revised and resubmitted to the engineer within 15 calendar days, at which time a new 15-calendar-day review period by the engineer will begin. Only upon approval of a change by the engineer shall it be reflected in the next schedule update submitted by the contractor.

Schedule Time Extension Requests—When the contractor requests a time extension due to contract change order or delays, the contractor shall submit to the engineer a written time-impact analysis, illustrating each change or delay on the contract completion date or milestone completion date, utilizing the current contract accepted schedule. Each time-impact analysis shall include a fragnet demonstrating how the contractor proposes to incorporate the change order or delay into the current schedule. The fragnet shall include the sequence of new and existing activity revisions that are proposed to be added to the accepted baseline project schedule or current schedule in effect at the time the change or delay is encountered, to demonstrate the influence of the delay and the proposed method for incorporating the delay and its impact into the schedule.

Each time-impact analysis shall demonstrate the estimated time impact based on the events of delay, the anticipated or actual date of the contract change order work preference, the status of construction at that point in time, and the event-time computation of all activities affected by the change or delay. The event times used in the analysis shall be those included in the current update of the current schedule in effect at the time the change or delay was encountered.

Time extension will be granted only to the extent that equitable time adjustments for the activity or activities affected exceed the total or remaining float along the critical path of activities at the time of actual delay, or at the time the contract change-order work is performed. Float time is not for the exclusive use or benefit of the engineer or the contractor but is an expiring resource available to all parties as needed to meet contract milestones and the contract completion date. The extensions will not be granted nor will damages be paid unless:

A. The delay is beyond the control and without the fault or negligence of the contractor and its subcontractors or suppliers at any tier; and

B. The delay extends the actual performance of the work beyond the applicable current contract completion date and the most recent date predicted for completion date and the most recent date predicted for completion of the project on the accepted schedule update current as of the time of delay or as of the time of issuance of the contract change order.

Time-impact analyses shall be submitted in triplicate within 15 days after the delay occurs or after issuance of the contract change order.

Approval or rejection of each time-impact analysis by the engineer will be made within 15 days after receipt of the time-impact analysis, unless subsequent meetings and negotiations delay the review. A copy of the time-impact analysis approved by the engineer shall be returned to the contractor and accepted schedule revisions illustrating the influence of contract change orders or delays shall be incorporated into the project schedule during the first update after approval.

First Schedule Update—Within the first 15 days after the acceptance of the contract by the director, the contractor shall submit a final update of the schedule with actual start and actual finish dates for all activities. This schedule submission shall be accompanied by a certification, signed by an officer of the company and the contractor's project manager, stating, "To the best of my knowledge, the enclosed final update of the project schedule reflects the actual start and completion dates of the activities contained herein."

Equipment and Software—The contractor shall provide for the state's exclusive possession and use a complete computer system specifically capable of creating, storing, updating, and producing CPM schedules. Before delivery and setup of the computer system, the contractor shall submit to the engineer for approval a detailed list of all computer hardware and software the contractor proposes to furnish. The minimum computer system to be furnished shall include the following:

1. Complete computer system, including keyboard, mouse, 17″ color SVGA monitor (1,024 × 768 pixels), Intel Pentium 200 MHZ microprocessor chip, or equivalent or better;
2. Computer operating system software, compatible with the selected processing unit, for Windows 95 or later, or equivalent;
3. Minimum 64 megabytes of random access memory (RAM);
4. A 2-gigabyte minimum hard disk drive, a 1.44-megabyte 3½″ floppy disk drive, 16 × speed minimum CD-ROM drive, and Ethernet card, 33.6 modem;
5. A color ink jet plotter with a minimum 8 megs RAM capable of 300 dots per inch color, 600 dots per inch monochrome, or equivalent plotter capable of printing fully legible time-scaled charts and network diagrams, in four colors, with a minimum size of 36″ × 48″ (E size), compatible with a selected system; and
6. Primavera Project Planner® CPM software, Version 2.0 for Windows 95 or later.

The computer hardware and software furnished shall be compatible with that used by the contractor for the production of the CPM progress schedule required by the contract and shall include original instruction manuals and other documentation normally provided with the software.

The contractor shall furnish, install, set up, maintain, and repair the computer hardware and software ready for use at a location determined by the engineer. The hardware and software shall be installed and ready for use by the first submission of the baseline schedule. The contractor shall provide 24 hours of formal training to the engineer in the use of the hardware and software to include schedule analysis, reporting, resource, and contract allocations.

All computer hardware and software furnished shall remain the property of the contractor and shall be removed by the contractor upon acceptance of the contract when no claims involving contract progress are pending. When claims involving contract progress are pending, computer hardware or software shall not be removed until the final estimate has been submitted to the contractor.

Payment—Progress schedule (critical path) will be paid for a lump sum price. The contract lump sum price paid for the progress schedule (critical path) shall include full furnishing for all labor, materials (including computer hardware and software), tools, equipment, and incidentals and for all the work involved in preparing, furnishing, updating, and revising CPM progress schedules as well as maintaining and repairing the computer hardware and software, as specified in the standard specifications and these special provisions, and as directed by the engineer.

Payments for progress schedule (critical path) will be made as follows:

- Interim baseline schedule will be accepted; then 10% payment for progress schedule (critical path) will be made.
- Baseline schedule will be accepted; then 10% payment for progress schedule (critical path) will be made.
- Monthly update schedules will be accepted; then 75% payment for progress schedule (critical path) will be made equally for each update.
- Final schedule update will be accepted; then 5% payment for progress schedule (critical path) will be made.

The department will retain an amount equal to 25% of the estimated value of the work performed during the first estimate period in which the contractor fails to submit an interim baseline, baseline, revised, or updated CPM schedule conforming to the requirements of this section, as determined by the engineer. Thereafter, on subsequent successive estimate periods, the percentage the department will retain will be increased at the rate of 25% per estimate period in which acceptable CPM progress schedules have not been submitted to the engineer. Retentions for failure to submit acceptable CPM progress schedules shall be additional to all other retentions provided for in the contract. The retention for failure to submit acceptable CPM progress schedules will be released for payment on the next monthly estimate for partial payment following the date that acceptable CPM progress schedules are submitted to the engineer.

The adjustment provisions in Section 4-1.03, "Changes," of the standard specifications shall not apply to the item of progress schedule (critical path). Adjustments in compensation for the project schedule will not be made for any increased or decreased work ordered by the engineer in furnishing project schedules.

Sample Specification 2

Terminal 18 Development Project
General Conditions

Article 2 Preliminary Matters

2.01 Delivery of Bonds and Other Information—When DESIGN/BUILDER delivers the executed agreements to owner, DESIGN/BUILDER shall also deliver to OWNER the following:

A. Such bonds as DESIGN/BUILDER may be required to furnish in accordance with paragraph 5.01.A, with effective dates no later than the effective date.

B. A cash flow projection to be used as a schedule for draw on construction funds and a preliminary schedule of values for all of the work which will include quantities and prices of items aggregating the contract price and will subdivide the work into component parts in sufficient detail to serve as the basis for progress payments during performance of the work. Such prices will include a pro rata amount of overhead and profit applicable to each item of work.

C. Certificates of insurance, with copies to each additional insured identified therein (and other evidence of insurance which OWNER or any additional insured may reasonably request) which DESIGN/BUILDER is required to purchase and maintain in accordance with paragraphs 5.02.A, 5.04.A, and 5.04.B.

2.02 Commencement of Contract Time; Notice to Proceed—The contract time will commence to run on the day indicated in the notice to proceed. A notice to proceed will be given on the day of the bond closing which will be the effective date of the agreement.

2.03 Starting the Work—DESIGN/BUILDER shall start to perform the work on the date when the contract time commences.

2.04 Before Starting Construction—DESIGN/BUILDER shall submit the following for review within 10 days after commencement of the contract time:

A. A preliminary progress schedule indicating the times (numbers of days or dates) for starting and completing the various stages of the work.

B. A preliminary schedule of required submittals and the times for submitting, reviewing, and processing each submittal.

2.05 Initial Conference—Within 20 days after the contract time starts to run, a conference attended by OWNER and DESIGN/BUILDER and others as appropriate will be held to establish a working understanding among the parties as to the work and to discuss the design concepts, schedules referred to in paragraphs 2.01.A and 2.04.A, procedures for handling submittals, processing for handling submittals, processing applications for payment, maintaining required records, items required pursuant to paragraph 8.01.A.6, and other matters.

2.06 Initially Acceptable Schedules—At least 10 days before submission of the first application for payment a conference attended by DESIGN/BUILDER, OWNER, and others as appropriate will be held to review for acceptability the schedules submitted in accordance with paragraphs 2.01.A and 2.04.A. DESIGN/BUILDER shall have 10 days to make corrections and adjustments and to complete and resubmit the schedules. No progress payments shall be made to DESIGN/BUILDER until the schedules are submitted to and acceptable to OWNER. The progress schedule will not be acceptable to OWNER unless it provides an orderly progression of the work to completion within any specified milestones and the contract time, but such acceptance will neither impose on OWNER responsibility for the sequencing, scheduling, or progress of the work nor interfere with or relieve DESIGN/BUILDER from DESIGN/BUILDER'S full responsibility therefore. The format and structure of the progress schedule shall be as set forth in the contract documents. OWNER'S acceptance shall not be deemed to confirm that the schedule is a reasonable plan for performing the work. DESIGN/ BUILDER'S schedule of submittals will not be acceptable to OWNER unless it provides a workable arrangement for reviewing and processing the required submittals. DESIGN/ BUILDER'S schedule of values will be subject to acceptance by OWNER and independent engineer as to form and substance.

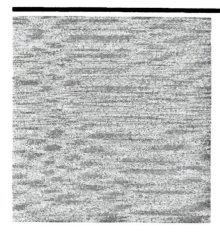

Index

Page numbers in *italics* indicate figures.
Page numbers followed by *"t"* indicate tables.